INSIDE PAUL HORN

INSIDE PAUL HORN

THE SPIRITUAL ODYSSEY
OF
A UNIVERSAL TRAVELER

PAUL HORN

WITH
LEE UNDERWOOD

HarperSanFrancisco
A Division of HarperCollins*Publishers*

To order recordings by Paul Horn, contact Celestial Harmonies,
P.O. Box 30122, Tucson, Arizona 85751, phone number (602) 326-4400.
His latest release is *Inside The Taj Mahal II*, available on
compact disk and cassette.

FIRST EDITION

LIBRARY OF CONGRESS CATALOGING-IN-PUBLICATION DATA

Horn, Paul.
    Inside Paul Horn : the spiritual odyssey of a universal traveler / Paul Horn with Lee Underwood.
       p. cm.
    Discography: p.
    ISBN 0–06–250388–X
    1. Horn, Paul, 1930–   .   2. Jazz musicians—United States—Biography.
I. Underwood, Lee.   II. Title.
ML419.H67A3   1990
788.3'2165'092—dc20
[B]
                                      89–46443
                                         CIP
                                         MN

90 91 92 93 94 HAD 10 9 8 7 6 5 4 3 2 1

This edition is printed on acid-free paper that meets the American National Standards Institute Z39.48 Standard.

———

TO THE BEST MAN
I'VE EVER KNOWN
MY FATHER

JACK L. HORN

1895–1981

CONTENTS

CONTENTS

PART II   THE JAZZ YEARS

PART III   THE TRANSITION

PART IV   A NEW LIFE IN CANADA

CONTENTS

PART V   THE TRAVELER

ix

ACKNOWLEDGMENTS

Special thanks to Jim and Rosalie Heacock of the Heacock Literary Agency, who believed in this project from the start; to my co-writer, Lee Underwood, for his talent, friendship, and dedication to this project; to Denise Brethour, for her tireless and excellent transcribing; and to Alex Crespi, for his invaluable assistance in the computer and printing area.

I would also like to acknowledge the following people who in one way or another influenced my life and became a part of it: my mother, Frances Horn; my father, Jack Horn; my wife, Tryntje; my sons, Marlen and Robin; also Maharishi Mahesh Yogi, Swami Satchidananda, Swami Muktananda, Gina Cerminara, Baba Hari Dass, Haida (the killer whale), Miles Davis, Chico Hamilton, Fred Katz, Lee Hardesty, Bob Willoughby, Fred Wilkins, Emil Richards, Lynn Blessing, Bill Plummer, Bill Goodwin, Paul Moer, Chuck Gregory, David Kapralik, Shorty Rogers, Henry Lewy, Nadine Lewy, Duke Ellington, Tony Bennett, Frank Sinatra, Tony Curtis, Eckart Rahn, David Friesen, Leonard Feather, Joachim-Ernst Berendt, Frankie Nemko, Chungliang Al Huang, Shelly Siegel, Eddie Sauter, Bill Finegan, Donovan, George Harrison, Paul McCartney, Ravi Shankar, Ramtha, Jack

Herschorn, David Greene, Chris Paton, David Amram, Buddy Rowell, Ralph Dyck, Patricia Willard, Chick Corea, Buddy Rich, Dick Bock, Inka Jochum, Anne Gershman, Nat Gershman, Al Schmitt, Lalo Schifrin, and many others who are too numerous to mention.

PRELUDE

This book is more to me than a diary of geographical travels and personal experiences. It is a chronicle of my spiritual odyssey, of the ways in which music and meditation have transformed my thinking and my life. My hope is that it will bring some measure of joy and comfort and insight to all who choose to take this journey with me.

Heaven and hell do not exist "out there" somewhere. They exist in our own lives, now. Life is a trip, an experience. Like a good movie, it contains all of the elements of excitement and boredom, triumph and tragedy, grief and joy, love and anger. Everything in our lives is here to teach us certain lessons, which ultimately are spiritual lessons. Awareness must come through one's *own* experience of heaven and hell. Before we can emerge from the other end of the tunnel, we must pass *through* the tunnel. I passed through. I do not believe that suffering is necessary for awakening. But sometimes it proves to be a mighty catalyst.

The joy of my earliest musical experiences led to serious classical studies, which became painful. That pain led me to popular music, the clarinet, the saxophone, and dance bands. Then I heard bebop jazz and the music of Charlie Parker—another dramatic turning point. Jazz led me to Chico

Hamilton and those wonderful years in Hollywood. My first marriage was painful—but that union was necessary in order for my sons to be born. When the Hollywood life-style lost its charm, my world felt empty and meaningless. That suffering led me to India, Maharishi, and meditation. Through meditation, I discovered my higher Self. I became quiet and serene inside; I found a new dimension. This dimension led to *Inside the Taj Mahal*; it led to leaving Hollywood; it led to a new life in Canada with my second wife, Tryntje.

Before learning how to meditate, I saw music primarily as a form of aesthetic entertainment, based upon excitement and emotional catharsis. After learning how to meditate, I valued emotional quietude and spiritual bliss as well. My vision expanded. Once consumed by ambition, I began to see that music has a higher purpose. There is more to being a musician than simply achieving fame and fortune, having one's name in the Hall of Fame or winning Grammys. I began to realize that music can be a powerful force on this planet.

The history of humankind is the history of war. By contrast, music has the power to heal, not only physically and emotionally, but politically as well. If two cultures or two large groups of people are in conflict and we come along and play music to both sides, the differences fall away in an instant. Through the universal language of music there emerges the bonding of brotherhood. And so I have traveled around the world, playing music for all who wish to listen.

Looking back over the past quarter century, we can see that the level of consciousness on our planet has changed dramatically. Music and meditation are very important parts of these changes. Slowly but surely we are coming to understand their value and power and constructive potential.

All over the world, an amazing transformation is taking place, particularly in the West and especially in the United States. We are beginning to see that meditative quietude—being centered and at peace within ourselves—has a valuable place in our culture.

There will always be noise, hyperkinetic activity, excitement, anger, frustration, rage, greed, and desperation. And there will always be certain music that reflects these things, because they are a part of life itself.

Now, however, a recognition of the value of psychological integration, meditative awareness, and inner peace is emerging. There is also a growing awareness that these states of inner well-being are *practical*. When people feel good within themselves, they are healthier and more productive. The hope for the future lies in this emergent awareness. Such perceptions, which are long overdue, are becoming more and more a significant part of the world. I do whatever I can to help.

I play many kinds of music, but I consider myself a jazz musician. The basis of jazz is spontaneous improvisation, which means one must be attuned with the living moment, fully open to its wonders, challenges, and delights. Jazz is a personal and exciting experience, always fresh, always new, always changing. Whatever I learn and experience today is added to all my yesterdays, and something a little different will come out of my horn tomorrow.

PART I

CROSSROAD

ONE

INSIDE INDIA

The plane's engines geared down for our landing in New Delhi. It was almost midnight. I looked over at my friends Henry Lewy and his wife, Nadine. They smiled and beamed. So did I.

As we walked down the plane's stairway, I looked over to the chain-link fence nearby. Dozens of poor people dressed in rags stared at us through the fence. Immediately, it felt as if we had landed on another planet. Everything was different. I could sense it in a second. Another place, another world, another time. It also felt strangely familiar.

"You're home," I thought.

I can't explain it. I had the feeling of being *home*. I remembered the psychic Betty McCain telling me that I was once a monk in India. Although I believe in past lives, I don't recall any of them. It was just some inner feeling that night, very comfortable—I had returned to a familiar place that I would relate to very well. The feeling was definitely there—that deep, unmistakable association with the word "home" and all that it connotes. I had arrived. India. Home. India.

Was I doing the right thing? Of course I was. Really? Back in Hollywood, everyone said I had to be out of my mind.

"Your name's in the paper all the time," the doctor told me when I got my inoculation shots. "You receive all kinds of promotion and publicity. That TV documentary about you—'The Story of a Jazz Musician'—was shown everywhere. The stores stock your records; you're playing in the top jazz clubs; you've got all kinds of studio work; you're famous—and yet you're walking away from it all. What's happening, Paul? Why are you doing this?"

"I don't know if I can explain it, or if I even care to," I replied. "I just have to do it. My career is not everything. In fact, success has not brought me happiness. Sure, everything is going well. I'm achieving all of my goals. Shouldn't I be happy? Well, I'm not. I have to find out why. Otherwise, my life is a waste. I'm going to India."

I hadn't lied to the doctor. Focused on my career, I was living in L.A., making a good living playing in studios and jazz clubs. The career was going well. At the same time, the rest of my life was in serious trouble. I didn't tell the doctor about that.

In 1959 my marriage to Yvonne had fallen apart, and a few years later the divorce came through. Marlen and Robin, our two sons, were growing up, and I wanted to be a good father, but studio and club work took away too much time. The fast-lane jazz life was profitable and fun, but I was losing control. Smoky nightclubs, late-night hours, marijuana, a heartbreaking affair with a beautiful actress—all of it was taking its toll. I had become a juggler on a tightrope, teetering, losing my balance, almost falling. Having lost my sense of purpose, I needed help.

Henry and Nadine Lewy introduced me to meditation, and near the end of the summer of 1966, they talked to me about their upcoming trip to India. Nadine was going to sign up for Maharishi's four-month teacher training course.

Back home that night after talking with them, I couldn't sleep. My head spun. An inner voice said to me, "Why don't *you* go to India?" Another voice said, "That's the craziest thought you ever had. You can't go to India. Look at all the recording dates you've lined up. And what about the kids? How can you leave all this?" The first voice said, "You ought to go to India. You ought to go to India." I didn't get any sleep at all that night. The next morning, I called Nadine and said, "How do you go to India?"

"This is a teacher training course," she said. "Most of these people have been meditating for years. You haven't been meditating very long."

"Is there any chance for me to come?"

"Make an appointment with Maharishi. Ask him. All he can say is no."

A month or so later, Maharishi arrived in L.A. He was staying at Mr. and Mrs. Olson's house. Nadine and I set up an appointment for me at ten o'clock in the morning.

I arrived right on time, actually a little early for a change. It was a nice old house. A lot of people were there, but they were very quiet. Around Maharishi, you don't feel like talking loudly. There's a reverence for quietude. Somebody served tea; people moved around. Some sat inside. Others sat outside on the lawn. Several people meditated while they waited.

It was ten o'clock—then eleven, twelve, and one o'clock. The day went on, but I wasn't bugged the way I normally would be. I didn't seem to be in a hurry. That was a change. I just sat quietly and meditated. Everything was cool, although when six o'clock came around, I began to get a little concerned. Maharishi's lecture was scheduled for eight o'clock. At six-thirty I was just about ready to give up, when somebody said, "Okay. Come quick. He can see you now."

Somebody led me into a small, dimly lit room where I saw this beautiful man, quietly sitting cross-legged on the floor. He was radiant. When I saw him, I lit up from within myself. There was such peacefulness about him. Time felt different in his presence. He was very busy but totally unhurried. Even if you were there only one minute, it was such a fulfilling minute, and so relaxed and unhurried, that you felt you had gotten everything done in just that one minute. I stayed perhaps three or four minutes; whatever it was, there was enough time.

His secretary introduced us. "Maharishi, this is Paul Horn." Of course, my name meant nothing to him. He did not follow the jazz trades, *down beat*, and all of that. Paul Horn was just a name. "How are you?" he said. "What can I do for you?"

"I would like to go to India in January and attend your course."

"Why do you want to go to India?"

I was not going to lie to him and say I wanted to become a teacher. I said, "I am unhappy in my life right now. Everything is confused. If I could be with you for a while, I think it would be very beneficial."

He remained quiet. Then he said, "How long have you been meditating?"

There it was. There was my fear. I hadn't meditated long enough. I figured it was going to end right there.

"Not very long, about six months. Already, I feel positive benefits."

"Are you married?"

"Divorced."

"Do you have any children?"

"Two."

"What kind of work do you do?"

"I'm a free-lance musician."

"Will your job be here when you get back?"

"A free-lance musician works for many employers. It is not steady work in a fixed job. There will be no problem when I return."

"Who will take care of your children while you are gone?"

He wanted to check me out. He wanted to make sure I wasn't escaping everything, running away from parental duties just because I was unhappy.

"I have saved some money, and I have a sense of responsibility. I have always taken care of them and will continue taking care of them when I return. I would not think of leaving them and not taking care of them."

Then there was a very long pause. Dead quiet. It seemed like an eternity.

"Okay," he said. "You come. It will be good. But *don't expect anything*."

He paused to let those words sink in. And then he said, "Are you attending the lecture tonight?"

"Yes."

"Ask some good questions."

He laughed. And that was it. That was our conversation. I felt really good, like I was floating above the ground. I was accepted. I could go. And what an adventure—leaving this whole L.A. scene, venturing out into totally uncharted waters with my friends Nadine and Henry, and I would be with this man whose presence was so powerful, even when with him for only a few minutes. In December 1966, I bought a round-the-world ticket and flew with Henry and Nadine to India to spend four months with Maharishi at his ashram in the Himalayas.

IN NEW DELHI

My first morning in New Delhi, I opened the curtains of my room at the Broadway Hotel and looked down into the marketplace. Unbelievable. "Where am I?"

Outside there were bicycles, horse-drawn carts, trucks, taxis, and people, people everywhere, buying, selling, bartering. Cows were walking all over the place, and I saw snake charmers, beggars, tourists, trained bears on chains, and acrobats. I grabbed my camera and started shooting like crazy.

Between thirty-five and forty people from a dozen different countries had signed up for Maharishi's teacher training course. I did not intend to become a teacher. I simply wanted to meditate and be with Maharishi. A great host, Maharishi wanted us to see New Delhi, and he especially wanted us to see the Taj Mahal, which is about a hundred miles from New Delhi, in a town called Agra.

This was the first time I had seen the Taj Mahal, an extraordinarily beautiful place, and we were in no hurry. During the day, and later that night, we walked in the flower gardens, sat inside, sat outside on the lawn, just gazing at the building and listening to the sound. The guide sang a note and stopped. His voice floated around the high dome like a dove, echoing again and again, so long, so lovely.

"If I ever return," I thought, "I will bring my flute. Perhaps I can play in here. With the echo, the flute will sound especially beautiful."

For about three days, we toured New Delhi and visited the Taj, and then things started getting serious. For the past seven years, Maharishi had held an event called the World Assembly. This year was the Eighth World Assembly. Even though he had no backing or support at that time, he always had the vision of a worldwide movement.

He thought in big terms, and he had infinite patience, a quality money can't buy. If you have infinite patience, you will always win—because you have infinite patience. You're not in a hurry for somebody else's decision or for things to go your way. You just plow straight through. And you can wait for eternity. That's the way Maharishi is. You can never wear him down. He doesn't get upset because things move slowly. He just goes ahead, just goes ahead, just goes ahead, little by little, straight ahead.

Maharishi envisioned the spiritual regeneration of the whole world, not through religious belief, but through meditation, which is nondenominational and has nothing to do with belief systems. If people meditate, they will find their own inner being, and the answers will come by themselves. Maharishi wanted to set people on the path of meditation and give them a technique. He neither challenged nor provided belief systems. It took time for people to understand this point, and many, of course, have never understood it. But that's where he was coming from.

So Maharishi held the Eighth World Assembly in New Delhi. He had a plan and a meeting place. Every night he gave lectures in an auditorium that seated about a thousand. Important people attended. We sat on stage with him. He sat in the center, in a big chair, with flowers all around. His Indian disciples, who were with him all the time, sat on stage with us. They sat on the floor around and in front of him. We sat in chairs. The men among us wore ties and sports coats, while the women wore saris.

Before each of these evenings, Maharishi met with us. He dictated individual speeches that we would make, having us write them down, refining every word. He did not want to leave it up to us to ad lib.

Then, at the lecture, he gave a talk about his intentions and about the promise Transcendental Meditation held for the world. After that, in parliamentary fashion, he had a person from each country stand up and say, "Maharishi, I would like to make a motion."

A medical doctor from Argentina, for example, stood up and said, "I am a physician from Argentina, and I can see where meditation would be of great benefit for people who are physically ill." He talked about stress reduction and physiologically refining the nervous system, which automatically leads to a higher state of consciousness.

Then a woman stood up and said, "I am from a different walk of life. I am a housewife, living in Montreal. I would like to second the doctor's motion to have Transcendental Meditation entered as a valid technique for improving a person's physical well-being."

Every night, people from all walks of life put forth motions. I got up and said, "Hi, I'm Paul Horn, a musician from Hollywood." (Maharishi specifically wanted me to mention Hollywood. Everybody knows Hollywood. They'll be impressed.) "I can see where meditation would be of great benefit in the arts. It stimulates creativity. Your mind becomes more settled. Creative energy, which is always there, is allowed to manifest itself, and the person receives more creative energy in a greater flow." Someone else got up and seconded that. Then there was a question-and-answer period. This went on for three days.

It was amazing to see the wide range of people there, a mixture of high government officials along with impoverished people just off the street. That's the way it is in India.

Some man in rags, literally living on the street, a man who had absolutely nothing, would raise his hand and get up and ask in English—not his native tongue—a very deep philosophical question that would blow all our minds. And Maharishi would answer him.

It was fascinating to hear the different types of questions. Typical questions from Westerners were, "Why are you charging for this? Where is all the money going? Why do you wear those long robes? What are all the flowers for?" By contrast, the Indians asked "good questions," as Maharishi called them, and raised high philosophical issues, perhaps challenging Lord Krishna on a point made in the Bhagavad Gita, their spiritual book.

These three days were very successful. The questions and answers were documented and printed out on Maharishi's primitive printing press.

Then it came time to travel north to the ashram, about 150 miles away. How were we going to get there? By taxicab!

AT THE ASHRAM

Traveling by taxi is normal in India, and it's very cheap. To go this 150 miles, it cost about five dollars per person, four people to a cab. We put our luggage in the trunk and on top of the car in a rack. It was like a convoy, with about fifteen cabs.

We drove on country roads, and it took ten hours to get to the ashram. We passed through Hardwar, a holy town, where we took a bridge across the Ganges River. We drove the bumpy, washed-out dirt road through the jungle, where we were in danger of wild tigers and elephants. After a long, noisy ride, we arrived at the ashram after midnight and began four months of life with Maharishi.

From the flatlands, you can see the snowcapped Himalayas rising up in the distance, continuing on for hundreds of miles, all the way to Kashmir, from where you can see the snow-covered peak of Manga Parbat. Maharishi's ashram sits on a knoll, about 500 feet above the Ganges.

The word "ashram" means two things—a place of learning, and a place of refuge. In towns like Bombay and New Delhi, ashrams are like Salvation Army centers, where homeless people can get a hot meal and a place to sleep at night. Maharishi's ashram is a place of learning.

The government granted Maharishi a lease for five acres of land in the Himalayan foothills, across the river from Rishikesh, a city that Indians consider holy because it is thousands of years old and mentioned in the Vedas. "Rishi" means wise, and "kesh" means city. It's a city of the wise men. "Maharishi" means "great wise man" or "great teacher."

Originally, there was nothing on the hill where the ashram now stands. Maharishi and his disciples—celibate monks in training called Brahmacharies—built everything. The disciples were there to learn from Maharishi, to be around him, and to work at the ashram.

There was always construction going on there, supplied mostly by Sikh laborers. At first, the noise annoyed us. All day long, we heard band saws and hammers and talking. The crows cawed in the jungle, and the monkeys chattered and jumped around, sometimes landing on the roof.

"Good God, Maharishi," we complained. "We've come thousands of miles to get away from big cities, where it's always noisy. We came all the way to the Himalayas to be quiet and to meditate. Listen to this racket."

He always said, "Yes, of course. I'll see what I can do." And he sent men to chase the crows out of the trees. It was sort of humorous, and you knew the noise was not going to go away.

From that incident we learned a lesson: silence is not a prerequisite for meditation. You should be able to sit in the middle of the intersection at Hollywood and Vine and go within yourself. It's just an attitude. If you set up the idea that it has to be quiet before you can meditate, then you're in trouble. It's almost impossible to find a quiet place. Even if you do, when you leave and go somewhere else, you won't be able to meditate there because it will be too noisy for you. After a while, our attitude changed. We accepted the noise, and eventually it didn't make any difference.

We had to make a number of internal adjustments, especially during the first few weeks. We were involved in the process of learning how to settle down and unwind. That sounds easy, but it isn't.

None of us knew just how wound up we had become over the years. Like twisted rubber bands, we had become tighter and tighter within ourselves. It took at least six weeks before we could unwind enough to be able to settle into longer meditations. As you slowly begin to relax, your nervous system starts to purify itself, gradually releasing stress. Then you are able to sit and meditate for longer periods of time.

Back home in urban society, it is dangerous, even impossible, to do lengthy meditations because there is too much tension in the atmosphere, and the demands from daily life are intense and extreme. You can't simply say, "I think I'll sit down and meditate for six hours."

Most people work from nine to five, looking forward to a two-week vacation once a year. Rarely, if ever, can they take even a brief time-out from their daily routine, and a two-week vacation does not even begin to unwind them. Besides, with all the tourists and hassles, vacations usually increase stress rather than decrease it.

Almost never do we get a time to ourselves, even when we fall asleep. The only reason we go to sleep is that we are too fatigued to maintain a waking state of consciousness. That kind of sleep does not take us to any deep levels, and we do not wake up feeling rested.

Back home, stress seems normal. Caffeine gets us up; tranquilizers bring us down. On the surface, these and other drugs temporarily give us energy or cool us out. On a deeper level, however, they only compress the emotional junk inside of us, which gets harder and tighter as it becomes more compressed. Our stress increases, and we wonder why we feel so lousy most of the time. The majority of us live with enormous tension inside ourselves—and we don't even know it. Meanwhile, stress accumulates, little by little, building up like cholesterol, until we are so stifled by it that we are literally ready to die.

But when you visit a place like an ashram and your daily activities are reduced to a comfortable minimum, then day by day, you begin to let go of accumulated stresses. After that, you can sit for longer periods of time. Activity and stress take us away from our essential nature. Meditation helps us rediscover it.

So I sat there for several weeks. Mentally, however, I was still grinding axes I had carried with me from back home. Trying to meditate, I'd find myself angry at some guy who had screwed me in a business deal. Or I'd recall some scene I'd had with my actress lover and find myself getting upset with her, as if she were right there in the room with me.

This is ridiculous, I thought to myself one day. Here you are, thirty-six years old, as far away from Hollywood as you can possibly get, literally on the other side of the world. You're sitting by the Ganges in the Himalayas, and yet you are *still* wrestling with problems that plagued you back home.

At that moment, it clicked in for me rather profoundly—you are where your mind is, not where your body is. That realization was not just somebody else's abstract idea. It came out of my own experience, directly, and it brought home full-force to me the reason I was here.

I came to the ashram to heal myself mentally and emotionally, not physically. The mind is tricky. You can't run away from problems or heartbreak, no matter where you go. Regardless of where you find yourself physically, you still carry all of your mental and emotional baggage around with you. To me, that was a revelation.

There was another adjustment I had to make, and it, too, led to a beneficial insight.

Maharishi never forced anything at all upon us. He just talked. We accepted whatever we wanted and discarded the rest. He gave wonderful philosophical discourses, and my listening time was very precious to me.

One English fellow, however, was not interested in listening and receiving. He took great pleasure in continually arguing. Whenever Maharishi made a statement about karma or something, the Englishman popped in with his heavy British accent and debated the point, apparently trying to prove to himself that he could intellectually match wits with Maharishi. He constantly disrupted Maharishi's flow of thoughts and our concentration. Instead of simply accepting or rejecting Maharishi's ideas, he fragmented the atmosphere and wasted everybody's time. This went on for several weeks, and all of us were getting bugged at him.

After a month or so of this, I was walking back to my room after the evening lecture, talking with a very nice lady from Montreal. She had been with Maharishi the year before, and this was her second time at the ashram. She was a TM teacher. Her husband was in the diplomatic corps, I believe, and she had been teaching meditation in Laos. I confided to her that I was upset with this English guy, who was driving me crazy with his pseudo-intellectual game-playing.

"Just keep remembering why you are here," she said. "You are here to be with Maharishi, to *just be* with him. Don't let these other things sidetrack you. Forget about the Englishman. Focus on Maharishi."

It was great advice, very meaningful to me. From that time on, whenever the Englishman did his thing, I watched it as a dance.

The woman from Montreal also helped me learn what it meant to "just be" with Maharishi. He said important things, but ultimately those things were secondary. The truly important thing was the sheer beauty and power of his presence. These matters are true, and very subtle. The important thing is to experience them—which I was learning to do.

As I reflect back, I now see what was perhaps the most important thing of all for me. I was freed from the daily routine and allowed to unwind from accumulated stress in the protective presence of a sensitive, intelligent, enlightened man who loved me and understood what I was going through.

At the ashram we stayed in *puris*, U-shaped apartment blocks that accommodated about eight rooms. There were some six *puris*, about forty-eight rooms, equipped with Western-style toilets and showers. It's unusual to see a Western-style toilet anywhere in India. A few of the rooms had bathtubs. The rooms were simple, with a cement floor, throw rug, bed, desk, chair, and lamp. That was it. Most people hung a picture of Maharishi on the wall.

We even had hot water, which was unusual in India. A five- or ten-gallon tank stood behind each *puri*. A worker kept a fire going. So, at certain hours of the day, we had hot water.

We enjoyed a view of the Ganges on one side of the ashram. That's where the dining hall was, an open area with wooden latticework for walls and a ceiling. It never rained while we were there.

The kitchen was primitive, just a pit in the ground with a big fire in the bottom. You never drank unboiled water. Boiled water was always available. We dipped in our thermos jars and brought the water back to our rooms.

Food was simple—rice, vegetables, and *dal*, a kind of lentil dish. They also had Indian bread, sort of like Mexican tortillas, called *chapati*, and fruit, cheese, butter, and milk from water buffaloes. They always served tea in the afternoon, a custom left over from the British. Coffee was available for those who wanted it. All kinds of flowers grew in the gardens, which were nicely kept by the workers.

Maharishi had a house, a luxury by Indian standards, built for him by his disciples. It was made of brick, well constructed, with a meeting room large enough to hold twenty or thirty people if they sat on the floor close together. Maharishi's bedroom was small and simple and plain, visually attractive, built with love.

People came to see him constantly. He held private audiences in his house. Every day, you'd see people coming up from New Delhi, often important government people. There were Japanese faces, German faces, American faces, Indian dignitaries. His days were always full, but he stopped those appointments when it came time to meet with us because his primary focus was on the people who had come to be with him for the training course.

Maharishi was always concerned for the comfort and well-being of visiting Westerners, taking time out from his various meetings to ask, "How is everyone? Is everybody comfortable? Are there any problems?" If a person raised a hand, Maharishi discussed the problem, taking as long as necessary—maybe a few minutes, maybe an hour, sometimes more, never hurrying. "We don't have enough fruit, Maharishi," or "We need more blankets at night," or "Lucy is sick and needs medicine." He took whatever time was needed and was a very considerate man. He'd take off on some amazing philosophical discourse and then come right back to the mundane—"You need a hot water bottle?" It was a real lesson to watch him.

He discouraged people from leaving the ashram and going out into the jungle. Tigers don't usually walk into places where there are people, but they do roam the jungles.

And there were a lot of monkeys. One kind was brown. The others were gray-white, with black faces and hands and feet. Families with little babies climbed the trees and sat there, or jumped from branch to branch, sometimes landing right on the roof above us while we were meditating.

Occasionally, we walked down to the Ganges and went swimming. The water was cold and very clean. Fine sand with mica in it covered the banks. It sparkled and glistened and felt good to walk on.

MAHARISHI

We tend to think that important people will be big and tall. When I first met Maharishi, I was surprised to see that he stood only 5′4″ or so. Although he is deceivingly short, he is a powerfully built man, with broad shoulders, thick chest, thick arms, and very strong forearms.

He wears a dhoti, or two white sheets, wrapped in a certain way. The lower cloth is wrapped around the waist and forms a long, ankle-length skirt. The upper cloth is draped over the shoulders and across the chest to look like a shawl that leaves the forearms exposed. Seen from a distance, it looks like one long white covering.

Some Indian men wear saffron-colored dhotis, but Maharishi wears a white one. That color has to do with the monastic order and caste he's in. Maharishi is a Shastria, a member of the warrior caste. Indeed, he is a warrior, not in the physical sense, but in the sense that he is battling to raise the consciousness of humankind. He's been out there doing it every day for the last thirty years or more, with only two to four hours' sleep a night. For the first fifteen years, he traveled constantly around the world. Then he settled down to form the organization that exists today.

When I met him, he had long straight hair, about shoulder-length. His dark beard was beginning to turn white in the center, and he had a dark moustache. Today, his hair is all white, thin on top, long on the sides and back.

Maharishi is a handsome man, really beautiful looking. He has dark skin, full lips, a broad nose, widely set eyes. His eyes grab you. It is said that the eyes are the windows of the soul. Love and intelligence and a twinkle of humor flow out of Maharishi's eyes continuously. His eyes pull you toward him and make him extremely attractive.

I love Maharishi's sense of humor, something I wish I could develop more in myself. I do love a good laugh, and I've noticed that the great teachers I've come across always incorporate a good sense of humor into their talks. It's fun to listen to them, and it's fun to learn from them. It's not a chore, something you have to work hard to plow through.

Maharishi is always laughing. Indeed, gales of laughter is sort of his public trademark. It's a kind of cosmic humor. He sees everything as being funny. Once in a while I've reached that point. When things get really bad, sometimes you laugh. You think to yourself, "Am I going crazy? What am I laughing at?" But when your situation has become ludicrous and you can get far enough up to look down at it, it's actually funny.

Maharishi seems to be that high. He looks at life and sees the plan. He also sees what people have set in motion for themselves—and he laughs at it. He sees the humor in it. Not that he is an unconcerned person. Just the opposite—he is extremely concerned. But he has attained the perspective where he can laugh at things and not take them too seriously. He's fully aware of the problems we have on earth, but he does not let it permeate his being, nor does he go around all day with a heavy head. He laughs a lot.

He does a tremendous amount of work. And yet, when you are with him, you never feel rushed or hurried. With other people, you often feel as if you're taking up their valuable time. With Maharishi, who is always busy with a full schedule, you feel as though he has given you full time, even if it's only a minute or two.

True, you have to learn how to wait for him, which is typical of all the gurus I've been around. They make appointments, but you shouldn't expect them to be anywhere near on time. Maybe that has a dual purpose. On the one hand, they *are* busy, and they do take time with each person, and they cannot adhere to a rigid schedule. On the other hand, it teaches you how to be flexible and patient.

He seemed to be tireless. I once watched how he slept. At the World Assembly in New Delhi, he spent all day with us as a group. He spent time with us individually, helping us write out our speeches for the formal presentations. Then he led the evening meetings, which lasted about four hours, with us sitting on stage feeling physically uncomfortable.

The meetings ended around midnight. Maharishi went back to his room, where he began speaking with the next day's people. That's when I had the chance to watch him.

I was in his room with three other people. We were going to speak in the meeting the next day, and he was writing our speeches. He semi-reclined on his bed, which was on the floor. It was nearly three o'clock in the morning. We were fading, but there was Maharishi, still going strong.

He was talking; then suddenly he stopped talking. We waited. We looked at him. He had dozed off. We sat quietly for twenty or thirty seconds. He opened his eyes and continued talking, picking up exactly where he had left off. It wasn't "Where was I?" If his sentence had stopped in the middle, he picked it up precisely there, right at the word where he'd stopped. He hadn't lost his train of thought. He had just faded for a few seconds.

He continued talking, then he stopped and dozed again, maybe forty-five seconds this time. The breaks got longer and longer, with him still picking up the sentence without missing a beat. Finally, it reached the point where he was out. He never said, "I think I'm tired now, folks. Time to go to bed. Excuse me." He doesn't do that. He works until he can't work anymore, and then he falls asleep. That's when the people leave. In two, three, maybe four hours, he's up and going again. He's been doing this consistently for thirty years.

This is an example of the kind of energy that can come through a person who has this kind of awareness. When you use your full mental and spiritual potential, you are in a state of cosmic consciousness, also called enlightenment. When you use 100 percent of your mind, you also gain incredible physical energy. That's where Maharishi is. He is a living example of what he talks about philosophically. He's a human being, a person just like everyone else, but he's different because he is using all of his potential. All humans have the capacity to develop themselves to this extent, but few of us do it. And that's what meditation is about—learning how to connect with your higher inner Self, how to discover and develop your full potential.

As a bandleader, I found it fascinating and instructive to see how Maharishi incorporates other people into his decision-making process. During that first year, there were some forty people around him; the second year, maybe a hundred. Most of them would have been content if Maharishi solved the problems or made the decisions himself simply by saying, "Here's what you do. . . ." But he never did that.

Instead of just telling people what to do, he said, "What do you think? Should we do this? How about this? What do you think about that?" He often involved the whole ashram, not just the particular group who had to solve the problem. Pretty soon, everyone participated, adding their own thoughts on the matter under discussion.

Now, he might already have the solution clear in his mind, and in the final analysis, he would work it so that it came to his way of thinking. He'd say, "Oh, that's very good, but don't you think maybe we could do it this way?" And he turned it around. He took what you said and agreed with you, and then cleverly worked it so it ultimately came out the way he wanted it. At the same time, everyone had contributed something, and they felt important. If you're an employer and you treat your employees that way, you will probably run a successful business, because that's good management.

The whole point is that Maharishi is a practical man. Here he is, a reclusive monk from the Himalayas, a man who spent thirteen years of his life in isolated existence with his master, much of it in a cave. And yet he is deeply knowledgeable about ways of becoming successful in the material world. He's a good businessman.

Being around him, I learned many things spiritually, but I also learned a lot about life and how to handle people. It was fascinating and very beneficial for me to observe him at work and to be a part of that process.

Just before Maharishi's master, Guru Dev, died, he called his disciples around him and told each one what he wanted him to do. He was in good health, but he was in his eighties and felt his mission had been accomplished. It was time for him to go. Like many Indian masters of the past, he knew how to withdraw his life energy, how to condense it and release it. He called his disciples to him and said he would be passing away the next morning at 11:00 A.M. This is called Maha Samadhi.

He bestowed his monastic authority on one disciple, choosing that man to take his place. Many thought Maharishi would have been the one chosen for the post, but he wasn't.

To Maharishi, Guru Dev said, "I have something for you to do that I feel is more important. I want you to bring the knowledge of meditation to people all over the world. People suffer and they are miserable. With meditation, they can emerge from their misery. They can begin to evolve. They can experience more joy in their lives. I want you to develop your knowledge of meditation into a system and go out into the world and bring it to people everywhere."

Maharishi hesitated. He felt reluctant and inadequate. The enormity of the challenge was overwhelming. He didn't know if he had the energy, the strength, or the capabilities to live up to such a commitment.

Guru Dev saw Maharishi's concern. He brought Maharishi closer to him and said, "You have thousands of lifetimes. Could you not devote just one to this?"

The next morning, at precisely the time he had predicted, Guru Dev took his Maha Samadhi. For the next two years, Maharishi wandered around India, developing the system known as Transcendental Meditation. Guru Dev taught him how to meditate, but Maharishi devised the ways of presenting it to ordinary people as a technique. For the following fifteen years, with very little money, he traveled around the world, talking to people everywhere, and successfully built his present organization.

GIVING UP EXPECTATIONS

There is an ancient Zen story about a bright young student being introduced to the master. While the master pours tea, the student is expounding, trying to impress the teacher with his knowledge and insight.

The master is pouring the tea—and pouring and pouring. The cup fills up and overflows and spills out all over the table. The dumbfounded student says, "Master, the cup is full and running over. None of the tea is going into the cup."

The master replies, "The cup is full. So are you. Before I can teach you anything, you must empty your cup. Only then can I put something into it."

This is true for everyone. Before any guru can teach you, you have to be able to receive his teachings. If your mind is full of ideas, expectations, and preconceptions, how can the guru put anything new into your head? The Bible says, "Before you can enter the kingdom of heaven, you must become as a child." The word "child" does not mean one who is selfish, immature, or silly. It means being open and empty. It means you enter a state of receptive innocence.

Most of the people in the ashram wanted to become teachers. That was their aim. In no way did I have that in mind, and thus I was not anxious about anything, which was a kind of blessing. Maharishi had said to me, "Come to India, but don't expect anything." I have continued to learn from that phrase over the years, applying it to all facets of my life.

The premise is valid. If we harbor preconceived ideas, then we are bound by those preconceptions, and we limit our capacity to experience life directly. Expectation is bondage.

All of us resist change. We can free ourselves considerably, however, if we allow some leeway for change. "Don't expect anything" simply means, "Be open to the moment."

You can't preconceive a moment. How can you be open to the moment when you hold a preconception about what it should be? If that moment does not fit your preconception and expectation, then you miss it. You don't see it for what it is, and it isn't what you thought it would be, and therefore you are disappointed.

The majority of us don't wake up for the day when we get out of bed. We open our eyes, but we don't really *show up*. Because of our fixed ideas and preconceptions and expectations, we remain asleep. Showing up means arriving each day, fully present, filled with enthusiasm about our lives. Showing up is an attitude, a perspective —a willingness to be open and receptive, a willingness to experience the living moment in living time.

If you visit a new country and you just show up, without expectations, and whatever is there is okay with you, then wonderful things happen and you gain the experience of what that country truly is. If you love hamburgers but they don't serve hamburgers, right away you're bummed out. But if you forget the hamburgers and just enjoy the food they do serve, then you are free. Instead of experiencing misery over disappointed expectations, you experience the delight of surprise. You're free because you're open.

Maharishi and other gurus are always changing their minds. They'll say, "Tomorrow we'll have a picnic." You go to bed excited because tomorrow you're going on a picnic. The next morning the guru says, "We're not going to have a picnic." He doesn't give a reason. We're just not going to have a picnic. There you are, disappointed.

Maharishi constantly changes his mind, and he does it on purpose, throwing you off-base, teaching you not to expect. He can't just say it because mere intellectual understanding of this concept is not enough to change it. He changes expectations by constantly frustrating you.

When he was a disciple, his master sent him all over the Himalayas. "Here, take this over to that guru," his master would say. Maharishi would walk thirty miles and give it to him. Then the guru would say, "I don't want this. You brought it to the wrong place. You should go over there," and Maharishi would take it another twenty miles somewhere else.

This sort of inconsistency and reversal goes on continually in the ashram, until you come to the point that you *surrender* your expectations. Once you give them up, then you are open and can receive new information.

It is very difficult to progress in this world. We are all fixed in our perceptions. We are all brainwashed. We are all conditioned. When we encounter real knowledge, it is almost impossible for us to receive it because we are too full, like the teacup. It is a rare opportunity, a great experience, to be with a teacher who can show you how to empty your teacup, how to become open and receptive to new insight, new knowledge, and new wisdom.

DISCOVERING THE INNER WITNESS

When you meditate, you are not blanked out, as some people think. Your mind continues, and your thoughts stream by. In meditation, you learn how to become detached from your thoughts. You watch them, like a movie, without getting emotionally involved with them. You just observe—you watch how your mind is working; you pay attention to how thoughts arise, what they do, where they go. You watch the whole process and learn how to be a witness, how to be detached, how to observe without judgment.

This is an important state of awareness, and we rarely experience it. Of course, we are participants in life. But we can also be observers or witnesses. That witness part is usually submerged, and it may never emerge, not even in a lifetime, because we are constantly caught up in life's activities. In the activity of life we lose the awareness of who we are through the process of identification. When we rediscover the detached, nonidentified witness within ourselves, we regain an important part of our nature.

The course at the ashram followed a kind of curve. At first, two hours were set aside for meditation after breakfast. Following meditation, we met with Maharishi for a lecture, which lasted about an hour. Then we ate lunch and met again with Maharishi from two o'clock until four. After another two-hour meditation, we ate dinner, then met again with Maharishi for his evening lecture.

As I mentioned, Maharishi never asked us to believe anything. He simply exposed us to certain knowledge, and we accepted whatever we could. If we couldn't accept something, we discarded it. After a while even that

Englishman I mentioned began to see this principle. If we chose to enjoy Maharishi's insight and make use of it, fine. If we chose not to, that was all right too.

There were times after those evening lectures when I felt higher than I could get in any other way. Maharishi blew away preconceptions. He opened our minds. He unveiled deep knowledge that has been around forever, passed from teachers to disciples since the beginnings of civilization.

Two weeks into the course, Maharishi cut out the morning lecture. We devoted that time to meditation, about four hours. In another month, Maharishi eliminated the afternoon lectures. Most of the day was now devoted to meditation, after which we met in the evening.

Then Maharishi started a little competition. He put a chart on the dining room door. It had everyone's name on it, and the question, "How many hours did you meditate today?"

After a while, you felt guilty if you meditated only six hours, because here's some other guy who meditated twelve hours, another who meditated eighteen hours, still another who meditated the whole day, twenty-four hours. Maharishi was pushing us to get into that state of transcendental consciousness a little longer.

I started to get frustrated. One day, I said, "I can get up to eighteen hours, but I can't get past that. How do these other people do it? What is the secret?" Maharishi's answer: "Simply sit and meditate." In other words, "Stop making excuses—just do it."

In long meditations, certain things happen. You're in your room, sitting with your eyes closed, and you don't come out. People bring you food, but you keep your eyes closed. You sit on the floor or on the bed or in a chair. You don't have to sit cross-legged. The food they bring you is light—fruit, tea, cheese, bread, butter. You're not expending a lot of physical energy, so you don't have great hunger pangs, but the food is there for you. Things are arranged ahead of time. "Look, I'm going to meditate for a couple of days. Would you bring my food?" They take care of you.

Even when you're sitting with your eyes closed, you can feel sleep coming on. You don't resist it. You just lie down and go to sleep. When you wake up, you wake up in your mind, but you don't open your eyes. It's very important to keep your eyes closed. That way, you maintain a quieter state. If you open your eyes, visual information floods your mind and draws you to the surface. To maintain the deeper state, you keep your eyes closed, even when you go to the bathroom. That's the way we did our long meditations.

Once I got through the first twenty-four hours, it was easy. I sat for eighty-five hours. I wanted to go a full week, but someone came to me and said, "Maharishi wants you to come out now. You should attend this evening's lecture." Well, I didn't want to come out, but I did. It's like jogging. That first mile is hard, but pretty soon something kicks over in your body; you get your second wind, and then you can jog for a long time. It's the same thing with meditation. Once you pass a certain point of resistance, it's easy. Sitting there and doing nothing—that was one of the most interesting experiences of my life.

In meditation, you become aware of other senses. For example, I could feel the weight of certain times of the day. Twelve noon feels different from twelve midnight. We all know this, but now I know it from a different angle. I can feel the atmosphere. Everything settles down and gets quiet at midnight. The early morning hours are very peaceful. There's not much activity. When I'm just sitting there, eyes closed, I become sensitive to this.

Normally, I wouldn't notice, because if I'm awake at one o'clock in the morning back in L.A., I'm playing a jazz gig in some club, or I'm out with people getting something to eat. That's my normal experience of one o'clock in the morning. Now, however, I have the experience of just sitting there, experiencing what one o'clock in the morning truly feels like, without noise, activity, conversation, or any other distraction, and it's different.

Four o'clock in the morning is the time when the air is richest with energy, a life-energy called prana. That's when the dew comes out, awakening the flowers and plants for the day. That's a high energy, and it happens around four o'clock in the morning. This is why the yogis do their breathing exercises and meditations at that time, four to five, when the prana is the heaviest with creative, uplifting energy.

And then you begin to hear sounds—animals with bells around their necks, monkeys chattering, birds singing, people waking up and getting ready for work. I never took time out to hear these things before. In fact, I never took the time to truly feel what each hour of a twenty-four-hour period feels like.

As you sit there, you can feel the energy of the day pick up. It's nine o'clock in the morning, ten o'clock—you feel the changing temperatures. Around noon, things are really bustling, and it's warmer. About five, things start to settle down, and then evening arrives. There's still activity, but things are getting more gentle—animal sounds in the jungle, people coming home, children playing.

After that eighty-five hour meditation, I wrote these entries in my diary:

First day: So-so. Many thoughts. A little difficult to settle down. Slept six hours at night.

Second day: Much easier. Fewer thoughts. Many periods of absence of everything, including the mantra.

Then, in the evening for about three hours, a feeling of great joy. Seems as though I was in the Transcendent continuously. Smile always present, with many periods of laughter. Very rewarding experience.

All events of our life, if viewed from a great enough distance, are extremely funny. We must get beyond personal feelings to experience this. From this vantage point, life is viewed objectively as a fantastic voyage.

Third day: Many hang-ups in my personality and in past actions became clear to me in an objective way. A good indication for change in behavior patterns for the future. A clearer perception of basic truths. The realization that liberation is possible in this lifetime took hold of me, and I experienced more fully than ever before the enormity of Transcendental Meditation.

The late afternoon and evening are restless for me. Mostly physical— so I am lying down quite a bit and not forcing anything. Slept nine hours.

Fourth day: Now I know the fullness of life. I need never feel lonely or empty again because I know how to contact Being, my own source. I now feel purpose flowing through my veins again.

Seeking personal recognition is shallow and ultimately nonrewarding. But it is a forerunner of higher purpose, and a necessary phase of evolution.

One need never force decisions. They never come out right that way anyway. The thing to do is sit down quietly and meditate, and, having reached the field of Being for a few minutes, the answers come unbidden.

Through these means, it is not the "I" who makes the decision. It comes from the field of the Absolute, not the ever-changing world of the relative.

Whatever actions we take should be done with purity of heart. Then all the forces in nature support us.

Formula for a happy life—

1. Don't worry.
2. Keep smiling (with joy).
3. Send out good vibrations.
4. Meditate morning and evening.
5. Take life easy in between.
6. Sit in patience (all seeds planted grow in their own time).

When people emerge from long meditations, it's almost difficult to look into their eyes. There's something there, in their eyes, like a beam of light. It looks almost unreal. After you sit that long and have all these inner experiences, it shows up in your eyes.

After meditating for eighty-five hours, I walked into the evening lecture that night, and everyone said, "Man, you ought to see your eyes. They look like two searchlights." Of course, if I looked into a mirror, my eyes wouldn't necessarily look that way to me. Nevertheless, when deep internal transformations take place, you can see them in a person's eyes.

After you have completed a long meditation, Maharishi likes to visit with you to discuss your experiences and answer any questions you may have. When I went to see him this time, I felt enormous love for him. I felt transformed through him, through his being there, through his setting up the conditions and methods for me to experience these things. I had great, great love for him. That is the only way I can put it.

At that moment, I think I experienced what is called surrender. I felt that he was a master—not a superman, not a god, but a truly enlightened, high human being. Bowing down and touching his feet, my heart full of love, I surrendered to him. Whatever resistance I might have had toward him, or toward anything, had melted away. I was totally open. My cup was empty.

A huge weight had been lifted and flung away. I was free. I felt great happiness. I think I was feeling what is called bliss, so good, so true, so radiantly joyous.

The problems that racked my brains two months ago when I was sitting by the Ganges now seemed like nothing. I felt completely cleansed of business hang-ups and neurotic preoccupations about the ways of love and need. My mind and heart felt clear and clean and full of joy. To me this was a miraculous event.

In the West, we think in dualistic terms. We regard you-me, us-them, spirit-flesh, nature-human, war-peace, and so forth as separate, often conflicting opposites. Dualistic terms are military terms. Somebody wins; somebody loses. As a result, the word "surrender" nearly always means "defeat" to the Western mind. When you surrender, you have lost the war. You surrender because you are in a losing situation.

From a spiritual point of view, however, the word "surrender" means just the opposite—you are liberated from the ego, freed from bondage to the personal self.

I continually marvel at the way we are as human beings. I also marvel at the game of life—and life *is* a game, a tremendous and mysterious game, an incredible game.

God created us out of Himself. Every cell in my body is individual and has a life of its own, and yet each is all Paul Horn; similarly, all individual human beings are cells in the body of God. God has manifested Himself as us and as everything else that exists.

He created us and gave us *free will* to choose and create our own lives, and then He set us in motion. The catch is, we are responsible for our choices; like the law of physics, every action has an equal and opposite reaction. In metaphysical terms, this is called karma.

We live our life and make many choices and build up much karma. Then we die. But the soul's journey is incomplete. For the soul, there is unfinished business here, situations that remain unresolved. Therefore, our soul reincarnates and continues on, making more choices and building more karma, until somewhere along the way we realize how lost we are—how separate and far-removed we are from God, our Source, our Father, our Selves. As soon as we realize how lost we are, we begin trying to find our way home again. This is the game, the wonderful game of life, the purpose and goal of which is to know and realize who we truly are (Self-realization) and to go home again—like E. T.: "home . . . home . . . home."

No matter who we are, we still look in the mirror in the morning. We shave or put on makeup. We are involved with ourselves on every level.

That preoccupation goes on and on, and it all revolves around our identification with our body and our identification with who we think we are.
We have a name; we have brown, blonde, or black hair; we have height and
weight; we are male or female, white or black, red or yellow. Whatever we
are, we have a self, an ego, an identity. It is miraculous to think beyond
those terms, of course, but most of us do not.

Some do, however. When we wish to explore this phenomenon called
the Self, we embark upon a journey. It is the inner journey, the journey of
the psyche and the spirit. As we travel this path, we soon encounter a seemingly insurmountable paradox. In order to find out who we truly are, we
have to lose ourselves, who we *think* we are. We have to shed this ego. We
have to give up our sense of personal identity. How do we do that? How
can we possibly get rid of ourselves and still be here? This is the paradox.

The whole thing comes down to the word "surrender," not in the Western sense, but in the spiritual sense. A moment arrives when our particular,
individual personality is no longer important to us. A much greater love
wells up inside. Because of this expansive, all-encompassing love, we suddenly have an infinitely wider view of life—an eternal perspective, if you
will.

That is the moment of surrender. No longer do we cling to our personal
identity. We let it go. And when we do, we experience an exhilarating sense
of freedom, an exuberant lightness of being. The weight of this burden we
were carrying—that heavy ego—is lifted from our shoulders, not because
we don't care about it anymore, but because we are not attached to it.
When we lose our personal self, we discover our higher Self, which is who
we truly are.

We need a person we can look up to when we are children, someone
greater than ourselves who understands and forgives us. These people are
usually found among our parents and teachers.

As we mature and become concerned about spiritual matters, we still
need a father image, but for many people, including myself, "God, the Father" is too abstract. Where is this God? Is He sitting on a cloud in heaven
somewhere? I found a man who in my view is the living presence of God
in a pure form. Maharishi doesn't say he is, but I feel that he is, and that is
why I selected him to be my guide on the spiritual journey.

There are any number of authentic gurus around. They don't necessarily
have to wear white robes and be Himalayan monks. A guru might be some-

one who just comes along in our life, perhaps our mate. It doesn't have to be a registered holy person who carries a diploma and wears a certain dhoti.

A guru can be any human being who mirrors where you are not; who lets you be safely vulnerable and constructively open; who has enough insight to understand you; who loves and respects you as a self-fulfilling divinity in your own right; who can forgive you under any circumstances because, not only are you divine, you are human as well. And I bow down to that.

A guru is a spiritual guide. When you bow down to him, you are not bowing to him personally. You are really bowing down to your higher Self. Of course, you could bow down to yourself, but it is easier to touch someone else's feet. It is also easier to bow down to someone else than it is to say, "I am bowing down to myself." In essence, however, you *are* bowing to yourself, your higher Self—which is the same as the guru's higher Self, and the same as all of our higher Selves. On this level, we are unified as One.

Each day at the ashram we took little walks. One morning soon after my arrival, I watched as the men working at the ashram stopped whatever they were doing. They went over to Maharishi, who was taking his morning walk, and bowed down to him and touched his feet. They did this whenever Maharishi took his walks.

"I can accept their doing that," I thought, "but I would never do it myself."

Maharishi has a nice gentle way when people bow down to him. He knows why they bow, even if they don't, and he knows what bowing is about. He does not ask them to bow, nor is he trying to play God. He allows bowing because that is what people in India do to acknowledge holy men and their own higher Selves.

When anybody bows and touches his feet, Maharishi reaches down with his hand and very gently moves his fingertips across their forehead in a little fluttering motion, as if he were playing the piano. "Come on," he says. "It's okay, come on," and they rise up. I thought this was a sweet way of handling the situation. Otherwise, they would stay down there for five or ten minutes.

Whenever I saw them bowing, I thought, "Indian traditions are fine, but I can't see a Westerner doing it."

A famous neurosurgeon was staying at the ashram, a retired Englishman. He had met Maharishi many years ago and had become his disciple. When this man bowed down and touched Maharishi's feet, I still thought, "Isn't that amazing. Here is a British aristocrat, a gentleman, a famous surgeon from a very conservative Western country, and yet he is bowing down. Well, fine, but I really can't visualize myself doing that."

I resisted the whole idea because, like nearly all Westerners, I was full of pride. In a free society, we are raised with certain attitudes. "Look, I am free, and nobody tells me what to do. I am an individual. I can stand on my own two feet. I am separate and complete, powerful in my own right. I don't need anybody, and I don't bow down to presidents, kings, gurus, or anyone else." That kind of pride is really arrogance, one of the strongest karma builders of all.

When I finished my long meditation and visited Maharishi, I found myself bowing down and touching his feet. He touched my forehead with his fingertips and gently said, "Come on, come on." It was one of the most beautiful, sensitive, and healing experiences I have ever had.

Inner pain disappeared. I felt as if I were flying. I have flown many, many times in my dreams, often as a bird. This was not a dream, and yet I felt such lightness, such freedom. It was as close as I have ever come to that remarkable dreamlike feeling of flying.

I didn't say after my long meditation, "When I see Maharishi, I'm going to bow down." It was not premeditated. It was spontaneous. I had tears in my eyes as it happened. The whole thing felt so healing, as if my soul were being washed clean; it was one of the most beautiful, fulfilling moments I have ever experienced.

That is surrender.

For all of us, mother and father figures are strong. You may do something wrong and get punished for it, but then they forgive you because they love you. You know you did something wrong, you know you were punished, you know you were forgiven, you know they love you, and you know you are safe—all of which gives you the courage and confidence to continue exploring your surroundings and your life, mistakes and all. Good parents do not inculcate fear or shame, which create low self-esteem and lead either to greed and lust for power or to rage, withdrawal, and self-destruction. Good parents, like authentic gurus, inspire confidence, exploration, and creative courage.

As you get older, of course, you don't keep holding on to Mommy and Daddy. You become a mature person. But you can still learn and grow, and a father or mother figure can still assist you. When your evolution takes you on the spiritual journey, you might ask a guru for guidance. He can help you give up your little self to gain your higher Self, which is what surrender is. By giving up your illusory sense of individuality and becoming nothing, you gain everything. When you surrender the self, you merge with the whole of existence, which is infinitely greater than any of its parts.

An individual raindrop falls from the heavens into the ocean. When it hits the ocean, it becomes the ocean. It is no longer an individual, but look how vast and powerful it has become as part of the ocean. It doesn't know itself anymore. It has just become the ocean. Surrender is as simple as that.

After you surrender your sense of isolated individuality, you are still in this world, of course. You are aware of yourself. You still look in the mirror. You still shave and comb your hair and do your daily things, but now there is a difference. You are not attached to them or to yourself because now you know there is something more than yourself. You are still here, and you still live your life, but instead of feeling tense and uptight about it, you decide to enjoy it. You've been given this body and this identity, but now you *like* what you see in the mirror. You look at your reflection and say, "Great. Thank you very much for this vehicle. This time around, I will enjoy it."

You now know that this body is not "me." You know and understand that there is much more to yourself than your physical identity, much more than your personal ego and your particular name. After surrendering yourself and finding your Self, you now have a degree of wisdom.

Wisdom is distilled knowledge. It is the fine little fleck of gold that remains in the pan after you have washed away the mud. This little nugget of gold is what is left after the search. It is the sparkling essence of Truth, with a capital *T*. That is what I found on my spiritual odyssey.

FRIENDSHIP AND MUSIC

As a rule, Maharishi did not get too close with the people at the ashram. But with a few, especially those he had known for some time, he became more personal and friendly, and those people could get closer to him. I never expected that relationship—and even if I were in that position, what would I say to him? How would I be? A lot of people had a million specific questions for him. I just came here to be with him and hear him talk—about anything at all.

After my long meditation, he connected with me. He invited me to come along with him when he took walks. He let me hang out with him, which felt like an extra bonus, like icing on the cake.

Once in a while I played flute. Maharishi would say to somebody, "I didn't know he played that well." I never said who I was, nor had I brought any recordings with me. After he heard me play for a few people, he asked me to come along to this or that lecture. Before he began his talks, I played a little flute solo. That made me feel good, and I felt close to him. It was like getting a few extra strokes, pats on the back.

In one of my meditations, a certain thought came by. "Wouldn't it be great if somebody made a TV special about Maharishi? People back home could see what we are experiencing here. It wouldn't have to be a heavy thing, and it wouldn't be about converting anybody. We could show how people from all walks of life and from many different countries around the world come together here. Who are these people? What is our common denominator? Why are we here? Who is Maharishi? He's a happy person, a good person, and we're all having a good time. This isn't all serious learning, and he's a wonderful teacher. What a terrific TV show this would make." I spoke to him, and he thought it was an interesting idea. He encouraged me to follow up on it when I got back home.

At the far end of the course we came back to daily life. You can't go into a long meditative hibernation and then leap immediately back into activity. That would be psychologically dangerous. So at this point Maharishi said, "Okay, I don't want you to meditate so much now." He had us meditate only four hours a day, then two, then one, then even less.

Instead of meditating so much, we went on those picnics he had promised earlier. We visited nearby towns and took trips up to the source of the Ganges. We had a good time, and it eased us back into activity. He's a very smart man, totally aware.

Toward the very end, the specific training for teachers began. The first part of the course was designed to deepen our inner experience through meditation. Now it was time to impart to the teachers what they were supposed to know.

One day someone came to me and said, "Maharishi wants to know if you would like to become a teacher." This came as a complete surprise. He had told me not to expect anything, and I had not thought about becoming a teacher, not in a million years.

But something else was happening over in the States. The year before, a fellow named Jerry Jarvis had taken Maharishi's course and began teaching at Berkeley and UCLA. The response had been incredible. Who would have thought that kids would be interested in something like meditation? But this was the 1960s. The drug culture was happening. People were taking psychedelics, deconditioning themselves, trying to expand their minds. And these same kids were interested in meditation.

Jerry told Maharishi that he needed help. He couldn't handle the numbers of students he had, and he recommended me to Maharishi. "Paul's young, and the students can relate to him. He's a musician; they know him."

When Maharishi asked me to become a teacher, I said, "Can I let you know tomorrow?" I was happy he asked me, but what was I letting myself in for? What does it mean to be a teacher? Do I have time for it? If I don't have time, will I feel guilty?

The next day, he said, "There is no pressure. If you have time and you have the desire, then teach. If you don't, then don't teach. Just go with the flow. There is no pressure on you."

That eased things for me. I relaxed and started learning how to be a teacher. I was behind because the course had already begun, but I studied hard and became a teacher.

We spent the last two weeks of the course in Srinagar, Kashmir, because the weather at the ashram had become too hot. It was beautiful in Kashmir, up near Pakistan, on Dal Lake, where the elevation is 8,000 feet, and the mountains go up from there. That's where we had our convocation. We were officially declared teachers.

After that, most people departed and went back home. I planned to travel around the world. Before I did that, however, something else happened, involving Dick Bock, an old friend of mine.

Dick was ahead of us all. He became interested in meditation when almost nobody else had even heard of it. He was one of the original New Agers, embracing Eastern philosophy, gurus, meditation, and vegetarian health foods long before these things became well known and popular. He was also one of the first Americans to meet Maharishi.

Before passing away at the beginning of 1988, Dick was a great benefactor of mine. I had known him since I originally came to California with the Chico Hamilton Quintet in 1956. Along with a lot of West Coast guys, including Gerry Mulligan and Chet Baker, Chico recorded for World Pacific Records, then called Pacific Jazz. Dick Bock owned the label.

Dick came to India at this time to negotiate a contract with Ravi Shankar. On the way, he stopped off at the ashram to see Maharishi. He needed a place to stay, but we were full-up. I had a room that was a little larger than the others, however, and Dick stayed with me for about three days. It was good seeing him again. We took some nice walks, meditated together, shared some time.

On the day he was going to leave, he came out of his morning meditation and said to me, "I've been thinking about something, Paul. While you are still over here, I would like to set up some recording dates for you," and he told me what he had in mind.

There it was again. Don't expect. Just show up. I did not go to India expecting to record anything, or even to play my flute. I was lucky I brought my flute along at all. And suddenly, here's a man who comes out of nowhere and wants to set up a recording date for me to play with some of Ravi Shankar's disciples, many of whom lived in New Delhi. Ravi himself would write a couple of compositions for the album.

Dick left the ashram and later that day called me from New Delhi. "Everything's set up," he said.

Immediately after completing my teaching course at the ashram, I got together with the musicians in New Delhi. We rehearsed a little and then recorded *Paul Horn in India* at the United States Information Service, which broadcasts around the world, like the Voice of America. They had a four-track recording board in the New Delhi station, probably the only four-track in the whole of India.

Another flute player attended the rehearsals and the recording session, not to play on the album, but to coach me and help me along. We also had a violin, vina, sitar, tablas, and tamboura. Ravi wrote two compositions for the album, just as Dick said he would.

Some Western musicians think Indian music is simple, but it's not. It is very complex. Nobody expected me to play those ragas. Learning them is a life-long process. We shared a common denominator, however—our ability to improvise.

The compositions were written out, leaving room for all of us to improvise, and when it came to me, they freed me up even more. I did not have to stay within the strict ascending and descending scales of the ragas. I could play outside the scales, like I do in jazz. We related to each other very well, and *Paul Horn in India* came out quite nicely.

While still there, I recorded a second album, *Paul Horn in Kashmir*. For this one, it was I who suggested the project to Maharishi.

When we were up in Kashmir for the final three weeks of the course, I met several Indian musicians who had played for Maharishi during this part of the course every year for the past four years.

"These are wonderful musicians, Maharishi. Maybe I could do a recording with them. On the liner notes, I could tell the listeners about meditation. I could talk about meeting you, about what TM is, about what it has meant to me. An album such as this could bring your message to a lot of people. What do you think?"

He said nothing. Then, about a week later, he called me into his room. I couldn't believe what I saw. There, sitting around Maharishi on the floor, were all of the musicians. Maharishi sat in the middle, designing the album cover, laying out what music should be on the recording, planning the whole thing.

The next day we took cover photos. We sat on top of a houseboat. Maharishi was beaming. The musicians sat around him. The snow-capped Himalayas rose up majestically in the background.

Dick Bock released *Paul Horn in India* and *Paul Horn in Kashmir*, which in the mid-1970s were combined into one double-album and reissued on Blue Note as *Paul Horn in India*.

After recording these albums, I left India and continued my journey around the world.

L.A. REENTRY

Right off the bat, L.A.'s freeways blew me away. I couldn't handle them. After I got back from India, friends drove me around for three months; it was six months before I could drive on my own. I couldn't keep up with the pace of my personal life either.

Other people moved as fast as always, but I had slowed way down. I was operating at about one-tenth of my previous speed. Even then, everything seemed rushed. Musicians in L.A. are oriented toward their work and their answering machines; they're concerned with establishing contacts, making appointments, who's got which gig, who's high in the jazz polls, all of that stuff.

Before my ashram experiences, I too was an ambitious go-getter, making phone calls, meeting people, pushing, hustling, climbing the ladder. Now, no longer motivated by the work ethic, I found this life-style to be as hectic and difficult as it was absurd. My focus had changed. My life now revolved around things having nothing to do with ambition, money, or prestige. I wanted to get the documentary on Maharishi launched; I wanted to teach meditation; I wanted to play music for the joy of it, not just to win Grammys or pay the rent; I wanted to lie on the beach in the sun and listen to the waves.

Sensing some of these changes before leaving the ashram, I asked Maharishi what to do. "I feel so different, Maharishi. Here at the ashram, I am having wonderful experiences. How can I possibly return to my old life?"

"This is a test to see how much you have grown," he said. "You do not meditate simply because you enjoy it. If that were the case, then your meditations would be mere escapes. You test your progress by returning to the marketplace and your previous environment.

"People suffer in their lives," he continued, "because they work so hard to accomplish so little, exhausting themselves in the process. They feel fragmented instead of whole, harrassed instead of challenged, miserable instead of happy. For them, life is no longer joyful. It is drudgery. They cannot focus their attention. They cannot give inner power to their thoughts, or spiritual richness to their dreams. Having lost this power, they cannot manifest their goals in smooth, effective ways. If they meditated, they could accomplish much greater things by using less effort. You have the ability to focus. You have the power. You can do this, too."

"How, Maharishi?"

"Work less and charge more."

I laughed aloud. He did, too. What eminently practical advice—from a Himalayan monk, no less.

Leaving India, I continued around the world, visiting friends in Israel, Italy, and England; initiating my first meditator, in Switzerland; lecturing in Málaga, Spain, where I also founded the first Spanish Transcendental Meditation center.

In no way did I want to return to L.A.; I was having a great time being away. But money was running short—and I had a commitment to perform a concert at the Pilgrimage Theater, an outdoor amphitheater across from the Hollywood Bowl, today known as the John Anson Ford Theatre. We were performing the Jazz Mass, which had won two Grammys in 1965, and Lalo Schifrin would be conducting. Money aside, I wanted to play this gig, and I wanted to get Maharishi's documentary moving. It was time to return.

HOLLYWOOD BACKSTAGE

To my surprise, it took less than a week to rebuild my chops when I returned from India. Once you've played long enough, you know your instrument, and you don't forget it. In the conservatory, I had practiced thousands of hours. When I went to India, I didn't touch my clarinet or sax for six months and rarely played my flute. To record those two albums in New Delhi, it took only three days to get my fingers loose and my embouchure back.

Nine-tenths of being in shape is mental, not physical. Once you know what you're doing and how to do it, you don't have to kill yourself practicing. Like walking after a long hospital confinement, it comes back quickly. When I returned to L.A. less than a week before my big concert at the Pilgrimage Theater, I practiced a few hours a day for five days, and my chops were fine.

I eagerly looked forward to performing the Jazz Mass again, live, in Hollywood, in front of the most sophisticated audience this side of New York. Sunday rolled around, a sparkling sunny day, and the amphitheater was sold out. People packed the regular seats, while others sat up in trees or behind the stage or in the aisles. Lalo Schifrin, who wrote the music, conducted the choir, the orchestra, and my quintet.

It felt so good to see my friends again, especially vibist Emil Richards. He too had been initiated into Transcendental Meditation. Although he had not come with me to India, we corresponded while I was there. The first thing he said when I saw him backstage was, "Man, there's a lot of light around you."

Lalo Schifrin and I warmly greeted each other. Although L.A. is hectic, particularly backstage before a concert of this magnitude, nothing seemed rushed that day. My mind did not feel agitated or fragmented. I was able to focus clearly on people as they spoke, talking with them, smiling, giving and receiving a lot of love.

I felt as if I were two people. One was the professional musician who walked out onstage to play in front of 3,000 people. The other was an observer or witness, who was centered and calm, just watching things happen. I was an integral part of the event but serenely detached from it.

Around me, the pace was fast, but I didn't experience it that way. From my observer-perspective, time moved slowly; events occurred easily.

We played a marvelous concert. This was the first time I had performed since returning, and I noticed a change in the music. I didn't perceive the change directly and consciously the way I did later, recording *Inside the Taj Mahal*. I noticed it indirectly, intuitively. It wasn't a matter of new ideas popping out, although some did. No, it was something else, a different quality of feeling, something previously absent. Whatever it was, I felt it, the musicians felt it, and the audience felt it, too. The concert was an enormous success.

On this day, I began to see that separate areas of my life are not separate at all. They are one. My horns were not the primary instruments—I myself was the primary instrument. Whatever I did away from music did not diminish anything. Quite the contrary. While meditating and "doing nothing," I was not "wasting time." I was developing myself as a total human being. Whatever progress I made automatically spilled over into all areas of my life, including music. From that concert on, I no longer worried about spending time "away" from music.

A NEW WORK POLICY

In India, life had been slow and easy and quiet. We were there to meditate, to discover and explore our highest nature. We lived in a Himalayan jungle by the Ganges River. As I traveled Europe, staying with friends, getting wined and dined by RCA in Israel, Italy, and England, talking about meditation in Switzerland and Spain, I was not concerned about work, direction, or purpose. I simply drifted along, enjoying myself. I had discovered there is a lot to do, simply by doing nothing. Now, back in L.A., I had to think in terms of my former wife, my children, friends, the guys in my band, the studio people I had to work with, and the executives I had to deal with in setting up Maharishi's documentary.

When the phone rang for recording dates back in Hollywood, I took Maharishi's advice. I asked for double-scale. In those days, double-scale was almost unheard of. You were a studio musician who was glad to get the work. You made good money, but you did not ask for double-scale.

Now when contractors called, I said, "I have a new policy. If you'd like me to play your date, I want double-scale." There was always an awkward pause. I filled in with, "If you don't want to do that, I understand completely. Thank you very much for calling. . . ." Half the time, they went for it. And there I was—working less, charging more, and earning just as much as I had before.

Whenever I got a call for a job I didn't want, I turned it down. Quite often I chose not to work at all. I collected unemployment, some sixty dollars a week, and worked on Maharishi's film project, taught meditation, or lay on the beach, for none of which I got paid. Personally and professionally, I played music whenever I felt like it.

A NEW VIEW OF RELATIONSHIPS

I eagerly wanted to reestablish contact with my friends and tell them what had happened, what Maharishi and the ashram were like, and what some of my meditations had revealed to me. I especially wanted to talk with the guys in my band and with people like Emil Richards, Shorty Rogers, and Joe Mondragon. Before I'd left, all of us were on the spiritual path, and we had spent many hours discussing philosophical matters. India was still fresh in my mind and deeply meaningful. I couldn't wait to tell them.

To my dismay, however, I quickly discovered that my stories weren't getting through. I couldn't relate my experiences to anyone. I had pictures in my mind that they didn't have. When I told my stories, I was immediately transported back to India, but my friends remained in Hollywood. They could not possibly receive what I told them, not in the ways I experienced it.

When I talked about some of the deeper spiritual revelations I had during four months of isolation with Maharishi in the Himalayas, their eyes gradually went blank. Emil Richards listened. He cared. But most of the others did not. I am only speculating, of course, but I think they were afraid to know what I had discovered. Maybe it would be too upsetting.

Maybe it would reveal to them that some of the things they thought were so great in Hollywood really weren't so great after all. Except for Emil, they nodded their heads, smiled, and tried to get into it, but they couldn't. Pretty soon, their eyes glazed. Frustrated by my inability to communicate deeper personal things, I finally just told them stories about my first visit to the Taj Mahal, how nice the mountains looked in Kashmir, things like that.

I began to see that when we live in darkened rooms, we almost always claim we want the light turned on. But if somebody walks in and attempts to do that, we reject them. We *say* we want light, but we really don't—not until we are truly ready.

And we can't help it. When we suffer in psychic isolation, as I did for so long, we embrace the darkness that imprisons us, denying the light we claim we want. We protect our ignorance and maintain our inertia by denigrating anybody who might try to flip on the switch or open the drapes. Quite often, we call such people boring. And we shut them out.

Conversely, if we graduate from one level to the next and then come back and attempt to tell our friends the wonderful things we've discovered, our friends can only resent us. Consciously or unconsciously, directly or indirectly, they erroneously perceive our new values and insights, not as gleaming beacons of hope, but as criticisms of their present way of life, which used to be our way of life too.

In order for experience to have positive meaning, our listeners must be intuitively aware of the truth of what we're saying, which means they must already yearn to graduate from one level to the next. Otherwise, they only feel anxious and uncomfortable, and we feel frustrated, sad, and alone.

I also realized that it wasn't just my experience that couldn't be communicated. On a deep personal level, *nobody* can communicate experience directly. All of us would like to share deep experiences with people who are close to us; we know they would benefit if they could receive such things. But they can't. It's impossible.

As parents, we feel this dilemma intensely. We love our children, and we hope to save them grief. We tell them we have experienced what they are going through; if they continue in their present direction, they will have serious problems. They listen to us, but they won't take our advice, not because our advice is unworthy, but because they can't.

With friends, children, or anybody else, our life is not theirs. We are all on our own path. We can learn a little from other people's experiences, but never very much, and certainly not nearly as much as others would like us to learn. In order to learn, we must have our own experiences. Nothing else will do. Experience is the key to learning about life. Ultimately, it is the only key.

Major changes took place in other areas as well. Before I went to India, I attended Hollywood parties. We gathered together at a friend's house, passed the joint, got a little high, played some music, ended up with some chick, had a good time. Now when I went to parties and the joint came around, I didn't smoke. People started looking at me like, "Boy, is he weird."

Before, I defined high as being oblivious to problems and frustrations. A little grass or a couple of drinks gave a few minutes of euphoria, and I felt freed from my hassles. That's what's so alluring about chemical substances. For a short, temporary period, you sail beyond heavy burdens, and you're out there floating around, laughing and enjoying yourself. That is considered high.

Since experiencing the benefits of meditation, my new definition of high was clarity. With my mind clear and alert, I felt more in control and enjoyed life more. Pot had the opposite effect. It used to fog my brain.

When the joint came around, I passed it on, saying, "No, thanks, I don't feel like it." Everybody looked at me. "What happened to Paul? Wow, man, he doesn't smoke pot anymore."

I tried to ease matters by saying, "Please, I am not here to judge anyone. I'm not saying I'm right, you're wrong. I just don't feel like smoking." No matter what I said or did, my presence still made people feel uncomfortable.

After I'd attended a couple of parties, I found myself wondering if these people were truly my friends. What does "friend" mean? It seems to me a friend is one who knows and accepts and loves you for whatever you are. You don't worry about how a friend is acting today or might act tomorrow, because you love his or her essence. It seemed then—and it still seems—that a true friend relates to who and what you are deep down inside, as a unique human being, a special person. That's how I regard my friends. Shouldn't they regard me the same way? Well, they didn't.

I remembered when I first got involved with TM. I thought everyone in my band would want to participate. We had enjoyed many philosophical discussions about meditation, and yet when the time came actually to do it, I was the only one who jumped in. The others did not. That was the first puzzling thing. Now, nobody was interested in my India experiences; nobody asked serious questions or listened to the answers; and they felt uptight because I didn't smoke pot. Were these my friends? I began having doubts. I had not expected this kind of reaction at all. Before long, there I was, alone by myself.

Each one of us is alone. We seek friendship and love because friends and loved ones diminish loneliness. But my friends and I could no longer relate to each other. Our lives had taken different turns. I felt alone, but not lonely.

I recalled a profound insight I had during my long meditation in India when I realized that I never needed to feel lonely anymore because I had found God. My parents gave me this physical form, but God is my real father, responsible for all of life and all of creation. God is the creative force that brings the gift, the energy, and the miracle of life to each of us. That God is my father, and he is with me and inside of me and all around me, not just once in a while, but always. When I experienced this revelation back in India, tears rolled down my cheeks. It was so beautiful and wonderful to know I need never feel lonely again.

Back in Hollywood, recalling this insight, I began to realize I did not need people on a personal level. I could look at them from a more detached perspective. A lot of people were suffering the same way I was before I went to India. Instead of being angry about it, I could have compassion for their sufferings. It is no fun living in darkened rooms. Perhaps I could help them.

When you go deep within yourself and external experiences disappear, you are left alone with your real Self, which is God. The more often you realize this fact directly—not intellectually, not as an abstract idea, but directly, as an empirical, personal experience—the more you realize its ultimate reality in your life. Soon, you feel happier. You become more self-fulfilling. This is why teaching meditation became such a joy for me. I could be of service, giving people a way to experience meditation's ultimate realization: God lives within you *as* you. To know this is Self-Realization.

To this day, I view people and relationships differently. I do not base my relationships on day-to-day activities or on how people treat me in any given moment. I see in them their God-essence, which is the same as mine and yours and everybody else's. I respect and love their essential Self. God is within everyone. On this deeper level, I wish everyone well.

Sometimes people view this attitude as being cold and impersonal, because I don't get as emotional as I used to. Something great or small goes wrong, and I don't become extremely upset about it. I am not attached to it in a personal way. I went to India the first time precisely because I was tired of roller coasters. I was sick of highs and lows. I yearned for emotional balance and psychological stability. Well, I found it. That is where I am. I can't go back. And I don't want to go back. It feels good to be a whole person, centered and calm inside.

All of these things went through my mind as I looked at my friends getting high, asking me to get high, and then putting me down when I refused. Even after I returned from India the second time, I tried to be part of the festivities, but I wasn't. If anything, I just kept my friends from feeling free and enjoying themselves. I knew I could no longer hang out. It wasn't fun any more. In my heart, they remained friends, but on a social level it wasn't happening.

I gave up that circle of people and spent more time teaching meditation, especially to UCLA students. I loved that because I love to be around young people and never want to let go of youth's exuberance and enthusiasm.

Most of these students were high, not on drugs, but naturally. They got higher than dopers ever could. The majority of these people were products of the sixties drug scene. They had smoked pot and been involved with a variety of drugs, not cocaine or heroin, but psychedelics. They had experienced drugs and gone past them. They discovered that grass didn't get them high anymore, while meditation did. I felt good being around them. There was a lot of laughter, a lot of lightness, a lot of enthusiasm and creative energy. Among these people, I found a new circle of friends.

TM LECTURES

At Northridge, I gave my first public lecture on meditation. I felt nervous beforehand, the same way I felt before playing my first Oberlin concert. At

Northridge the day before, Timothy Leary had spoken. He was an experienced lecturer, a great speaker, and the students loved him. What was I going to say? How would I say it? I had no idea, and the butterflies in my stomach refused to let up.

The TM movement had grown enormously. First, the word about meditation had spread throughout college campuses, especially UCLA and UC Berkeley. Then photos of the Beatles and Maharishi appeared in all the magazines and newspapers. Now everybody knew about Transcendental Meditation.

Until recently, Jerry Jarvis had been the only teacher and lecturer on the college campuses. When he became inundated with students, he asked Maharishi for help. Maharishi initiated me as a teacher, and now I was giving my first public lecture.

Next to Maharishi, Jerry was the best speaker I had heard, and he became my model. For several months, I attended his talks and watched the way he presented himself, taking notes on how he got into things, what five or six points he addressed, and how he got out.

He did not stand behind a podium with a piece of paper in his hands, reading a prepared lecture word-for-word. He walked casually on stage and sat informally on a chair, the way somebody might sit down in your living room. He told jokes, laughed a lot, and enjoyed himself. Although he covered pretty much the same territory, he changed things each time he spoke. Now it was my turn, and I felt nervous.

Maharishi had told me something very interesting. "You will never get tired of teaching this subject, because you are talking about the fundamental truth of life. The subject will reenergize you because it is always fresh and new. You are delving into the source of creativity itself."

As I took the podium, I told myself, "Hey, man, relax. This is like jazz. You showed up. You're here. You know your subject. Now trust the moment. Let your ideas sing as if you were playing the flute." And that's what I did. Once I got into it, the butterflies vanished.

I didn't try to guide anything or force it into uncomfortable molds. I lost my personal self in the subject and let my higher Self do the talking. The words flowed like music. When I finished, I felt as good as I do when I complete a concert.

The kids enjoyed the talk, and many signed up for the meditation course. As I became a better lecturer, I started having more and more fun.

I never got paid for lecturing, teaching, or initiating, but after each talk I felt so high, so incredibly awakened by clarity and insight. That was my payment, far more than enough reward.

As I became busier, lecturing and teaching and initiating seven days a week, twelve hours a day, my music slipped into the background. For a long time, I didn't miss it. Eventually, I became concerned but figured I'd just go ahead with whatever made me feel good, knowing that everything in life is connected with everything else, and evolution in one area leads to evolution in all others. To pay the rent, I still played in studios, but by this time studio life bored me to tears. I detested the L.A. environment in general, Hollywood in particular. To get away from the smog and traffic and noise, I often drove down to the Santa Monica beach, where I lay in the sun, just letting my mind float.

THREE

THE EARLY YEARS

Carrying a towel and a bottle of lotion, wearing only my bathing suit, sunglasses, and sandals, I walked through the crowd on the boardwalk at Santa Monica beach onto the sand, passing by volleyball players and hundreds of cheering people. I ambled down to the shoreline and spread my towel near the pier. It was midafternoon, a typically sun-splashed California beach-day, complete with gorgeous bikini girls, laughing children, romping dogs, and blond surfers. At first, I heard merry-go-round music from the boardwalk pier, but as I let the sun soak into my body while I lay on the sand, the music gradually faded away and disappeared.

I held my hand up to the sun at arm's length, moving my fingers slowly, one at a time, the way I did as a child in New York, where I was born on March 17, 1930, the same day the steel structure of the Empire State Building was completed, or so my father said. Even as a very little kid, I had certain questions in my mind. Why am I here? Where did I come from? Where did everything else come from? What is life about? At that time, of course, I didn't have the language to express such things, but I felt them.

Lying on the beach, I marveled once again at the fact that I could wiggle each finger simply by the power of a single thought. At age two, I had held up my hand and wiggled my fingers and tried to feel the process that transpired between the thought and the movement, but of course there is nothing to feel. Meanwhile, I had observed the miracle that my mind could move an object—this finger, that finger—simply by *thinking* about movement. I felt as if I were someone else, watching a strange and marvelous hand that did not "belong" to me.

This event, which felt extraordinary, created in me a profound sensation of detachment. I regard it as my first out-of-body experience. There I was, two years old, moving a finger, which obviously was mine, wondering who the "I" was who was moving it. Who was living inside my body that could do this? I had sat for hours moving my fingers, contemplating the mystery and wonder of it all. I began to realize, however dimly, that my true self is separate from the image of the self I see in the mirror. Beyond that "ego-self," which feels as if it resides in my body and which I call "me," there is a deeper and higher Self. Who and what is it?

Throughout my life, I have been able to detach and be an observer. Although I experience things directly, there is always a part of me that watches myself participating in that experience, as if the events and sensations were scenes in a movie. As I watch the movie, I enjoy it immensely. Life to me is fun. Fun does not mean things are always cheerful, or every event has a happy ending. Fun is the adventure of living, in and of itself. Life has always been exciting to me, and much of the excitement revolves about the mystery: Who is it that experiences all of this?

SPIRITUAL AND FAMILY BEGINNINGS

I have been on the spiritual path many years. The mystery of who we are has always been with me. My life has led to adventures and to many different kinds of music. This fact seems to be almost a logical outgrowth of that early experience of looking at my hand and my self and my whole life as if it were a big adventure. I have always wanted to see and taste as much of life as possible.

God bless Maharishi for helping me to discover my higher Self, I thought, slowly moving another finger in the sun. That higher Self has

TOP LEFT: Paul Horn, age 4, with his mother and father in Washington, D. C.
TOP RIGHT: The "Count" Williams Quintet, Oberlin, Ohio, 1950
BELOW: The Oberlin Conservatory Woodwind Quintet (plus piano), 1952

ABOVE: Paul's first wife, Yvonne, in Hollywood, California, 1957

ABOVE RIGHT: Paul's first group, the Paul Horn Quartet, in 1958. *From left to right:* Gene Estes, Paul Horn, Lyle Ritz, John Pisano, and "mascot"

BELOW RIGHT: The Chico Hamilton Quintet, 1956. *From left to right:* Fred Katz, John Pisano, Chico, Paul Horn, and Carson Smith

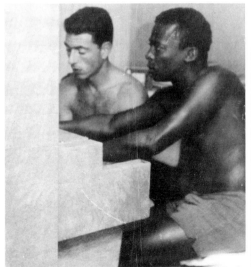

TOP LEFT: With Miles Davis in Los Angeles, 1961

TOP RIGHT: With "Cannonball" Adderley, Los Angeles, 1963

LEFT: With Tony Curtis at Paramount Studios, coaching him for a part in the movie *Wild & Wonderful*, 1964

TOP LEFT: With Tony Bennett at the Playboy Club, Hollywood, 1966
TOP RIGHT: A recording session with Ravi Shankar, Hollywood, 1965
BELOW: A Hollywood studio recording session, 1964

Paul's wife, Tryntje, on the
MGM lot in Los Angeles

A photo session in 1967 for Artley Flutes, with sons Marlen (10) and Robin (7)

With George Harrison (*top*) and John Lennon (*bottom*)
at the Academy of Meditation, Rishikesh, India, 1968

TOP: With Donovan on a 1969 U. S. tour at Madison Square Garden in New York,
performing for a crowd of more than 25,000

BOTTOM: With His Holiness Maharishi Mahesh Yogi on Mt. Gulmarg, Kashmir,
India, 1968

TOP LEFT: With Maharishi and musicians in Srinagar, Kashmir, India, 1968

TOP RIGHT: At the Taj Mahal in India in 1968 for the recording of his best-selling album, *Inside*

BELOW LEFT: In front of the Great Pyramid of Giza in Egypt, 1976

BELOW RIGHT: Recording *Inside the Great Pyramid* in 1976 in the Queen's Chamber of the Great Pyramid

On the Great Wall of China, 1978

Performing at a commune in
Guangdong Province, China, 1982

At a 1983 concert in Kaunas, Lithuania, with David Friesen on bass and son Robin on drums

An Indian-style greeting from a Russian fan in Moscow, 1983

A duet with Haida the whale at Sealand of the Pacific, Victoria, British Columbia, Canada, 1971

From his weekly network television show, "The Paul Horn Show," on BCTV in Vancouver, 1973

At Machu Pichu, Peru, 1987

 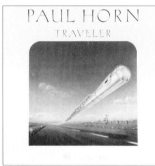 

TOP ROW FROM LEFT: *The Sound of Paul Horn* (first album for Columbia Records, 1961), *Cycle* (Grammy award nomination in 1965), *Jazz Suite on the Mass Texts* (winner of two Grammys, 1965)

MIDDLE ROW FROM LEFT: *Inside (the Taj Mahal)* (1969, over 750,000 sold), *Inside the Great Pyramid* (1977, over 300,000 sold), *China* (1982, partly recorded in the Temple of Heaven in Beijing)

BOTTOM ROW FROM LEFT: *Live from Russia with Love* (recorded during Paul's first tour of the USSR, 1983), *Traveler* (Grammy Award nomination, 1987), *The Peace Album* (1988, a flute choir of up to ten voices played by Paul and overdubbed) been trying to emerge for decades. What fun I had as a four-year-old child, playing my mother's piano, running these same fingers over the keyboard, listening to those wonderful sounds emerge, singing along with them, feeling the power of music beginning to stir my soul, awakening me to the higher realities within myself. Music was my first portal.

Or lying in bed at night, first in New York, then in D.C., where I graduated from Roosevelt High School, and listening to Mom play the piano. Frances Sper was her maiden name. In the 1920s, she was totally into music, a professional, and had her own weekly radio show in New York, playing piano and singing. She was the first person to sing "When the Red, Red Robin Comes Bob, Bob, Bobbin' Along" and "Blue Skies," recorded on the Cameo label. She could sight-read anything and transpose music on sight, which made her valuable to Irving Berlin's publishing company. When composers brought their songs to audition for Berlin, Mom accompanied them on piano. She was the only woman pianist Berlin ever had. She gave up her career when she married Dad in 1929. I don't think she had any regrets about that. She was a devoted mother and wife and treasured her family. I'd lie in bed at night, listening to her play music, beautiful music.

I took after my mother perhaps a bit more than my father. Their personalities were quite different. Mother was an intellectual who read a lot and had a very good vocabulary. She was also an emotional person, quick-tempered, high-strung, hyperenergetic, a go-getter, an achiever, creative, goal-oriented. I used to be very emotional, too; I had a quick temper, cried easily, and was very energetic, impatient, and subject to outbursts. Later, I sought a balance between mind and heart, intellect and emotion. Because of my temper, I eventually realized it was best to reason things out, and I did.

I also took after Paul Sper, my mother's father, a Frenchman who came to America at an early age, learned how to speak nine languages fluently, and became a Supreme Court interpreter. He was a bright man, a talented carver and designer, an avid reader who loved nature and music, even as I do.

My father's parents lived in Hungary. They came to New York in 1893 and set themselves up in the restaurant business. Dad's mother died when Dad was two years old. His two brothers and one sister went to an orphanage, and Dad grew up in foster homes. His father visited him on weekends. Dad had to work while attending night school, completing high school and two years of college before he was drafted into World War I. As an infantry sergeant on the front lines, he had to lead soldiers out of the trenches, over the top, through no-man's-land, into hand-to-hand combat with the Germans. He spent two years in a sanatorium after the war, suffering tuberculosis as a result of breathing mustard gas. During this time, he recovered completely and met and married my mother. As a child, I often read the diary he kept in the war.

Dad was an honest and charming man. He liked people, as I do, and people liked him. He was quiet and humorous, rather low keyed, a bright man, but he did not read very much, and he was not an intellectual. He knew very little about music, but he was a very loving person. Things touched him deeply because he was quite sensitive. Tears came to his eyes easily, not from sadness, but from the beauty and poignancy he saw in life. He was a straight-ahead guy who did not like arguments, violence, or anything upsetting. We were not rich by any means, but we always had plenty of whatever we needed. His emphasis was not on money but on providing a decent life for us, which he did.

He was a wholesale liquor salesman, and his company transferred him to Washington, D.C., when I was four. They set us up in an apartment downtown. We arrived at night. In the morning when we went outside, we saw that we lived in a totally black neighborhood. That was okay with us, but not with our neighbors. D.C. is a bloody prejudiced town. I got into a lot of fights.

We moved a few times that first couple of years in D.C. Whenever we looked for apartments, the "Are you Jewish" question inevitably reared its ugly head. My father never denied being Jewish, and then the landlords said, "Sorry, we don't allow Jews here." We'd drive to Chesapeake Bay to swim at the beach and see a sign "No dogs or Jews allowed." In school, other kids called me a damn Jew, and I fought them.

The height of prejudicial absurdity came when I got into an argument with a Jewish girl who lived next door. In the heat of the squabble, I got so mad I said, "You're just a damn Jew." She said, "When you call me that, you call yourself that, too." I realized how utterly ridiculous the whole thing was.

When I was thirteen, we moved to an all-Jewish neighborhood, and things settled down. I made a lot of friends and enjoyed those years. I couldn't understand racism then, and I still can't. Prejudice is the dumbest thing on the face of the earth. It reveals and exhibits total ignorance, arrogance, and stupidity.

Music was always a relief for me, and Mrs. Miller, my first piano teacher, made music fun. On our living-room floor, she spread out a big scroll with a five-line staff on it. She brought metal notes and sharps and flats and clefs, which I placed on the staff by hand. What a wonderful way to teach a four-year-old how to read music. She made it a creative, physical game, and I loved it.

The Washington College of Music was a conservatory for young people, which I entered at age five. They had national piano-playing contests, with judges and committees, and they graded us. Things started getting serious, and music was not as much fun. I began to get nervous before playing, something that never happened before. The syndrome of the educational system was setting in—the competition, the judging, being aware that there is a right and wrong, that mistakes are bad, all of that stuff. Before, I just played. Now, I started losing interest.

Then I took lessons from Mr. Spear, an excellent musician, but a strict teacher. We went into Bach and Chopin, very heavy stuff, and I developed good technique, but by now music had lost its magic. I looked out the window on Saturday afternoons, wishing I was out in the sunshine playing baseball with the guys, but there I was, stuck with this demanding piano lesson, too young to appreciate Bach, Mozart, and other great Western composers. Besides, I wanted to get into pop music, things like my mother played, songs like "Embraceable You" and "Stardust."

At nine or ten, when I told my parents I didn't want to play classical music anymore, they said okay. What did I want to play? I wanted to play pop music. They said yes to that too, and once again music was fun. I listened to Artie Shaw and Benny Goodman; by age twelve, I wanted to drop piano and play clarinet. My parents did not fight me. They were willing and able to let me be myself. They did not try to force me into molds of what they wanted me to be. They just loved and nourished me and wanted me to be happy, supporting my efforts all the way.

To buy a clarinet, I needed money, so I worked as an usher in the Earl Theater during the summer of 1942, where for fifteen or twenty cents people could see a first-run major feature, short subjects, newsreels, and cartoons. Then the lights came on, and the pit stage rose up with an eighty-piece orchestra on it. For an hour and a half, dancers, singers, comedians, and balancing acts thrilled us. I got to go backstage and meet the artists and get their autographed pictures. It was tremendously exciting to be in a show business atmosphere. By the end of the summer, I had saved enough money to buy a $200 Selmer clarinet, which I have to this day.

Lee Hardesty played in the orchestra at another theater in town, the Capitol Theater, where he gave me clarinet lessons. He was a jovial, heavy-set man. He was only in his thirties, but he had a huge beer belly, and he laughed all the time—a very loving, gentle man, an excellent teacher who made music fun. When I walked in, he'd say, "Come over here, lad," and give me a big hug, pulling me up against his great belly, and then say, "Okay, let's see what you got for me this week." I couldn't wait for my lessons, which took place backstage.

To get there, I walked through a long alley to the backstage entrance and down the steps to the musicians' room, where the orchestra guys hung out. Each musician had a locker, with girlie pictures pasted inside the door. I was fourteen and thought those sexy pictures were terrific. During the lessons, Lee played along with me, which I loved. After lessons, I could stay and see the movie and the show, meet the stars, and hang out with the musicians and chorus girls. I especially looked forward to the show's orchestral overture, because Lee always had a featured solo. I felt so proud. "That's my teacher playing. Isn't he fantastic?"

After a year and a half on clarinet, I got Lee to teach me saxophone, and I joined Al Rine's full-sized dance band, where I was the youngest member. With me on third alto, not lead alto, we rehearsed three times a week and played proms and dances and churches and country clubs.

I also played in combos. I wasn't improvising, but I wanted to. One night during a small-combo tennis-court gig I said, "I sure wish I could improvise." Jack Nimitz, a good alto player, respected by us because he once took a lesson from Charlie Parker, said, "Why don't you?" I said, "How?" He said, "The next time a solo comes up, you take it. Just do it."

By this time, Charlie Parker was my idol. I could appreciate the complexity and depth and excitement of his music, but he played too many notes for me to understand them fully. However, he often ended his solos with a little three-note phrase that I memorized (in the key of C, the notes would be E, G, D).

When it came time for the next solo, Jack said, "Okay, you got it." I jumped up, put the horn in my mouth, closed my eyes, blew hard, and moved my fingers as fast as I could, without the slightest idea of what I was doing. At the end, almost running out of breath, I played that little Charlie Parker lick. The guys in the band cheered and said I sounded great. "Good God, I did it," I thought. "I improvised a whole solo. Without any music in front of me, I stood up and played." I'm sure the solo wasn't any good, but I did it. The first time is always the hardest, and I had an indescribable feeling of elation.

On following gigs, I improvised more often, and better ideas came out. I began developing coherence and style, listening to Charlie Parker, Miles Davis, Dizzy Gillespie, Bud Powell, and other beboppers, playing along with their records as well as I could—a good way to learn.

In those days, they didn't have formal ways of teaching jazz like they do today. You learned on your own. Jazz classes are good to a point, after which they are self-defeating because the essence of jazz is spontaneous improvisation. Each person brings a different creativity to it. The more you analyze jazz, and the more you practice specific phrases and licks, the less spontaneous you become. It is a paradox. You can't practice who you are— you just are—and yet you practice anyway.

You practice becoming open to the flow of music that emerges from within you. You practice the art of disappearing, of getting out of your own way, of vanishing as an identity so the music itself, which has its own life, can flow through you unimpeded, using you as its vehicle, its instrument, its tool for realization. In this sense, the process of improvisation is similar to the process of meditation.

Spontaneity is the real secret to living a happy life. At its deepest, most fundamental natural level, life *is* spontaneity. To live a full, natural, creative life means being in the now, participating, responding, enjoying what is happening in the moment. You can't plan how to act in the next moment because you don't know what the next moment will bring. In this moment, you are you. When the next moment arrives, you are a new person. What is happening now? What do you see? What are you thinking? What is going on within and around you? I felt drawn to improvisation because it offered an excitement that appealed to me. When you improvise, you don't know what will happen next. Improvisation teaches you how to trust in the moment.

Most people think improvisation is a total mystery, and yet, at least on certain levels, we do it ourselves every day of our lives. We meet someone and carry on a conversation. Whatever the context, we do not rehearse its contents. We know the language; the other person knows the language; we interact directly and spontaneously. What are we doing? We are improvising. We are trusting in the moment. We are trusting that we will survive this totally unpremeditated conversational contact. Why not apply this principle to all of life? For one who lives life richly and fully, daily life and daily conversation are as spontaneous as improvised music.

In my senior year of high school, I got kicked out of music class. The class was designed for the average kid, and I had to take it, even though I knew so much more than the other kids. I was bored and fooling around, talking, causing a little disturbance, and the teacher sent me to the principal's office.

May P. Bradshaw, the principal, was an older woman—very severe, and a strict disciplinarian. I walked in, and there was no ceremony at all. She referred to some of my friends, compared me to them, and said, "Horn, you're just a bum. You will never make anything of yourself. You're kicked out of school until you bring your father here to see me."

That infuriated me to the point of tears. "Oh, yeah?" I said, trying to fight the tears back. "Well, you just wait. Someday you'll see my name in headlines." I walked out the door.

I was ashamed to tell my father, of course. He was not pleased about it, but he was understanding and listened to my story, and he took time off from work to go with me to the principal's office.

We had to wait because Miss Bradshaw was late. When she finally arrived, she walked right by us and into her office without saying good morning or even acknowledging my father's presence, not a nod or a smile, nothing. We were on time, she was late, and she ignored us. When she spoke with us, my father let her know how he felt. "I don't appreciate your attitude," he said. "I thought it was rude of you just to walk by and not say good morning." I was reinstated in school.

It was a terrible thing to lay on a kid, calling him a bum, but maybe that was where part of my early energy came from. I wanted to show her I was not a bum, that I *could* make something of myself. I resented her unjustifiable remark and worked hard to accomplish something in life, not only for myself and for music, but to prove my point. My name *has* been in headlines many times.

Both of my parents were totally supportive. They thought it was great I played in bands. They did not discourage me. They didn't fear my involvement with jazz. They didn't put down jazz musicians. They didn't tell me how insecure the music business is. They didn't tell me to "get serious" or suggest that I get a "real" job. In other words, they didn't plant failure in my mind. They let me go for my dreams and encouraged me every step of the way. Intuitively they knew a secret that all great teachers know: Find the good, and praise it. Just by being involved with jazz and spontaneous improvisation, I was already beginning to train myself for the spiritual things to come.

OBERLIN

I liked the idea of focusing completely on music at the Oberlin Conservatory of Music but I was astonished at how much we were required to do. We had to practice at least three hours a day on our major instrument and one on our minor instrument, which was piano for all of us during the first year. Besides that, I had courses in theory, ear training, sight singing, and music history and three or four hours of homework a night. I also played in an ensemble, which involved preparation and rehearsals.

During the week, I lived the life of the dedicated student. On weekends, I played sax in Frank Williams's jazz quintet, which had nothing to do with classical music or Oberlin. Frank was a heavy-set black man who looked like Count Basie, so they called him Count. It was a piano, trumpet, bass, drums, and sax group, and I was the only white cat. They were all great players, straight-ahead jazz, rhythm and blues, and a lot of down-home funk music. The clubs we played in were black, and I had a wonderful time. I felt no prejudice and saw no color. After five days of rigid, heavy schoolwork, the weekends were a refreshing change. Instead of strict discipline and critical evaluation, I could play music I loved for the fun of it.

I had no trouble with ear training but had a tough time with theory and harmony. It was also difficult for me to perform in school. That first year, we performed only once in a while just for the other woodwind players, but the pressure felt intense. It made us extremely nervous. I saw players whose legs shook so bad you could see their pants legs flopping back and forth as if there were a fan behind them making a breeze. I never got to the point where my pants flopped in the wind, but my mouth got dry and my foot trembled. I never had those feelings playing jazz on weekends. Many times, I said to myself, "No more. If I ever manage to finish this first year, I'm not returning. This is ridiculous."

In those moments, my father's words came back. "If you start something, finish it. Don't be a quitter." His words helped. I didn't want to be a quitter. I plowed through the work. By the end of the year, I had gotten used to the grind and decided to come back. I knew that someday I wanted to travel to Hollywood and do studio work, so I took up the flute at age nineteen, my second year at Oberlin.

Bob Willoughby, my teacher, played second flute in the Cleveland Symphony Orchestra. He was a nice guy, a lot of fun, an excellent flute player and teacher, who gave me a solid foundation right from the beginning. No bad habits. After a few months, I began trying jazz things on the flute.

In my second year, I played clarinet before the whole student body for the first time and got through it fine. But during my lesson a few days later, I told my teacher, George Waln, how I felt. It was torture, and I am not a masochist. Is performing always going to feel that way? If so, maybe I should reconsider my intentions about becoming a professional musician.

He said something very important, which I've never forgotten and which has held true all of these years—"Just get absorbed and involved in the music. When you do, you will forget about the audience and the stage and the fact that you are performing. Let yourself become absorbed, and your nervousness will either diminish significantly or completely vanish." He was absolutely right.

The musical challenges and difficulties I dealt with at Oberlin were far more demanding than anything else I came across during my whole professional career, including studio work in L.A. As I look back on it, I see the importance of accepting difficult challenges early in life. If you meet them, life will be easier as you get older. If you struggle to lift 200 pounds and you succeed, it's easy to lift 150 pounds from there on in.

I played a very successful senior recital on clarinet. By that time, I still felt pressure, but I could get involved with the music and enjoy it. I had conquered my nervousness. The conservatory director came backstage afterward and said, "Congratulations, Paul. That was one of the best woodwind recitals I've heard since I've been here."

That knocked me out. I had started school as a jazz musician, playing the last-chair clarinet in the concert band, not making the orchestra, not knowing anywhere near as much as everyone else, and now, four years later, the director was telling me my woodwind recital was one of the best he had heard since he had been at the conservatory. That made me feel pretty proud. Because of my performance level and my grades, I was elected to an honorary musical fraternity called Pi Kappa Lambda, the musical equivalent of Phi Beta Kappa. Part of my success was due to two teachers I had, Gustof Langenus and Simeon Bellison, both authors of several basic exercise books and both of them masters of the clarinet, widely known as two of the finest clarinetists of all times.

When I was twenty years old, home for the summer, my mother died of cancer. I could not understand my reactions to her death. It was difficult to cry. I didn't have those agonized emotions I had seen a thousand times in the movies, and I felt guilty. Did this mean I didn't love my mother? In my heart I loved my mother very much. So why wasn't I crying over her death?

I went to a nearby orthodox Jewish synagogue and talked to the rabbi. He asked if I was saying kaddish, the prayer for the dead. Yes, I said it every morning at home. That is no good, he said. You have to come to the synagogue to say it, and there must be a minyan, a quorum of ten, required by traditional law to be valid. If I didn't have a total of ten or more people saying this prayer, it wasn't going to be any good.

That really annoyed me. If nine other people weren't there, and if I didn't do it in the synagogue, does that mean God will not hear my prayers for my mother? From that moment on, I wanted nothing to do with organized religion. I didn't have much to do with it to begin with. Now I felt certain.

I certainly believe in the Power that is responsible for the whole of creation. I also believe that organized religions serve to separate humankind and to divide a person from himself or herself and from others. The great teachers and founders of religions did not come to earth to tell us there is only one route to salvation. They came to speak about the Father of us all, the universal Life Force that permeates and is responsible for the manifestation of all creation.

But because of the gap between the higher consciousness of the masters and the lower consciousness of the disciples, the profound messages of the masters of every era become locked into ritual and dogma. I was too young at the time to understand these things, but I began to see that when ritual exists for its own sake and its practitioners have no real understanding of its underlying basis, then that ritual exists only to preserve the hierarchy and perpetuate the dogma. As such, it has no value for the spiritual seeker. I began to see that all organized religions are far removed from the essential truth that gave them birth and that they are ultimately divisive.

I was deeply hurt by the rabbi's remarks—by the rigid position he took—but that hurt also served to open my eyes. The spiritual journey I took after that conversation proved to be enormously enriching, rewarding, and uplifting. It led me to India and Maharishi and meditation, and these things changed my life.

MANHATTAN SCHOOL OF MUSIC

After graduating from Oberlin in 1952, I attended the Manhattan School of Music. Simeon Bellison, one of the greatest clarinet players alive at the time, taught me clarinet, and Fred Wilkins, principal flutist with the New York City Center Opera and Ballet and with the Firestone Symphony, taught me flute. Neither bothered with basics, which we were supposed to know already. Instead, they spent their time discussing interpretation, musicianship, and phrasing. It was a great opportunity to be able to study with them.

I stayed at the Young Men's Hebrew Association (YMHA) at 92nd and Lexington Avenue in Manhattan, a huge building with many residential floors for men and women, small rooms, a good cafeteria, and a great in-house concert hall, famous for its series of classical recitals, chamber music, New York Philharmonic soloists, and a variety of ensembles. People came from all over the city to hear these concerts. As well, the YMHA had a music school of its own, where I got a job teaching. With my two teaching jobs and a scholarship, I made enough to sustain myself without having to ask my father for money.

Of course, I was in awe of New York. Here was the Big Apple, full of crazy musicians and famous people. At first, I was reluctant to play jazz, but when I went to sign up with the Musicians' Union, Local 802, I met a sax player named Tony, who said he could play faster than Stan Getz. I was just a kid. I didn't know this guy, and I was impressed. Since he was a jazz musician, he must play his ass off. He invited me to his apartment, and we talked, then went out and ate dinner. I asked if he knew any top musicians and he said, yes. In fact, there was a jam session in the Bronx that night— did I want to go with him?

I brought my horns with me, but I was nervous. I didn't know if I was going to play or not. Meanwhile, Tony was talking about how great he was and the recording sessions he'd been on. I couldn't wait to hear him play.

The club in the Bronx was a glorified bar with a good-sized stage and a lot of musicians sitting around waiting for their chance to play. The session began, and Tony jumped right up and started blowing. It was the worst sax solo I had ever heard. I couldn't believe how poorly this cat played. He moved his fingers very fast, all over the place, like the first time I improvised and didn't know what I was doing. Other guys played, too, and they weren't much better. The musicians I played with for four years in Count Williams's band at Oberlin were ten times better than all of these dudes put together.

I took out my sax and got up onstage and played. Compared to these guys, I was a superstar. Everyone came up to me afterward, saying, "Hey, man, what's your name? Where you from? Haven't seen you before. You sure play good, man."

That one night taught me a great lesson. There is nothing to fear about being in places like New York, Los Angeles, or Chicago. We build up an image in our mind—musicians in those places must be great. Well, about nine-tenths of them are shucking and jiving. There are thousands of mu-

sicians in little towns across the country that are every bit as good as players who live in big cities. There's nothing to fear. All we have to do is
change the image in our mind.

I played first clarinet in the Manhattan School Orchestra. There were a
number of excellent musicians in that orchestra, including Julius Watkins
on French horn, Joe Wilder on trumpet, Sam Most on second flute, and
Claude Monteux, conductor Pierre Monteux's son, on first flute.

Before one concert, Claude got sick, and I was asked to take his place—
playing first flute. Most symphony players do not double on other instruments. They don't want to damage their lip muscles. I regularly played first
clarinet, and now I had a chance to play first flute, highly unusual. It also
validated my abilities as a doubler, which was encouraging.

On one occasion, I played for Eleanor Roosevelt. My accompanist was a
woman named Zita Carno, a true genius, a very young pianist, about nineteen years old. She could sight-read anything—Stravinsky, Bach, anything
at all. She was an incredible pianist and technician, whose dedication to
music had rather warped her social development. She was strange, but we
all understood and accepted that.

Zita hated jazz. Whenever we rehearsed, I'd fool around with a little jazz,
and she got furious. She slammed her hands down on the keyboard and
said, "Stop playing that jazz." I'd laugh and play on, teasing her a bit. Interestingly enough, she developed an interest in jazz in later years and became a writer for a number of jazz magazines, including *down beat*.

The school received a request to select one or two students to perform
for an occasion honoring Eleanor Roosevelt. I was chosen and took Zita
with me. We were to play after Mrs. Roosevelt's speech.

Zita sat in the front row and listened to the speech. I waited in the back
of the auditorium. When Mrs. Roosevelt finished, a woman came on and
said, "Now, ladies and gentlemen, from the Manhattan School of Music,
Mr. Paul Horn on clarinet and Miss Zita Carno on piano."

Zita stood up, put two fingers in her mouth like a baseball player, gave
a tremendously loud whistle, peered at the back of the auditorium, motioned to me with a big wave of her arm, and yelled, "Hey, you!" That was
my entrance to Mrs. Roosevelt's party.

People onstage, including Mrs. Roosevelt, tried to muffle their laughter
and cover their smiles. I was embarrassed, of course. I had to come down

the aisle, holding my clarinet—the longest aisle I've ever walked. We got up on stage and played, and the people settled down and enjoyed it.

It was a terrific year. It opened my eyes to some of the realities of being a professional musician in a big music center like New York, and I met a number of first-class musicians.

Most of all, I came to realize that the classical music experience was more than mastering complex techniques. It exposed me to our entire Western cultural heritage, which has survived hundreds of years, and it took me far beyond Western traditions, into cultures thousands of years old.

The study of classical music also helped me build a vocabulary for jazz, and it helped me become a disciplined player. Jazz is the spontaneous expression of who you are, what you are, and what you know and feel. Your own life is an integral part of whatever you play. To play your life well, you must discipline yourself. Charlie Parker was a disciplined player. You can't play jazz like that unless you have enough discipline to gain total command over your instrument. He chose to live a hard life, all of which came out through his music. Instrumental virtuosity is not the goal of discipline. You and your instrument are simply tools through which you give expression to your deepest, highest Self. At the time, of course, I was not fully conscious of these things. I was developing an intuitive awareness of them as I progressed.

I knew I did not want to be a professional classical musician. In school, I gained information, learned new musical forms, connected with Ravel and Debussy and the other Impressionists who have influenced me so much. I expanded my knowledge, my mind, and my sensibilities. In other words, I prepared myself for jazz.

WE'RE IN THE ARMY NOW

As soon as I graduated with a master's degree in June 1953, I received a notice from the draft board to report for army induction. I knew I had to go, but I had options. I could be drafted for two years, or I could enlist for three and choose my assignment. I decided to enlist. After basic, I was assigned to the Navy School of Music in Washington, D.C., where I taught five or six hours five days a week, lived off-base at home with my father, and had the weekends off. I also played in the army field band. During the two years I spent with that band, I became a very good flute player. If for nothing else, I am indebted to the army in general and to the band's principal flutist, Jessie Campbell, in particular, for the opportunity to develop my flute playing.

During this time I met Yvonne at an off-base Sunday afternoon jam session in Washington, D.C. Up onstage playing, I looked at the crowd and saw a very pretty blonde out there dancing. When I stopped jamming, I introduced myself to her. We danced a few times and had a couple of drinks, I got her phone number, and we began dating.

Marie, Yvonne's girlfriend, came from the same hometown—Boonville, Mississippi. They left together and came to D.C to seek their fame and fortune. Marie went with a guitar player named John Pisano, an air force man stationed in D.C. Later, when Jim Hall left Chico Hamilton's band, I recommended John as Jim's replacement. John's career took off when I brought him to California. If I hadn't met Yvonne, I wouldn't have met Marie, and I wouldn't have known John. It is interesting how our lives are intertwined.

Yvonne was a very beautiful woman. The previous year, she was a runner-up in the Miss Washington, D.C., contest. Our relationship continued, and the next year, in 1955, we got married. We lived in a nice little apartment, and my tours were neither long nor frequent, so I got to spend time with her at home. The beginning years were good, as beginning years always are. Later on when we were living in Hollywood, she traveled with me to some of the West Coast gigs, like San Francisco, or sometimes met me on the road. She and Marie got together and kept each other company. Fred Katz and Chico Hamilton's wives were warm and hospitable and good friends, too. Our marriage worked out nicely for a while there.

About six months before my exit from the army, I played a game with myself. I've done this several times in my life, but this was the first. I asked myself, "If I had my choice of any band in the country I would like to be with, which band would that be?" I thought of Woody Herman and Stan Kenton, bands I loved as a boy, but I had changed a lot. I was a good classical musician and a good flutist. Woody and Stan might not utilize all the musical potential I felt I now had, but Eddie Sauter and Bill Finegan would.

The Sauter-Finegan band had magnificent arrangements, merging contemporary classical music with complex jazz. As a woodwind player, I would get to play all of my instruments and utilize all of my knowledge and skill. I looked on the back of one of their albums and noticed the names of two or three musicians I knew from the Manhattan School of Music. I called them, got an audition, and landed the gig—my first job with a major band.

At first, I played only on weekends, because I was still in the army. I drove to New York on Friday, a seven- or eight-hour haul in those days, arriving early afternoon, then hopped on the Sauter-Finegan bus and traveled to Ohio or some other state. We'd play the Friday night gig, then travel again the next day, play the Saturday night gig, then come back to New York, arriving around midnight. I then got in my car and drove all the way back to the army base, where I reported for work at nine in the morning. I didn't get much sleep on weekends, but I sure had a good time.

After getting out of the army, I joined Sauter-Finegan in New York City, where I worked with them only two nights on weekends for twenty-five dollars a night. Fifty dollars a week was tough to live on, especially with a wife. Luckily, an aunt of mine had vacated her Brooklyn apartment for the summer, so we stayed there, and I made regular trips to the union, where I established myself with new people.

The last recording Sauter-Finegan made for RCA Victor was *Under Analysis*. Usually, major bands used certain musicians on the road, but for the recording they hired top studio players. It is a tough decision for leaders to make, and it always upsets the musicians, but you have to do what you have to do. You can't always get the best players for the road, but it's easy and important to get them when you're cutting a record that is going to be out there for the whole world to listen to. Of all the players in the road band, Eddie and Bill selected only two for *Under Analysis*. I was one of them.

This was my first recording session. It was very scary for me, and not all of it went well. A band on stage usually sets up with the instruments close together, and everybody can hear everybody else quite well. In the studio, they spread us out all over the place. They had to separate the instruments so the sound of the trumpets and trombones didn't spill over into the mikes of the saxes or the rhythm section. By miking the sections separately, they had flexibility when it came time to raise or lower the volume of each section for the recording, a process called mixing.

But the separation of sections created a time lag in the studio. By the time I heard what the rhythm section was playing on the other side of the room, it was a fraction of a second late. If a tune has a fast tempo, that lag becomes critical.

On a fast-tempo arrangement of "Liza," I had a tenor sax solo, and I must say I did not pass that test. My ideas were there, but not the time. I couldn't anticipate, and the time-lag drove me crazy. In order for it to come out right, I had to think wrong. I had to rush to be slightly ahead of the beat in order for my solo to come out exactly on it. We tried three or four takes, but I had no experience in this area, and I couldn't cut it. The piece itself was acceptable, but they gracefully passed on my solo and edited it out.

There was another tune called "How Am I to Know?" and that was no problem. I had a nice sax solo on it, the first solo I ever recorded. That was in September 1956. Right after that, I met Chico Hamilton and joined his quintet. By the end of the year I was living in Hollywood.

Here I was now, back on the beach in Santa Monica, watching the sun turn to a deep, rich red. Reviewing these years, I felt good about my progress, a little misty-eyed about the wonderful people I had known and left. Their voices and their music and their smiles echoed in my mind like the laughter of schoolchildren down a long and distant hallway. We can cling to nothing. We can only remember and cherish. Meanwhile, life indeed goes on, each step leading to the next.

I picked up my towel and walked back up the empty beach to the parking lot. Time to return to Hollywood and launch the documentary. That should be fun to do, and Maharishi was going to love it. I couldn't wait to get it going.

FOUR

INSIDE THE TAJ MAHAL

When my inner life back in Hollywood disintegrated into chaos, I made my first trip to India. I wanted and needed to be with Maharishi for a while. My experiences during those four months of intense and inspiring introspection transformed me forever.

I returned to India the second time in 1968, not as a meditator or student, but as the producer of a film about Maharishi and the ashram. On this occasion, the conditions at the ashram were vastly different. Maharishi and Transcendental Meditation had gained enormous popularity because of the celebrities who were there—the Beatles, Shirley MacLaine, Donovan, Mia Farrow, Mike Love of the Beach Boys, and several others.

Instead of forty people taking the course, now there were a hundred. Before, a simple gate stood at the entrance. Now, a fence surrounded the entire area, with guards posted to keep people out. Reporters from all over the world tried to get in. Denied entrance, they climbed trees and took pictures with telephoto lenses. Of course, they desperately wanted shots of the Beatles, but any celebrity would do.

Because of these things, the energy of the ashram was busy and hectic. I felt fortunate I had attended the year before, when we were simply interested in meditation. Now, the gaping crowds and celebrity atmosphere turned everything into a circus. This was the Himalayas? It felt more like Hollywood. However, most of the people at the ashram quickly got used to the fact that the celebrities were there, and they did not stand in awe of them.

The Beatles themselves attended because they were sincerely interested in meditation. They didn't expect any preferential treatment; they ate in the dining hall with everybody else; they went to the same lectures. We hung out together in a relaxed way, and pretty soon it was "Hi, George," "Hi Paul," just normal daily life, which is the way we all wanted it to be.

During this time, I had the opportunity to renew my acquaintance with George Harrison. We had met through Dick Bock of World Pacific Records a year or two before. George and I became friends at the ashram and played some music together in a special little music hut that Maharishi had set aside for the Beatles and Donovan and anyone else who wanted to play there.

Nevertheless, I could not help feeling a bit sorry for the new people. They couldn't go for walks away from the ashram down by the Ganges, for example, because the premises were heavily monitored for security. That first time had been very special for me. Although the new people would undoubtedly benefit from the course, they were not getting the same shake as I; my experience had been so pure and innocent and quiet. This time, there were just too many interruptions and too much underlying energy from all of the activity.

I felt the difference, but of course the new people had no basis for comparison. They were happy to be with Maharishi, and Maharishi stuck to his schedule. He spent time with the meditators and gave his lectures and did all he could to share himself with the people in attendance.

A FILM STILLBORN

The year before, everyone came for the purpose of meditation. This year, many people were not meditators. Most of my film crew, for example, had never heard of meditation. Others had heard about it, but they thought it was all nonsense and did not believe in it.

Four Star Productions committed to the film. I was the producer, and Gene Corman was the executive producer, which made him my boss. I had chosen Maharishi to be my master, my guru, my spiritual guide, but Corman didn't believe in meditation, and he thought Maharishi was a fraud. Corman created a lot of problems. In fact, he became a total drag.

Meanwhile, I was responsible for a $500,000 budget and for seeing that the film got made. I had a responsibility to Maharishi and a responsibility to the Four Star film company. Corman didn't believe in Maharishi's integrity or authenticity, and yet I had to work with him.

Initially, Corman's arrival was delayed, which meant I was the one who had to get everything rolling. Corman had made many films. I had not made even one—but now I was in charge. It was totally up to me. Following my original idea, I had us film Maharishi as he gave his lectures, and we shot footage of the meditators as they went through their daily routine. The whole idea was to film things spontaneously, having fun with the documentary, presenting Maharishi and the ashram and the meditators in a loving, natural light—*cinema verité*.

When Corman arrived, he wanted nothing to do with that approach. He wanted everything planned and set up, even though we had no script. As Corman took over, I lost control of the project. He and I clashed on nearly everything. Several times, I was pushed right to the edge of my sensibilities, and yet I had to hang in there because of my responsibilities, forced to watch as my premises and intentions for making the film flew right out the window.

Pretty soon, my beautiful dream turned into a nightmare. Corman and his crew were completely insensitive to the significance of Maharishi, meditation, and the ashram. Ultimately, the spontaneity and feeling I envisioned were lost. The film had no heart, and it was never released.

A number of good things came out of this trip, however. It was like a spiritual journey, in which I encountered innumerable trials that tested my patience, goodwill, and intelligence to the limit. From these tests I learned more about karma, detachment, self-control, and timing. I learned how to cope with some incredibly complex business affairs. And during the filming, I traveled to Agra and recorded *Inside the Taj Mahal*.

THE TAJ MAHAL AND THE RECORDING

Of all my albums, *Inside the Taj Mahal* is perhaps the most special. In terms of performance and intention, it was a magical moment, absolutely spontaneous, completely pure and innocent. I simply wanted to play solo flute music in that gorgeous environment and thought it would be nice to bring a tape home for myself and a few friends.

The original concept of the Maharishi movie was washing down the tubes; my disagreements with Corman frustrated me daily to the point of anger; throughout the production, I was surrounded by incessant conflicts and endless turmoil. Given that kind of context, one might think I would play rage music, not the music of serenity and inner peace.

Retrospectively, however, I can now see how it was possible to record that particular album in that particular moment, nor do I feel amazed by its gentle, uplifting spaciousness. The *Inside* recording session was a kind of test. Happily, it turned out well, but it was still a test. It clearly showed the degree to which my meditations had helped me adapt to chaotic, upsetting situations like those in which I was embroiled with Corman.

Every event in our life has an impact upon us. Of course, the degree and depth of that impact varies considerably, depending upon how far we have evolved within ourselves. Maharishi uses an analogy that I like, in which he talks about experiences and the ways they affect us.

Picture a chisel carving a line into some hard object, like a stone. If we have little or no awareness, our consciousness is very much like stone. When life's negativity carves its line upon us, the scar remains forever. It is fixed. It is with us all the time. It nags us continually, never letting us alone. In extreme cases, it leads to nervous breakdowns, even to suicide.

Imagine a stick drawing a line in soft sand. As we develop a bit of awareness, our perspective begins to widen. We become a little more detached and flexible, a little more like sand. Negativity still affects us, but less so. The stick of life leaves its line, but the line is lighter. A breeze comes along and blows new sand across it, or you can brush the line away with your foot. Sand is more receptive, more accepting, less resistant, and thus a line drawn in sand is neither deep nor permanent.

Now picture a stick drawing a line in water. The more evolved you become, the more fluid you become. You resist nothing, absorbing all that happens, enfolding the whole of the experience, and you do it without personal attachment. When the stick draws a line in water, it leaves behind but a shallow wake that vanishes in an instant.

If you are psychologically healthy and you have advanced well along the spiritual path, then you start noticing certain changes in your life. Whatever happens does not leave as much of a mark, not because you are insensitive, but because you are no longer identified with your outer self, with your physical ego-self that you see in the mirror.

You are still you, aware of everything that happens. You are sensitive to every nuance; you feel every feeling. But you respond differently because now you are established within your inner Self, your higher Self, your eternal, spiritual Self. This is your foundation and your home. This is where you reside. This is where you make your stand every day. You take your view of life from here. You feel centered instead of vulnerable, whole instead of fragmented, confident instead of insecure. No matter what happens, life's activities do not disturb your fundamental equanimity.

When you meditate long enough, that inward center begins to develop. It grows stronger over a period of time, and pretty soon it becomes an ever-present reality.

Maharishi emphasized to us that meditation is not a goal, not an end in itself. It is an ongoing process, designed to help us in our daily life. Progress in meditation is not measured by what happens during meditation. Yes it is wonderful to have insights and revelations and realizations, but they are not the measures of progress, not in themselves.

To test the effectiveness of your meditations, you ask yourself how your life is going. Are negative things affecting you less severely now? Are your relationships better? Do you have more creative energy? Do you feel calmer and more centered in the marketplace? Do you feel more loving at home? Are you basically a happier person?

I had been through several long meditations the previous year at the ashram, one lasting eighty-five hours. During the year between my first and second trips to India, I meditated every day; I taught meditation to others; I attended meditation meetings and took courses regularly, occasionally going on weekend and five-day retreats.

When it came time to record *Inside the Taj Mahal*, how was I going to meet the test? All about me, swirling like a cyclone, personalities clashed. Loving, creative ideas got ripped to shreds. I was not immune to that context. Yes, I became angry with Corman—not once, but many times, eventually to the point of wanting to punch him out. I am human. I was involved in the cyclone, and I was reacting to it. But there was now a significant difference in the quality of those reactions.

The negativity around me was not affecting me deeply. It wasn't touching me way down inside, where the center is. Like lines drawn in water, my reactions did not disturb anything fundamental, and they did not last very long. While events about me raged, I stepped inside, to the center of the cyclone, where everything was calm. In the act of recording *Inside the Taj Mahal,* I saw how my spiritual practices had helped me evolve.

Changes on the outside reflect changes on the inside. This recording was the first musical verification of the psychological and spiritual changes that had been taking place within me. The music on *Taj Mahal* was different from any music I had ever recorded before.

When I started playing piano as a child, I had no teachers, I had no fear, I had no ambition. The music was just there, and it was fun to play. I simply ran my hands over the keys, and beautiful sounds came out. It was fun, and above all, it was innocent. When formal education took over, I lost that innocence. With *Taj Mahal,* I regained it.

The Bible says, "In order to enter the kingdom of heaven, you must become as a little child." As I said earlier, that passage does not mean you are supposed to be ignorant or silly. It means becoming open and innocent, feeling awe and wonder. It means taking delight in life, although you may already be a mature person.

I had passed through the fires. I had the mature awareness of a man who has lived in the world for a while. I knew something about life. In that sense, I was not innocent. And yet, I was able to let go of it all. I was able to free myself from the intellect's concerns and just be simple and childlike, open and egoless, receptive to the music of that particular moment.

It was a moment of peace that had nothing to do with the film. I was away from Gene Corman, and I was among friends, with Earl Barton and John Archer, sound man on the film, and an Indian boy named Shankar. Here we were, in this beautiful place together. I was able to pick up the flute and play, transcending the problems, conflicts, and frustrations whirling around outside.

I felt no separation between me and the music, no awareness of myself playing. There was no desire to prove anything, no desire to record an album, no desire for approval. Here I was, just with the music, totally absorbed. As I began to play, I disappeared. I dissolved like a raindrop in the ocean and became one with the music. At that moment, only the music existed. It was an exceptionally peaceful event in my life and a very special evening.

The Taj Mahal stands just outside the city of Agra, on the south bank of the Jumna River. It is one of the most splendid monuments ever created. The majesty of it staggers the imagination, and the hushed atmosphere throughout the environment makes the soul glow deep within.

It is a tomb, erected by the Mogul emperor Shah Jahan in memory of his beautiful and beloved wife, Arjumand Banu Begum. The emperor affectionately called her Mumtaz Mahal, the Jewel of the Palace.

In 1631 Mumtaz died giving birth to her fourteenth child. Overwhelmed by grief, the emperor decided to build a monument immortalizing his lost wife and her exceptional beauty. He summoned the finest designers and craftsmen in the world. Working twenty-four hours a day, 22,000 men completed this architectural masterpiece in the year 1648.

Its white marble walls are inlaid with imported Tibetan turquoise, Chinese jade, Ceylonese sapphire, Arabian coral, Persian amethyst, Punjabian jasper, and fourteen other kinds of precious and semiprecious stones. When the full moon ascends, the marble domes seem to rise and unfold like pure white lotus flowers suffused with a blue-white glow. When you are there, it is easy to see why the majestic splendor of this memorial has inspired lovers, artists, and the general populace for more than three hundred years.

A man always stands guard in the central dome where the shah and his Jewel are entombed. He explains the inscriptions and magnificent floral inlay work in the marble, and every few minutes he unexpectedly bursts forth with a vocal call, demonstrating the remarkable acoustics that emanate from the dome, which is solid marble, sixty feet in diameter, eighty feet high. You hear his call at the beginning of the album.

This particular guard was a young man, quite proud of his job. His pride stemmed from the fact that he was the fourteenth generation of the family that did the original inlay work. He and his family still did any repairs that were needed because of vandalism, neglect, or natural causes.

The first time I heard his voice, I couldn't believe my ears. Each tone hung suspended in space for twenty-eight seconds. The acoustics are so perfect that I couldn't tell when his voice stopped and the echoes began. Individual tones did not spread out and decay as they do in other large halls. They remained pure and round to the very end. When I had visited the Taj Mahal on my first trip to India, I didn't bring my flute. This time, I did.

On this occasion, which was a month before we recorded anything, I visited the Taj with my friends Larry Kurland, a free-lance photographer from New York, and Shankar, a fourteen-year-old Indian boy.

When I had arrived for my second visit with Maharishi, I stepped from a ferryboat which had taken me across the Ganges to a small Himalayan town called Swargashram. Almost immediately, I heard a small voice say, "Carry your bags, Sahib? Are you going to Maharishi's ashram?" It was Shankar. He carried my bags, and we got acquainted. He sort of attached himself to me, and soon we became good friends.

Shankar was a bright boy who spoke English quite well. He had lived in the streets since he was ten years old, teaching himself English. At fourteen or so, he already knew how to survive in the world and how to wheel and deal. I liked his charm, humor, and intelligence, so I took him on and paid him ten rupees a day to run errands for me and the film crew. He also served as my interpreter and guide, saving many a rupee whenever he felt someone was trying to take advantage of me. He had never seen the Taj Mahal, so I brought him along and let him carry my flute.

The central dome was too crowded with tourists that day, so we stepped inside one of the outer chambers leading off the central dome. It was quieter there. Shankar handed me my flute and said, "Play, Sahib. Here is Lord Krishna's flute." (Lord Krishna is a Hindu god, an avatar who descended to the earth-plane some 5,000 years ago; he is always portrayed as either playing or holding a flute.) Shankar and I sat together on the floor in the antechamber, and I began to play.

Even here, where the ceiling was rather low, the sound was amazing as it bounced off the marble walls. A few people came over and stood above us. They smiled with delight at the sound and were fascinated with my gold-plated flute. A couple of Hindu monks talked with us. We remained for a while, hoping the tourists would leave the central dome, but they didn't. Before long, it was late afternoon, and we had to return to New Delhi. The sounds of the flute still rang in my head.

A month later, we came back, this time to work on the movie. In addition to the Taj Mahal, we were to film the Agra Fort, Akbar's Mausoleum, and Fatehpur Sikri (the "Ghost City"). The first day, bright and early, we arrived at the Taj Mahal to prepare for our next day's shooting.

How good it was to be back in that enchanted place. I closed my eyes and felt a warm glow inside. "How lucky I am to be able to visit so often," I thought. When Shankar and I walked into the mausoleum, I felt a sense of familiarity that gave me a strange feeling, similar to the feeling I had the year before when I arrived in India, almost like being home.

A marble screen surrounds the tombs. In itself, this screen is a work of art. It stands as high as a man; it is carved from a single block of marble, and yet it looks as delicate and translucent as blue-white lace.

The man guarding the tombs was the same young man we had seen the month before. Every few minutes he gave his call, which thrilled me. His voice seemed to hang in the air forever, floating, echoing, spiraling. I introduced myself, and we talked. He had that warm, beautiful openness that so many Indian people have.

I told him how much I liked his voice, that I was a musician, and that I would love to play my flute in here. He said to meet him that evening, around 8:30. Few people would be there then, and I would be able to play for an hour before they closed at 9:30.

That night, April 25, 1968, I returned with Shankar, Earl Barton, and John Archer, who brought a microphone and a small Nagra tape recorder. The evening was warm and humid, and the moon was out. We were not lucky enough to have a full moon, which is supposed to be the most magical time in the Taj Mahal. But there was enough moonlight and warmth in the air to create a feeling of intimacy and suspension.

Filled with excitement and anticipation, I mounted the stairs two at a time to the marble platform upon which the tombs rest. We entered the arched entrance—and found no tourists. Empty except for us, the room felt silent and still, soft and eternal.

Incense and a single candle burned on Mumtaz Mahal's tomb. The candle flickered, casting phantasmagoric shadows through the marble-laced screen onto the blue-white circular walls. In the tomb adjacent to his wife, Shah Jahan seemed to be watching over us.

From behind, I approached my friend, the guard, and greeted him. When he turned around, the smile on my face froze. This wasn't my friend.

It was someone else, a different guard. John Archer, not knowing this, began setting up his recording equipment.

"Namasté," I said to the guard, holding my hands together politely, Indian fashion.

He just nodded. He didn't smile. As I opened my flute case, he was not friendly, courteous, or inviting.

"What are you doing?" he asked.

"I'd like to play my flute here."

"You can't do that," he said.

"Why not?"

"This is a tomb."

"You sing in here, don't you?"

"Yes, of course I sing—but I sing to God," he replied emphatically.

"Well, I play my flute to God," I said, just as emphatically. "What is the difference?" I took my flute out and started putting it together.

I wondered how far I'd get, but the guard had no reply to my rebuttal, and John Archer was almost set up, so we went ahead as if the guard wasn't even there. Right between the tombs, I sat down with my alto flute and played a low C, which sailed out, filled the entire room, and hung suspended in air, reverberating, echoing, spinning, and spiraling like a gentle bird. It was a completely different sound from the guard's voice, with different vibrations and different overtones. It was the most beautiful sound I had ever heard.

The guard stood transfixed, his eyes full of wonder. He had never heard anything like this either. I played a few more notes. The guard said nothing and made no moves to stop us, so I motioned to John, who now had his headset on. "Roll it."

I played whatever came into my head, letting the notes hang in the air, listening to them as they echoed and multiplied, turning into whole chords, returning to my ears like choirs of angels. On top of each phrase, I played another, leaving long pauses between phrases so the music did not become cluttered. Pretty soon, the music sounded as if a whole orchestra was invisibly suspended among the shadows in the highest reaches of the dome. Magnificent, so beautiful, so true.

After a few minutes, I stopped and looked at the guard. He smiled ear to ear, clearly enjoying himself. I told him to give his call, which he did, and signaled John to keep the tapes rolling.

At 9:30, the guard said it was closing time. He had to make his rounds. I started dismantling my flute, but he turned and said, "No, that's okay. You stay." We were delighted, and I continued playing.

Earl and Shankar sat in back of me, a little to one side. Every once in a while, they slapped mosquitoes. After a few minutes of playing, I opened my eyes and looked at my arms holding the flute. They were covered with the biggest mosquitoes I had ever seen. I just closed my eyes and kept on playing. I didn't get one bite all night long.

However, a funny thing happened. Later, back in the hotel room, we listened to the playbacks. Right in the middle of one of the improvisations, we heard a mosquito go Bzzzzzzst! That cracked me up. He wanted to get in the act! He's got to be the only mosquito who ever "made it." You can hear him on "Agra," about forty-two seconds into it.

Also as we recorded, we heard a fireworks explosion that came from a nearby wedding celebration. Although the wedding took place at least a half-mile away, the explosion sounded like it was there in the room. You hear it on "Mumtaz Mahal," one minute and thirty-four seconds from the beginning.

The hall was completely emptied of tourists when the guard came back. This time, he brought two men with him, one of whom was my friend, the guard who said it would be okay for us to play here. He apologized for being late and introduced us to the other man, a close friend of his, a superb singer.

I said to the guard's friend, "I'll play, you sing." I then played a brief phrase and stopped, motioning for him to do the same. He caught on immediately, and we improvised a beautiful duet. The piece had so much empathy and warmth that I called it "Unity." He spoke very little English, and I spoke very little Hindi, and yet we were able to create this music together without knowing each other at all. Truly, music is the universal language that can unite the spirit of human beings everywhere.

The tape was used up around 11:00 P.M., by which time I was played out anyway. We packed up and slowly walked downstairs to the garden. As we headed toward the exit, walking beside that long, rectangular alabaster pool, my mind flashed to Richard Halliburton, one of my childhood heroes.

Back in the twenties, Halliburton wrote a book called *The Royal Road to Romance*. When he was a kid, he felt a burning desire for adventure. He was one of those people who would do anything once. Finally he became so bored with school that he walked out of his college economics class and never returned. Instead, he followed his dreams and traveled all over the world, doing and seeing as much as he could. He took odd jobs—cook, bus boy, deck swabber, whatever—not for his next meal, but to get him from country to country.

During the course of his life he wrote many books, but in *The Royal Road to Romance*, his autobiography, he tells of his adventure in the Taj Mahal. When the guards closed down for the night, Halliburton hid behind some trees and escaped their notice. He spent the whole night alone in the Taj Mahal, undetected, and swam in this same alabaster pool.

Looking at the moonlight in the pool and my reflection in the waters as we walked toward the gate, I thought about his experience, which was quite extraordinary. I smiled at his memory, as if he were a distant friend. And I could not help feeling that perhaps on this night I had done something even more extraordinary than he. With that thought in mind, I returned with my friends to the hotel.

THE SELLING OF *INSIDE*

It was not until I returned to Los Angeles and played the music for my friends that I thought of releasing *Inside* as a commercial album. They thoroughly enjoyed what they heard and encouraged me to take it around to record companies.

The first person I thought of was my old friend Dick Bock, the founding president of Pacific Jazz Records, which later became World Pacific. I had known him from the beginning of my jazz career, when I recorded on his label with Chico Hamilton's Quintet. It was also Dick who had visited the ashram my first year there and set up those two recordings I did with Indian musicians.

I took *Inside* to Dick one evening after the hectic business day had ended and telephones had stopped ringing. We sat quietly in his office and listened to the music undisturbed, which was good. When you listen to music that is this quiet, interruptions shatter the listening experience.

He was a sensitive man, receptive to quiet, gentle music, and he enjoyed what he heard. "Let me run it by my marketing people and see what they think."

When I first met Dick many years before, he was a one-man company. He did everything himself, including recording, editing, mixing, promotion, and marketing. He made up his own mind about everything, and matters were comparatively simple. Now he had a promotional division. He sent the tape to Massey Lipton, his marketing man.

A couple of days later, I talked again with Dick.

"Massey said he has doubts about *Inside*," Dick said.

"Oh?"

"In order to sell records, we've got to have airplay, and he's not sure we can get it with this album."

"Why not?"

"The music's too sparse and low-keyed, not exciting enough. Who will listen to something this quiet and spaced-out? Who will play it on the radio? Massey suggests you go into the studio and add a few percussion sounds, maybe some bells, gongs, a few finger cymbals—you know, jazz it up a little, make it more commercial."

I just looked at him. This point of view sounded very strange, especially coming from Dick. Then I said, "The only reason I'm here is because my friends thought it would be wonderful to get *Inside* released as a commercial album.

"This was a special moment, pure and pristine, and you know that, Dick. Frankly, I don't care if *Taj* comes out commercially or not. I never intended it to be an album, and I'm not attached to it that way. However, if it does come out, it must be as pure music, with pure echoes, and nothing added in the studio. *Inside* contains the living feelings of the living moment in which it was inspired. Bells and percussion would make it contrived. There's no way I will let that happen."

Dick went along with his marketing man, and I did not feel uncomfortable with the fact that *Inside* would not be released. I couldn't think of anyone else to bring it to in L.A., so that was it.

When Dick and I talked about it years later, he said, "You know, I turned down your *Inside* record, and it bothers me to this day. *Inside* was first-rate music and a commercial hit. You were right to keep it pure. But what could

I do? What's the point of hiring marketing people if you don't take their advice? Still, I wish I had taken *Inside* when I had the chance."

In a way, I also had regrets. Dick would have been much more aware of what he had than Epic and Columbia ever were, and he would have sold many more records. To this day, Columbia and Epic still don't know what they had in that album, and they don't care, either. Their company is too big, and *Inside*, although it sold over 750,000 copies, never sold as much as Bruce Springsteen or Michael Jackson, so what the heck. I, too, wish Dick had picked it up.

Nothing happened for about a year. Then one day I met an old friend in Hollywood, Chuck Gregory, a wonderful person. When I first met him, I had just signed my first Columbia contract, and Chuck was a Columbia salesman. He took me around to radio stations when my records came out, lined up interviews, helped me plug the albums. He was a happy person who laughed a lot, a big fan of mine, a very sociable guy, and we became good friends. Because I'd left Columbia and gone with RCA and then took off for India, I hadn't seen him for perhaps five years.

"Things have changed," he said. "I'm not a salesman any more. I'm West Coast director of Artist and Repertoire (A&R) for Epic." That meant he was in charge of signing new talent to the label. "You got anything for me?" he asked.

"I recorded a solo flute album inside the Taj Mahal."

"Oh, yeah? Bring it over. I'd like to hear it."

I played it for him, and he loved it. He sent the tape to David Kapralik, the number-one A&R man in New York. Kapralik also liked it and signed me with Epic, one of Columbia's subsidiary labels. In a sense, I was now back with Columbia.

"How much do you want up-front?" Chuck asked me.

Throughout my previous albums, it had never occurred to me to ask for an advance, which shows how naive I was. Even if I had asked for an advance, I probably wouldn't have gotten it. In those days, jazz musicians never thought of themselves as big sellers, and they weren't. If a jazz artist sold 5,000 copies, that was good. It was a big deal to sell 10,000, even though nobody made anything from it, as it barely covered expenses.

Perhaps Miles Davis earned something of an income from his early records, but Charlie Parker certainly didn't. Very few jazz musicians made any money at all. They were just happy to get their music out for others to hear, and to some extent, an album increased opportunities for concerts and club work. That was about it. Nobody asked for advances, including myself.

Record companies always gave musicians a line, and musicians always bought it—"Forget the advance. Keep the costs down. That way, you'll get out of the red faster and start collecting royalties sooner." Well, out of my thirteen albums prior to *Inside*, I got paid double-scale only for being the leader; I never got out of the red; and I never received any royalties.

Now here was Chuck Gregory asking me how much I wanted. The figure $5,000 came to mind, and that's what I told him. A couple of days later, he said, "Okay." Of course, I immediately wondered if I shouldn't have asked for more, maybe $10,000 or $20,000. However, you can see only as far as you can see, and $5,000 seemed like a big figure to me at the time. That's what I asked for, and that's what I got.

Compared to today's standards, the advance wasn't that much, but I received a big break on the publishing. I got to keep all of it, 100 percent, which was not the normal procedure. When I recorded my first album, I had set up my own publishing company, which meant I owned the copyrights to all original material, and that paid me full publishing royalties, which are called mechanical rights. Most record companies try to get the publishing rights, because then they pay only 50 percent of the mechanicals to the composer, keeping 50 percent themselves.

Somewhere in the beginning of our contractual talks, Epic mentioned they would like to have the publishing. For some reason, they did not pursue the matter, and I never asked why. Over the years, I've made more money from the publishing royalties than from the album royalties, which were only 5 percent per copy. Today, I make two or three times that much. In any case, I got to keep the publishing rights for *Inside*, which was great.

"ARTISTS" AT WORK

On the album jacket, I wanted to tell the story of how *Inside the Taj Mahal* was created, but the story would be too long to print on only one side.

Therefore, I asked for a gatefold cover, which opens up like a book. We could print the notes on the two inner surfaces. Usually, gatefolds were reserved for double-LPs, but I had only one LP, and this caused problems.

"Why is it a problem?" I asked.

"Because we have to charge an additional dollar for the record."

"What's wrong with that?"

"It's against our policy, and we hate to go against our policy. Your album is part of the regular line, and for our regular line we charge only $3.99 per album. Now you come along and want us to charge $4.99."

"How is one more dollar going to keep anyone from buying this record? I mean, if somebody likes me and the music, and they really want to hear this album, I don't see how an extra dollar is going to stop them."

They didn't go for it. I stepped over the business affairs department and went to the top. I attended a convention in Los Angeles and talked to the head of Epic Records. He heard me out and said okay, and I got my double-album gatefold and won the battle.

However, when I received a copy of the artwork from New York, I freaked out. I had wanted a picture of the Taj Mahal on the front, but they put a shot of my face on it, an extreme close-up from the top of my eyes down to my chin. It was huge. It filled the whole cover, and I didn't like it. They, of course, thought it was "catchy."

Also, they wanted to entitle the album, *Paul Horn Inside*. I wanted to simply call it *Inside*, not *Paul Horn Inside* and not *Inside the Taj Mahal*. Yes, I played inside the Taj Mahal, but the experience was also a quiet, inner experience. I was deeply within myself, as well as inside the Taj Mahal. The music is inner music, and I wanted that connotation in the title. We compromised. The album was called *Paul Horn/Inside*, and I had to get used to seeing my huge face on the cover.

They did include a nice picture of the inside of the Taj Mahal on the back, but I freaked out again when I opened the gatefold and looked at the two inner surfaces. One side was beautiful, and I had no objection to it. I had given the art director a nice picture of the Taj Mahal in moonlight. He used it, and that was fine.

He used the same picture on the other side, too, but—can you believe this?—he also overlayed pictures of little toy cars driving along the edge of the reflecting alabaster pool and had little puppets walking around all over the place.

First, Massey Lipton wanted to add bells, gongs, and finger cymbals, and now this guy was laying the same trip on me graphically. He said the album wouldn't sell with a cover that was just simple, plain, and direct. So let's be cute and create this little montage with the cars and the puppets. I groaned. Poor Richard Halliburton must have groaned in his grave along with me.

I flipped out and got on the phone and complained to people in the Hollywood branch of the company, but it was impossible to convince them. I said, "Okay, if that's how you want to play. . . ."

I bought an airplane ticket, flew back to New York, entered the big CBS building at 51 West 52nd Street, took the elevator up to the sixtieth floor, walked right in, and said, "Who is responsible for this?"

A graphics man was there, directing a slew of artists who sat at drawing boards all day long, pumping out this kind of stuff for their albums.

I introduced myself and said, "How can you do this?"

"What do you mean?"

"Look at my album. You're laying your personal trip on it, and your trip has nothing to do with the music. Did you listen to it? Have you heard it?"

"No, I haven't."

"Jesus, man, if you don't listen to the music, how can you know what to do with your graphics?"

He was not accustomed to this approach, of course. Like so many record company people, he just figured it was pop music. And if it's pop music, what difference does it make what's on the cover? If it's rock 'n' roll, let's put on some rock 'n' roll. And if it's rock 'n' roll, then it's rock 'n' roll, and we don't have to listen to it anyway—because it's rock 'n' roll.

"Well, it's not rock 'n' roll," I said. "This is a sensitive, introspective album, as far removed from rock as you can get. What you have done with this cover is totally contrary to the music. As far as I am concerned, the cover should reflect the music's content. Otherwise, you completely misrepresent me and the music to the buying public."

"I don't make the final decision," he said. "See my boss."

I spoke to his boss, the head of the graphics department, but he wouldn't make the decision either. I had to speak to *his* boss. It cost me a dozen sleepless nights, a plane ticket to New York, and all of the aggravation with the company people, but I finally won the battle. They took out the cars and the puppets.

The war, however, was not over.

I wanted the gatefold covers so I could write liner notes, telling listeners how the album transpired. But Epic wanted to use the inner surfaces for pictures. I said, "Okay, but the story still isn't there. Print the notes on both sides of a separate piece of paper and glue it in." They agreed, and I finally got the album out. But even then, after all of those hassles, they still didn't do it right.

Pressing plants print albums twenty-four hours a day. Unless someone calls attention to the fact that a specific album is a special order, and a piece of paper with notes must be glued in, the album will just go through the regular process and emerge without the paper. At least half of my records sold without those liner notes glued inside.

I didn't even know it until several people said, "What a wonderful album. Did you really record inside the Taj Mahal? How did it come about?"

"Didn't you read the notes?"

"What notes?"

Today, *Inside the Taj Mahal* is reissued on Kuckuck Records by Celestial Harmonies. There is a lovely picture of the Taj Mahal on the front; the notes are on the CD booklet so they can't get lost; the whole thing is beautifully packaged; and it includes *Inside II* as a bonus.

COSMIC TIMING

An impressive number of people bought the album, which startled all the record companies, not just my own. They were surprised that any market whatsoever existed for this kind of music. As I said, it was not my intention to create a commercial record, nor was it my intention to create a new style, and yet people bought *Inside*, and that album set a new course and a new direction, certainly for me, and to some extent, for music itself.

At the time, I still considered myself a jazz musician. I had a fusion band that vibist Lynn Blessing formed for me, and we played many styles of music. My quiet solo flute playing now became a regular part of our presentation.

Of course, I had played and recorded with Chico Hamilton, and over a dozen albums of my own were out, but to my surprise, I suddenly found myself with a whole new audience that was totally unaware of me as a jazz musician. They thought *Inside the Taj Mahal* was my first recording and perceived me as a "meditative" musician. By 1970 and 1971, probably the majority of people who attended my concerts thought of me solely in terms of *Inside the Taj Mahal*.

That proved to be a little bit of a conflict. How could I play an entire solo flute concert? Eventually I did that, but in those days I didn't think in solo terms. I wanted to present my musical personality in all of its facets, so we played jazz tunes, blues, ballads, fusion numbers, and then, once or twice a night, I improvised a long solo flute piece, using an electronic device called an Echoplex, which repeated my phrases, simulating the echoes in the Taj Mahal.

In the period during which *Inside* was recorded—the late 1960s through the mid-1970s—a new genre of music was born, today called New Age music. Because of *Inside the Taj Mahal*, many people have referred to me as the father of New Age music. In certain ways that is true, although no one person creates a whole new type of music.

Internationally, many musicians began exploring, not only forms of music that were new to the Western ear, but states of mind that were new to the West as well. Paul Winter, Terry Riley, Henry Wolff, Iasos, Constance Demby, and numerous others lived in America; Tony Scott lived in Japan; Peter Michael Hamel and Deuter lived in Germany; Vangelis and Jarre lived in France. During the sixties into the mid-1970s, these and many other musicians all over the world picked up on essentially the same vibration, which they expressed through inner music, serenity music, introspective music, quiet music, meditative music. Whatever you want to call it, musicians brought it through them and passed it on. Eventually, people began calling it New Age music.

It's true that *Inside the Taj Mahal* had an impact on music and the marketplace. It was an innovative album, and it pointed the way toward new styles and new states of mind. It caught on and made an impression, but never once was that my intention. As I said, I gave birth to it in total innocence. In no way could I have predicted its reception or controlled its influence. I call it timing, cosmic timing. Nobody has control over that.

NEW AGE MUSIC

One reason *Inside the Taj Mahal* and some of the other "Inside" albums became successful is that my level of awareness, extended through music, paralleled the general transformation of awareness in society at large. Along with a number of other musicians, I was giving voice to what many other people were beginning to feel. I needed and wanted quiet moments in my daily life, and so did they.

Even if it wasn't conscious for most people, the desire was still there. We need some kind of balance in our existence. We live hectic, fast-paced, anxiety-ridden lives. To balance that out, we need to slow down and relax; we need to become quiet and still within ourselves; once in a while, we need to shift from left-brained, intellectually oriented thinking to spacious, intuitive, right-brained, creative thinking.

In its higher forms, much of so-called New Age music helps us enter psychological and spiritual comfort-zones that revitalize us. So does meditation. By the late sixties and early seventies, interest in both of these things was growing, and it has continued to grow, naturally, without being forced.

People became more aware of stress and how it affects us, for example. Even the medical profession finally acknowledged stress and its deleterious effects on the body, mind, and emotions. As more and more people became aware of stress, so they also became aware of meditation and New Age music. All around us in society, awareness of these things grew by leaps and bounds, and it continues growing today. Traveling around the world for over twenty years, I've seen this awareness spread to other countries, including China and Russia. Wherever I have gone, I've seen increasing interest in meditation and quiet forms of music.

Back then, I felt the same need for balance and inner quietude that others felt, and that need manifested itself through my music. It was not necessarily a conscious act; it was a natural unfoldment of who and what I am.

Music can satisfy every mood, but in our society we have chosen to focus almost exclusively on exciting music—music that gets our feet tapping, our body moving, and our adrenaline flowing, either through intense emotional catharsis, as in rock 'n' roll, or through dazzling intellectual complexity, as in jazz or classical music, both of which often contain profound emotions and astonishing technical virtuosity. These forms of music are valid and worthwhile because they too answer listeners' needs. They are stimulating musics, exciting and satisfying. Above all, they are entertaining.

New Age music, particularly in its more serious forms, answers different needs. More often than not, it is neither intellectually complex nor emotionally exciting. It is usually not satisfying on those levels, which is why some people do not understand it and cannot relate to it. In terms of source and intention, New Age music is quite different from most Western music.

Often, as in my case, this kind of music is derived from the feelings and states of mind experienced in meditation. Its intention is to relax the listener, to calm him or her down, and then to offer an aural context that is serene, spacious, blissful, nourishing, and uplifting. It does not take listeners out to the dance floor. It takes them on an exploratory journey within themselves and helps them begin to experience their own higher consciousness.

As both a player and a listener, I have always enjoyed the benefits of quiet music, even as I have enjoyed the benefits of meditation. As part of my daily routine, I sit down twice a day for about half an hour each time and go inside myself, where I become quiet and still. I know this is absolutely necessary for my mental, physical, and emotional health. It enables me to stay in top mental and physical condition; it gives me additional energy; it keeps me creatively productive. The essence of meditation and the essence of responsible, high-level New Age music is the same. Meditation is what serious New Age music is all about.

Of course, the marketplace soon diluted New Age music, just as they diluted rock and jazz. Major labels waited until small independent labels proved the music's viability. Commercial radio refused to play it. Only National Public Radio and college radio stations saw the music's value and potential. For years, the only syndicated New Age music program in existence was Stephen Hill's "Music from the Hearts of Space," which still airs on NPR stations. At first, only a few listeners enjoyed the music, then many. Through this decidedly noncommercial grass-roots movement, the music proved itself. As soon as it did, major record companies and radio stations stepped in and commercialized it. Today, all kinds of music are marketed as "New Age." A lot of it has everything to do with rhythmic pop entertainment, little or nothing to do with meditation.

As a result, I really don't know how to come up with clear definitions anymore, but I'm not sure definitions are important. When music of any kind expands beyond its original intentions, sooner or later all categories break down.

Unfortunately, not too many writers out there understand what's going on in New Age music. Lee Underwood, coauthor of this book, is one of the few who has looked deeply into the genre. He has made a number of perceptive distinctions between New Age pop forms and New Age meditation music, which he calls New Age contemporary classical music.

In *Pulse*, for example, Underwood described the kind of New Age music that I consider to be authentic: "New Age musicians often compose from psycho-spiritual states of mind resembling those experienced in meditation. Their music makes us feel good by awakening our own centers of higher consciousness. It takes us away from the busy emotional and intellectual surface of our being. It gently leads us deeply inside ourselves to the still-point center. As we relax and resonate with the music's visionary beauty and compassion, so we resonate with these same qualities in ourselves. At its best, New Age classical music reawakens all-embracing, transcendental love—for ourselves, for others, for all of nature."

That seems to be a pretty good description of what I'm talking about. To me, the essence of New Age music is its quietude. That does not mean it has to be absolutely still or totally spacious like *Inside the Taj Mahal*. Maybe somebody adds a little rhythmic percussion or some synthesizer backgrounds, but the music itself can still be quiet and sensitive and introspective. It can still help us slow down and elevate our awareness.

No matter what it may be called in the future, there will be music that helps the listener become quiet inside, music that is intended to bring peacefulness and loving feelings into a world racked with pain and confusion and greed. To me, this kind of music will always be New Age music.

When I left India the first time and returned to L.A., I played the Jazz Mass in a concert. I felt different, and the music sounded different. I attributed the difference to my experiences with Maharishi and meditation. That was one of the earliest indications I had that I was changing. At the time, I was not fully conscious of it. I just felt it.

However, *Inside the Taj Mahal* was a major verification of the spiritual changes taking place within. That was also the first time I began to grasp fully what was happening. Over the years, those changes carried through in my music, and I became fully conscious of them.

Playing the flute in the Taj Mahal, I was able to free myself of my egoistic personality. I was able to go inside myself quickly and easily and simply disappear. That carried over, and throughout the years I have been able to do it consistently. Before concerts, I do not perform any rituals, such as the puja ritual I did inside the pyramids. I don't have to meditate before performing. I can just close my eyes and go inside, or leave my eyes open and do the same thing. It doesn't make any difference.

When I start playing music, I am immediately inside and at one with it. I am out of the way. My ego and my personal concerns do not interfere with the music's flow. I have no anxieties about whether this is going to be a good night or a bad night. In such a moment, there is no good or bad or right or wrong. The moment just is. I am playing music, I feel good, and that's it.

The "at one with" experience is at the core of all spiritual teachings and is available to everyone, not just to gurus. It can be a fleeting moment, or it can sustain itself for life, depending upon our spiritual evolution. It can happen through meditation or through music. It can happen when we're standing on a mountain or viewing a sunset across the ocean. It is not a state of mind reserved for an elite minority. Although relatively few of us develop it, *all* of us have the capacity to transcend the lower self and discover our all-encompassing higher Self. And through our higher Self, all of us have the capacity to be at one with humanity and nature and God.

PART II

THE JAZZ YEARS

FIVE

CHICO HAMILTON

When Tryntje, Marlen, Robin, and I moved from Los Angeles to Canada in 1970, we had no idea what kind of a life lay before us. I had no money to speak of, and Victoria is not exactly a world center for music. As I think about my journey, I can see clearly how the Victoria move emerged out of my India travels, which, in turn, emerged directly out of my jazz years. I suppose the very beginning of it all was the gig with Sauter-Finegan, but the real launching took place with Chico Hamilton.

A BURNING TIME

Opening night. Hollywood, USA. My first gig with the Chico Hamilton Quintet. Jazz City, right on Hollywood Boulevard. People waited in line outside. Inside, the place was packed.

Cigarette smoke and the scents of alcohol and expensive perfume filled the room. The music of Shorty Rogers and his Giants played over the sound system. Good-looking men in suits and ties clinked glasses with beautiful women, whose perfect teeth sparkled almost as much as their jewelry. A classy crowd, upbeat, fast, and glamorous.

Chico stood by the EXIT door, just offstage. "Come here, Paul. Take a look." I peered at the waiting audience. "See that guy over there?" He pointed to the third row. "That's Leonard Feather, the famous jazz critic and author of *The Encyclopedia of Jazz*. See those two guys next to him? That one's from *down beat*. The other writes for *Metronome*." Chico pointed out saxophonist Benny Carter and bassist Red Mitchell, too. Then he grabbed my elbow. "Hey—over there. See her?"

I followed the line of his finger. In a corner booth near the front of the stage sat movie star Rita Hayworth. Three handsome men stood around her table, nodding and smiling at her every word.

My heart jumped.

Chico laughed. "You're in the big time now, kid."

Carrying my tenor sax, I walked back to the dressing room. My other horns were already onstage. We still had five minutes. I rewet my reed, making sure it was perfect.

"Okay, so it's a challenge," I said to myself. "Relax. You know the music. Don't just dip your toe into this pool, and don't slide in gradually, either. Do it all the way. Jump in over your head, sink or swim."

The door banged open. A stagehand yelled, "You're on!" He disappeared. I clutched my sax, nervous as hell. Showtime.

Chico gave the crowd a big smile. He twirled his sticks, whacked his big cymbal, and laid down a beat on the hi hat. Carson Smith jumped in with a walking bass groove. Fred Katz joined him with a contrapuntal cello line. On guitar, Jim Hall painted a sonic rainbow with his elegant, full-bodied chords. As if in a dream, I started blowing my sax, playing the melody over the top. We were off and flying.

Chico had the radiant personality to lead and front our band, while Fred Katz wrote most of the music. Fred composed as if you were the greatest player in the world on *all* of your instruments. No mercy. Totally demanding. In order to cut it, you had to know your stuff. I knew my stuff, thank God. Now here we were, on stage at Jazz City, the music winging its way into the spotlight as if it had a life of its own.

Right from the top, I loved this group. Just before I got the gig, I had fantasized to myself the same way I had fantasized about Sauter-Finegan. "Of all the jazz groups in the country, which one would I like to be in?" Answer: the Chico Hamilton Quintet.

I wanted to be with Chico for a lot of reasons. Cellist Fred Katz wrote challenging compositions and complex arrangements. All of my horns and all of my classical training and jazz background would be utilized. In Sauter-Finegan's big band, I was one of five sax players in a section. In Chico's smaller group, we had just one cello, one guitar, one bass, one drummer, and one reedman. That meant considerably more exposure for all of us.

The audition took place one afternoon at the Blue Note Club in Philadelphia. Immediately, there were good vibes between Chico and me. I could sense that Fred was a very intelligent man and a warm human being. He and Chico were in their late thirties, while the other guys and I were in our twenties.

Nobody was threatening or hostile that afternoon. In fact, they sort of cheered me on. I felt some pressure, of course, because the music was difficult, and this was not a matter of simply gigging with the guys around D.C. or New York. Chico's quintet was an internationally famous group making records and riding high on their success. For them, it was just an audition. For me, it was nitty-gritty time.

They took out the charts, and we played. I'm a good sight-reader. No problem. The guys were very supportive of me, which I appreciated, but no decision was made. Chico thanked me for coming and said he'd be in touch from L.A. I let it go at that.

A week later, around midnight, the phone rang, waking me up. It was Chico. The gig was mine. He sent two plane tickets. My wife, Yvonne, and I drove down from New York to D.C. We said good-bye to my father and flew to L.A.

Buddy Collette, the regular reed player for the group, was leaving. He was an in-demand L.A. studio musician and didn't want to tour anymore. That gave me my big break. However, one thing upset me. For the first week of our opening gig at Jazz City, Chico wanted me and Buddy to alternate sets. I felt bad about that. Buddy was already established, accepted by the critics, on the recordings, a good player, and a total pro. There would be enough of a comparison anyway, with my getting up there after Buddy had been working regularly with the band. Now, I was going to be compared with him every set—he's there, then I get up; he's there, then I get up. I didn't feel comfortable with that, and I said so.

"I know how you feel, man," Chico answered. "But I've got to do it this way. A lot of people are coming to hear the same group they heard on record. It will give you more time to adjust to the music. People are going to compare anyway—and, hey, you'll do just fine. If you couldn't cut it, man, I wouldn't have taken you on in the first place. Besides, Buddy will alternate sets with you only for a week. After that, the gig is entirely yours."

We finished the final number of my first set. I had managed to relax and play well, and the audience loved us.

I was putting my horns back in their cases, the sweat still wet on my face. Buddy came over and wrapped his arms around me. "You were terrific, Paul," he said, giving me a big hug. "You sounded just great."

Buddy was supportive and helpful to me that whole time. He didn't come on like the big star, saying, "Okay, hotshot, let's see you cut this." He wasn't like that at all. He's a humble and generous person, secure within himself. He is his own man and doesn't feel threatened by anyone. To this day he's that way.

At that time, I owned my flutes and all the reed horns except an alto sax, which I needed. "Hey, man," Buddy said as I finished packing my horns. "I've got two altos. Come on over tomorrow and try them out. You can have either one you want." I bought one and still own it. It was really nice of Buddy to help me out that way.

At first, my alto playing was a little weak because I hadn't played one for a while, and the sound was weird. People didn't put it down, however. They thought it was unique. Over the years, it proved to be that way. I didn't sound like Paul Desmond, Bud Shank, or Art Pepper, all of whom I liked. I was a cross somewhere in between, my own man with my own sound and my own point of view.

From the first night on, I was learning things. That Jazz City gig lasted for one month, seven nights a week, twenty-eight nights in a row, three sets a night. That's a lot of playing. My chops got strong in a hurry, and by the end of that first week, I felt totally confident, just as Chico had said I would.

Onstage, Chico didn't hog all the limelight. In so many other bands, the leaders were just arrogant assholes. Not Chico. He didn't come on like The Leader, The Boss, The Main Man, The Big Star, treating the rest of us like nameless sidemen.

Eddie Sauter and Bill Finegan were good leaders, but they were older guys, and we didn't hang out much, nor did we expect to. In Chico's band, we were closer to the same age, and it was a small group, not a big band. It felt more like a family. We knew he was the leader, and we respected that, but we also liked him as a friend.

Chico gave me another image of a leader: one who cultivated mutual respect. We treated each other in a mature way, without ego trips or power trips. Outside of little differences that exist in any family, there were very few big problems.

Chico knew how to draw the best out of us. He let each of us have his own recognition and applause. We all got our individual pats on the back, which helped our confidence and self-respect. Chico got his share, too, and he didn't feel threatened by our popularity. He didn't need to steal my fans or Fred's fans or anybody else's fans. He allowed us to have our own praise. More than any other leader I had known, he mentioned our names on stage continuously, introducing each one of us before, during, and after every set. We loved him for that.

In later years when I had my own bands, I was inspired by Chico to pay attention to the needs of the guys, to give them their proper respect and their due recognition. Like Chico, I mention their names a lot onstage. A musician's reputation is the only security and the most valuable asset he or she has. As your reputation grows, you become accepted. The people who accept you are the ones who keep you going for the rest of your life. They buy your records. They come to clubs and concerts to hear you play. Mention the name, mention the name, mention the name, over and over and over again.

Chico did that, and his band became a kind of school. A lot of good musicians graduated from Chico's group and went on to establish themselves in their own right, including reedmen Buddy Collette, myself, Eric Dolphy, and Charles Lloyd and guitarists Jim Hall, John Pisano, and Gabor Szabo. These guys were good musicians, and Chico provided the context and gave them the recognition that helped them move up and become leaders themselves.

Backstage at Jazz City, I watched people as they gathered around Chico and Fred and the other guys. A lot of people gathered around me too. I watched how Chico handled himself when people praised him. He accepted compliments very graciously. I was impressed by that.

In New York, I once went backstage after listening to a great performance. I said, "Hey, man, you sounded terrific. I loved what you were doing." The guy sort of sneered and said, "It wasn't so great, man. Nothin's happenin'."

To me, that was like a slap in the face. In effect, he was saying I was either full of shit or a terrible listener. I loved his music and opened myself up to him—and he put *me* down.

There are reasons for that. He felt awkward when praised. He felt that he hadn't played well and that musicians like myself could see through it. If I or anybody else complimented him, it must be coming from ignorance, deceit, or pity. Because of his own self-doubts, he put me down.

After that, I swore I'd never make anybody feel that way when they complimented me, even if I thought I hadn't played particularly well that night.

At least twenty Jazz City people stood around Chico. Every time somebody said something nice to him, he smiled graciously, looked them in the eye, warmly shook their hand, and said, "Thank you." As simple as that. "Thank you."

Most people rarely get compliments in life. Chico cherished and appreciated them. So do I. It is not always easy to move somebody deeply. When they are moved enough to approach me, to make themselves vulnerable by complimenting me, I am happy to say, "Thank you."

It's not just music we're talking about. We're talking about the lessons of life in general. It could be an office situation or one concerning business or family. Learning how to say "Thank you" is learning how to be human, how to be sensitive to other people's feelings, how to communicate. It has to do with growing up, maturing, becoming aware. I never get tired of talking about music. When you're talking about music, you're talking about life itself, which is infinite.

In those days, the fall of 1956, there was a real jazz scene in L.A. It was a burning time, full of hustle and excitement. Jazz City was one of four or five full-time jazz clubs that featured big-name jazz seven nights a week.

"Hey, Paul," Chico called from the other side of the stage, waving his hand over the people between us. "Let's go hear what Chet Baker's doing."

That's the way it was. During intermissions, we walked across the street and heard Chet Baker—or André Previn, Shelly Manne, Hampton Hawes, Frank Rosolino, or any of a dozen other players in town. During their intermissions, they came over to Jazz City and listened to us.

I admit it: that first month in Hollywood blew my mind. I'd be up there playing, looking out through the spotlight into the smoke, and I'd see all sorts of famous faces, people like Lana Turner, Burt Lancaster, Tony Curtis. It was exciting to me—a lot of adrenaline.

After awhile, Burt and Tony came in regularly because they were getting ready to film *The Sweet Smell of Success*. They wanted to use Chico's band in it, and they wanted Fred Katz to write the score. About six months later, they started shooting *Success* at the Goldwyn Studios, and there I was, on-screen, an actor in the movies.

After Jazz City, we zipped up to San Francisco, where we played the Blackhawk, a famous jazz club. All the major groups played there—Miles Davis, Oscar Peterson, Art Blakey, everybody. And now that roster included the Chico Hamilton Quintet.

It was wonderful living in Hollywood, playing in a major band, going out on the road. I was really sailing.

Chico was busy then, and we did a lot of cross-country touring. Sometimes my wife, Yvonne, traveled with us to our West Coast gigs, like San Francisco, or joined me on the road, but not very often. There was no room in the car, and everything cost too much. I was making $150 a week now, not a lot, but better than the $50 a week I made with Sauter-Finegan.

For our first cross-country tour, we drove to New York in Chico's station wagon. We were to open for Billie Holiday at Carnegie Hall. Whenever we stopped at a restaurant, everybody could go in except Chico and his brother Bernie, who were black. When I got upset about this, Chico said, "Look, man, I know it's a drag, but there's just nothing we can do about it. This is America, and this is the way it is." I'd go in, order the food, carry it outside. We ate breakfast, lunch, and dinner in the car. In a few days Chico would be playing Carnegie's hallowed halls, celebrated as a star, and yet he and his brother couldn't even go into a restaurant to order a cup of coffee. Blew me away.

TIMING AND THE COSMOS

Timing is amazing. You can't plan timing. You might have all the qualifications and be somewhere at the right moment for you, but it could be the wrong place, or vice versa. As far as I'm concerned, timing is something cosmic. The most you can do is show up. If something happens, then it was meant to be.

Herbie Mann was at the right place at the right time. He was one of the first to take the flute, a classical instrument, and bring it out as a solo jazz instrument. People were ready for that, and Herbie became a star. Timing.

And it was timing when I happened to walk into the Musicians' Union, Local 802, that particular day in New York. I was just checking things out. The Sauter-Finegan band wasn't going to last much longer, and I needed to develop some new possibilities.

Herbie Mann hadn't seen me in years. We'd met only once before and didn't particularly care for each other. Usually you don't see musicians of Herbie's caliber at the union, but there he was. He walked right over. "Hi, Paul." Good. I didn't think he'd remember my name.

"Listen, man," he said. "Chico Hamilton is in town, playing Basin Street. I heard he's looking for a new reed player. Here's his hotel phone number. Give him a call."

Amazing. Just a few days before, I had been fantasizing about playing in Chico's band. I called Chico, set up the audition, and landed the job. Timing.

We can't entirely control timing because there are so many factors involved that are outside of ourselves. But we can control many of the ways in which we manifest our destiny.

First, you have to desire something. In my case, I wanted to be with

Sauter-Finegan and Chico Hamilton. Then you visualize yourself in the situation you want, as if it were already after the fact, and you visualize it in every detail.

The next step is practical. You remove yourself from visualizations, and you take action. You don't just wait for things to happen. You contact people you know who might be able to help you achieve your goal. Many artistic people fall short here because, by their very nature, they often are not temperamentally aggressive. But if you make the phone calls and get out and meet new people, establish contacts, and follow leads, almost surely the visualizations will begin to become real.

Once you desire something and visualize it and begin to take action, the rest is in God's hands, not in the sense that God is some external entity that will do things for you, but in a different sense. God is me. God is you. God is everything. The Life Force, the creative energy that runs through you, is your guide. From desire to realization, God is that creative force within you that can make things happen. Our job is to fulfill God's will. That is the way we fulfill ourselves in realizing our highest dreams.

If you are a creative person and you want things to happen, you have to be willing to follow God's direction, to take practical action, even if it means picking up your roots and moving someplace else. You can't just sit in the middle of nowhere and wait. You've got to be in Los Angeles or New York or some other major center. You don't have to be a super businessperson or brutally aggressive, but at least you have to transplant yourself to fertile ground. You have to put yourself into a context in which things can happen. Charlie Parker was broke and living outside of New York—in Kansas City. But New York was the place for jazz—so he went to New York, and the rest is history. He had talent, and desire, knew what he wanted, and took action.

I took action when I called Chico. After speaking with Chico, I said to Herbie, "Why did you throw this gig my way? Why me?"

"Because I want to get all the good flute players out of town."

Ha! That was an honest answer, and I took it as a compliment.

It was timing, for example, that got me into Chico's group while cellist Fred Katz was still there. Fred was a real teacher for me. His high musicianship pulled my own musicianship up a few notches. I learned a lot from him, talking about music, playing his compositions and arrangements, working in the band with him.

I learned other things from him, too. On road trips, when everything quieted down and everybody else in the car had fallen asleep, Fred and I often continued talking, getting into high-level philosophical conversations, which both of us enjoyed.

Along the way, Fred started talking about something I had never heard of: Zen. These conversations confused the hell out of me because Fred never gave any answers. In the past when I'd ask him a question, he'd always give me an answer. Now I'd say, "What is Zen?" and he'd say, "Well, it's this, but it's not this. It's really that, but it's not that, either." The conversations got abstract, and he'd never give me anything definite. By this time—it was 1957—Fred was the only one I had ever met who said anything about Zen. And we'd drive into the night, enjoying our talks, until one of us dozed off while the other continued driving.

After New York, we traveled to Chicago, where we played the London House down by the Loop. A very interesting thing happened on this trip. Lots of people attended opening night. During intermission, a good-looking Chinese gentleman invited the band over to his table for a drink. Fred and I joined him. The guy said he was a Zen Buddhist priest.

That blew me away. A week or two ago, there I was in the car talking with Fred about Zen, and now I'm meeting a Zen Buddhist priest—who didn't look like any priest I'd ever seen. He wore normal clothes, a suit and tie, and he had a drink in front of him. He was a dedicated jazz fan, especially of the Chico Hamilton Quintet. On Sundays he officiated at a small Buddhist temple. Outside of that, he was a dancer, choreographer, and teacher.

He came to the club just about every night, and he and I became good friends. His name was Kim On Wong. Several times before the gigs, I had dinner over at his house, and sometimes we'd get together in the afternoon just to talk. But every time I tried to bring the conversation around to Zen, he wouldn't talk about it. He wouldn't give me definitions or long raps.

He did say one thing. "Before you leave town, I'm going to see if I can create a little satori for you." I'd never heard that word before. "What's that?" "Well, it's an Eastern word for enlightenment." And he let it go like that.

One day I had a strange experience. All the musicians knew certain hotels. They weren't the Hilton, but they were clean, and you met a lot of other musicians there. Most of the bands coming through Chicago, for example, stayed at the Croydon Hotel, which cost eighteen dollars a *week* for a room with a kitchenette, where you could make your coffee or cook a little bit. There was a lot of life in a hotel like that—dancers, actors, musicians, other traveling entertainers. On this particular Chicago trip, however, I didn't stay at the Croydon. I stayed at a hotel on the north side.

We started playing at the London House around ten in the evening and finished up around four in the morning. Sometimes we'd go to an all-night movie until the buzz from the gig went down at seven or eight in the morning. Then we'd go back to the hotel and sleep until late afternoon. It was a totally backward life.

On this trip, two women friends from L.A., Roberta Bright and Lee Wilder, came to visit. About four o'clock in the afternoon, I got a call from Kim, which woke me up.

"Hi, Paul. Today at the Croydon I met some friends of yours."

"Yeah, I know. You and Roberta and Lee and I had breakfast together in the coffee shop this morning. Why are you telling me this? Of course I know. We sat in the corner booth. You sat on the right. I sat on the left. They sat on the other side. You and I ate pancakes. They had scrambled eggs and bacon."

"Okay, great," he said. "See you tonight at the club. Bye."

"Kim's an idiot," I thought to myself. "Doesn't he remember I was there?"

And then I realized, I had *not* been there. I was *here*, in the hotel, asleep that whole time. But I had seen everything. It was so real. How could it be?

I saw Kim at the club that night. "My God, Kim, after we hung up, I realized I had not been there at all. Did those things really happen the way I described them?"

"Exactly," he said, smiling. "What we ate, who was sitting where, which booth, everything—except you were not there."

Never before had I had an experience like that, and seldom since. I'm not psychic. I don't have visions or astral projection experiences. Obviously, however, I had been in two places at once. I was sleeping in a hotel on the north side, *and* I was there with Kim and the others in the Croydon coffee shop on the other side of town. I had seen the whole thing and been an accurate witness to it.

We had a good time in Chicago. True, there are a lot of temptations out there, and plenty of pretty women, especially for a young fellow in a jazz band. I tried my best to resist the temptations, but I was not always successful.

A lot of professional people enjoyed Chico's music. They had money, and they enjoyed spending it. Architects, lawyers, doctors, and people from *Playboy* magazine showed up at the London House all the time. Wine, women, and song. What can I say—beauty everywhere, on all levels. It was a real high for me. I couldn't have asked for more.

When it came time to leave, Kim was there, waving good-bye. A few Bunnies waved good-bye. Stan Kenton was just arriving. As he got off the bus with his band, I met him for the first time. He waved good-bye. Ramsey Lewis was just starting out, and he was there. He waved good-bye.

There is a real love for each other among jazz musicians. Sure, the music business is insanely competitive at the lower levels. You want to get better than the other guy. You want to cut him in jam sessions. You fight your way to the top.

Then, just as in business or anything else, once you prove yourself, once you are successful and accepted into the higher echelon where everyone is an acknowledged pro, then it becomes a matter of mutual respect and shared appreciation. You become part of a brotherhood. You've all made it. Why not hang out together ? Why not enjoy it? And that's what we did.

So we said our good-byes and hopped in the car and drove on down the road to our next gig. I found myself thinking, "Wow, I feel great! I feel really high. No questions left in my head. It seems like I know the answers to everything. Don't ask me anything and expect me to verbalize it, but within myself there are no questions. I've got all the answers I need. I'm at peace."

This feeling stayed with me two or three weeks. Back in L.A., I contacted Kim again, telling him of my experience.

"That's what I meant when I said I wanted to create a little satori for you," he said. "Now you know what it feels like, that sense of well-being, that sense of having a centered, quiet place within yourself where you feel satisfied and wide awake and alive, connected with everything and every-one around you.

"You will not maintain this feeling. It will go away. Nevertheless, do not worry. This is what we call the path, and you are on it.

"When that feeling disappears, remember that you had it. Remember what it felt like. Remember, above all: you can attain it once again. As you travel this path, you can arrive at the point where you will be in that state of satori all of the time. Right now, it is new and fragile. You do not have enough experience to maintain it. Life intrudes, removing you from this state of mind.

"Continue on the path. Have this experience over and over again, until it becomes established within you. Then you will not lose it. In time, you can live this way every moment."

Everything has to do with timing, with the mystery and the magic of it—from classical music, to Sauter-Finegan, to the Musicians' Union and Her-bie Mann, to Chico and Fred Katz, to Zen, to Kim. The right place, the right moment, the right people, the right preparation, the right state of mind—when all of these things converge into a single instant, everything works.

Thomas Mann said, "An artist is one upon whom nothing is lost." Every day I was learning new and exciting things. My mind was wide open, and life was a joy.

PASS THE CIGARS

When Yvonne became pregnant with Marlen in early 1957, it was an ex-citing time. She grew larger, and I looked forward to fatherhood more and more, unconcerned about money or a hampered life-style. I felt too much joy. As the time grew closer to the birth, the gynecologist suggested that Yvonne have induced labor, which is more controlled, and we did that. The doctor was ahead of his time in feeling that the father should be a part of the birth process. He thought it would be a good bonding experience. Yvonne and I agreed.

On September 3, 1957, the night Marlen was born, I was onstage with Chico at a prestigious club on Sunset Strip called Ciro's, a showcase for famous singers and entertainers and musical groups. It looked like the birth might take place that evening. I let Chico know we might be interrupted. He said okay.

In the middle of the set, around 11:00 P.M., the hospital called the club, and the bartender immediately passed the message up to me onstage. I split, right in the middle of the set and dashed down to the Beverly Hills Doctor's hospital.

I rushed into the delivery room, but right away everyone said, "No, no, you can't come in like that. You're not sterile. You have to put on a gown and cap." They took me out, put a mask, a gown, a cap, and some gloves on me, and ushered me back in. I watched the whole birth, and it was a great, great experience. I encourage all fathers to participate in the process. It is truly grand to see your child emerge into the world before it even takes its first breath.

Although it was a wonderful experience, I felt faint because of the blood. I don't feel like that when I see my own blood, but I do when I see the blood of others. I get a little woozy and start spinning out. There I was, turning white and green, so they led me away and gave me smelling salts. Everybody felt fine except Daddy, who was ready to collapse.

I went back to Ciro's and finished the gig. All the guys congratulated me, and I passed out cigars and did the whole father trip. It was wonderful.

I wanted to be a part of raising Marlen, so I changed his diapers, cleaned him up, dried his bottom, held him. He sensed that these were Daddy's hands on him, not just Mommy's, and it definitely brought us closer.

I went on with my career. Yvonne took good care of the baby. My father came out to California and helped me with a down payment on a house we all lived in, and it was a happy time.

MY DEBT TO CHICO

My first recording session was *Under Analysis*, an album with Sauter-Finegan. The next time I went into the studio was with Chico. Over the year and a half I was with him, we recorded *The Chico Hamilton Quintet*, *The Sweet Smell of Success*, *South Pacific*, and *Ellington Suite*.

Chico encouraged us to write for the band, another thing we appreciated. He made no guarantees that we'd get our compositions recorded, but he gave us the opportunity to hear our music played and the opportunity to get constructive feedback. When it was good enough, he put it in the book, played it on gigs, and sometimes recorded it.

First and foremost, music is feeling. Music is emotions in sound. Too often, the more training and education you get, the more intellectually oriented you become. Technical perfection becomes primary, the feeling secondary. Mental gymnastics and perfect execution become the goal—no wrong notes. Unfortunately, so-called perfect music can also be very cold, devoid of heartfelt emotion.

Through the process of recording and editing and splicing, I came to understand these principles. The more I recorded, the less concerned I became with little goofs here or there. If the take really felt good, minor mistakes and all, then that was the main thing. Eventually, I reached the point where I refused to make any edits or splices at all, and I take the whole solo as is.

Chico was a different drummer. He was sensitive to colors in music. He played wonderful brushes and did some brilliant things with his mallets and hands. "The drum is like a woman," he said. "You caress it. You make love to it."

Chico couldn't read music, but he created beautiful colors and tones and blends. At times he dropped the snare wires from his snare drum and played with mallets, which made the drum sound like a different kind of tom-tom, with a unique timbre of its own. He took the front head of his bass drum off, an innovation years ahead of its time. He was an intuitive drummer, first-class. In all of the complicated compositions Fred wrote, Chico knew just what to do to support the music.

Chico and Fred's kind of jazz fit in perfectly with my nature, just as the Sauter-Finegan band had earlier. I didn't sit around at night dreaming up things just to be different. I was drawn to those bands because they fit my own temperament and musical personality. They made use of all my horns and utilized and expanded my knowledge of different styles of music, particularly classical music and jazz. Later, when I formed my own bands, we were experimental in similar ways, always blending concepts from various types of music, always pushing back the narrow, limited ideas other people have about what jazz is.

Chico was the leader of a trailblazing group. In a sense, he lived in a middle ground, a kind of no-man's-land between black jazz, which springs from the heart of America's black culture, and white jazz, influenced by European classical music, perhaps especially as written by Fred Katz. Chico led this group because he *liked* blending straight-ahead jazz with classical music and complex, European-influenced original material. He was willing to pay the price for being an innovator.

When you're a trailblazer, the glory usually does not come your way. If you do get some, you pay for it—you might not be accepted in the very circles in which you would like to be accepted. There's a thrill to being on your own in uncharted waters, because you are an adventurer. You blaze the trail. But those who later follow that trail are the ones who usually get the praise and rewards that should have gone to the forerunners.

Chico got his rewards and praise, but he is also a black drummer. In his heart of hearts, I think Chico would like to have been hailed as another Art Blakey and celebrated by the East Coast black jazz community, the people who liked and respected straight-ahead, bash-'em-out jazz. Chico has never been an Art Blakey, Max Roach, or Philly Jo Jones, but he is a damned good Chico Hamilton.

Yes, he inhabited a kind of no-man's-land. But what other group was doing what we did? We called it jazz. Our records sold in the jazz sections of the stores. But it wasn't traditional, straight-ahead jazz. We stretched the definitions as far as we could.

Recognition is wonderful, but that is not the primary motivation for true adventurers. Explorers and innovators don't concern themselves with recognition or ask: Am I going to win the polls? Will my album be record of the year? Are lots of people going to like it?

They do things because they *want* to—for the excitement, the danger, the risk, the challenge, the thrill of discovery, the adventure of creativity, the pride and satisfaction of coming up with something new. When you come at it this way, you feel truly alive. Working from this perspective, there is honesty, integrity, intelligence, feeling, and depth in what you do.

Without the presence of these elements in the work, you will never get the recognition. *With* these elements, however, you may very likely get the respect you deserve for whatever you have accomplished. There are no guarantees, of course. Nevertheless, the work will have within it the inherent power to move receptive listeners deeply—if not today, then tomorrow. The yearning for recognition is shallow compared to the creative adventure of it all.

In addition to the adventure of creativity, there is also the joy of seeing your fans watching you onstage as you perform. There is a light in their eyes, a love for you and for the music. Whether you're in an intimate club or in front of thousands of people, you *know* when you are communicating, when you are touching them on a real deep level, a soul level, an emotional level, a meaningful level.

Nobody can take that away from you, and money can't buy it. That connection, the communion between you and the people, is precious. When that happens, you don't need any critic or friend or peer to tell you that you are doing well. The reward is in the communion with the people through the music you and they are deeply experiencing together in the living, breathing moment. That is a fantastic feeling.

After Fred left Chico's group, the band changed, and it was no longer meaningful to me. It just wasn't happening, and by the spring of 1958 it was time to move on. Sad, yes, but inevitable. Eric Dolphy took my place—a great alto player, very exciting, very fiery—and the band developed a new personality.

I will forever remain indebted to Chico. He helped me develop as a musician and as a human being. He was my friend and my teacher. I have great respect for him. Presently, he is teaching percussion in New York and still playing. We haven't been in touch very much over the years, but he knows that I love him. I give him full credit for opening the doors for me. We had some great times together, and I thank him, from the heart.

SIX

HOLLYWOOD, U.S.A.

During the early 1960s, in a series of half-hour documentaries called "The Story of," TV producer David Wolper profiled individual people in a variety of professions. One of those segments was "The Story of a Jazz Musician," and the subject he selected was me.

Wolper presented his subjects well. He chose Elmer Bernstein to compose the main title. He selected the best camera crew, the best lighting people, the best sound people, the best editors, directors, and producers, and treated the whole thing like a major production. Sometimes subjects narrated their own show, as I did, or they narrated part of it and a professional announcer did the rest. It became a hit series, and when they aired "The Story of a Jazz Musician" in 1961, it did wonders for my career.

Before shooting the show, director Ed Spiegel wanted to hang out with me. "Whenever you go somewhere, Paul, let me know."

I liked to go down to the Santa Monica beach, so we went together. We lay in the sun and talked, with him getting to know me, how I am, what I think, what my moods are. He met my wife and children, my father and stepmother. He attended karate classes with me, went to Shelly's Mannehole and met the guys in my band. As soon as he got a clear feeling of who

I was, he wrote the script, highlighting different phases and aspects of my life.

As a thread throughout the story, they used a tune I wrote called "Count Your Change," showing how I conceived and wrote it, how the band rehearsed it, how we presented it in public. It was an interesting idea, taking one composition and following it all the way through. That piece, one of several with odd time signatures, was included on our spin-off album, *Profile of a Jazz Musician*. For this production, I had the leading role and composed and performed all of the background music. Here was my chance to shine.

It was a great opportunity. The show was syndicated all over the country and greatly enhanced my career. It was also dubbed in five different languages. I received strong positive reactions from viewers because Spiegel got inside of me and my life, which was a credit to him. That was the show's whole point and purpose. Strangers saw me on the street or in restaurants and said things like, "How are your kids? How's your dad? Did you ever get back with your wife?" I was amazed at how many people absorbed the details. "Do you still take karate? Have you quit smoking? I really liked what you said about jazz." The reaction to the show was strong for months afterward, and for many years people continued asking about it.

KARATE KID

Like tips of icebergs, the details of that documentary reveal a lot about me. Although the show's primary focus was my professional life, it said a lot about my personal life as well, not dwelling on things, just touching them lightly. They showed clips of some of the exhausting karate workouts, for example, touching on that aspect of my life having to do with physical development. It took some time before I learned how to feel comfortable in my body.

During my last year of high school and throughout college, I lifted weights. Young and vain, I wanted to have a good-looking body. I did not want to be the ninety-eight-pound weakling on the beach getting sand kicked in his face by the local bully.

I also felt somewhat self-conscious about my height, which is 5′7½″. I always wanted to be taller when I was a kid, because in our culture anyone under six feet is considered short. Napoleon was short, so was drummer Buddy Rich, but that is small compensation for a teenager significantly under six feet. I was good at sandlot football, baseball, and basketball, and I ran fast, but I was not good enough to make the varsity teams. I never got that big letter "R" for my Roosevelt High School sweater. When you're considered short and you're not an all-star athlete, you tend to compensate. You push harder for recognition and respect.

So I lifted weights to look good and to get bigger and stronger; I smoked cigarettes to be included among my peers, and for twenty years smoked a pack and a half a day; I dug into music, mostly for the music's sake, but also to ingratiate myself with other people and win their approval.

I never enjoyed hitting or getting hit and therefore have been in very few fights. It's a sickening feeling when your fist smashes into somebody's face. But it's important to learn something about self-defense, especially when working in nightclubs, so I took karate lessons.

John Leoning, a fifth-degree black belt from the Philippines, was a good teacher. "The last thing I want you to do is use this," he said. "First, you try to talk your way out of a fight. If that can't be done, walk away, even though other people might think you're a coward. If the guy insists on fighting, then go for him. Karate is the art of killing. If you must use it, use it all the way."

Karate built confidence and inner strength. If you know how to kill somebody, you don't have to do it in order to prove yourself. You know your body's lethal power. You know your fleshy hand can smash through three bricks. You know how to aim deadly blows to vital parts. You know every punch can kill. Once you know how to do it, you don't have to use it to prove anything. You have confidence in your ability to to defend yourself. You become a stronger person, and very seldom, if ever, will you be forced to use these techniques. I liked that.

IN PURSUIT OF BALANCE

I said in the documentary that for jazz to really happen, there must be an audience, meaning that jazz is a language in which you express feelings.

The purpose of language is to communicate, and similarly music needs to be heard by other people. When I was younger, I knew I had to practice, but it was boring. And yet when we had a Friday night dance coming up, I practiced hard and looked forward to playing.

When I first started out, I played mainly because I needed recognition and approval. Any young person needs these things in order to advance. We have to prove ourselves, and we do so by means of recognition and acceptance from others.

But if we are going to plumb music deeply, if the music is ever going to be of value, if we want the music to come through us in powerful, meaningful, and healing ways, then we must evolve beyond that phase. If our motivation continues to be ingratiation and approval, then the music is bound to be shallow, something I did not fully realize until I went to India in 1966.

At one time, music was my whole life. That narrow focus screwed me up. One of life's secret words is "balance." If any one thing takes over our life, then life is out of balance. There are many things to experience and enjoy. If we are fixed on one thing to the exclusion of everything else, our judgment becomes warped, even fanatical.

Life is not static. It is forever in flux. If we are rigidly fixed on one thing, like music, then we are out of balance. We can't flow with life's changes. When we are centered and balanced within ourselves, we flow easily and smoothly, and we are able to grow.

With meditation, we become so deeply centered that no matter what happens in daily life, no matter how traumatic the situation is, we remain inwardly connected to a solid foundation and do not lose our balance. When music ceased to be my exclusive focus, I became a more balanced person, and life became more meaningful. Music is not the total answer to everything.

I took my son Robin to a drum teacher in Toronto, a man named Jim Blackley. He asked Robin what his ambitions were. Robin said he wanted to be a great drummer. Blackley said being a great drummer was not the highest goal. First and foremost, you should want to become a great human being. He wanted Robin to integrate music into the larger scheme of life. I said to myself, "This is a good teacher."

On a daily basis, music is probably the single most important thing in a musician's life. But to become a good human being overall, we have to get beyond music and the need for approval. We have to get to the spiritual level, where we can appreciate life's deeper and more meaningful values. In turn, spiritual development expands and deepens the music. Robin became a fine human being *and* a fine drummer.

When we did the documentary in 1961, I was still vain and ambitious, needing applause and success. I wasn't anywhere near a state of balance. I was learning and growing.

Spiritual concerns were new and quite inviting. I remembered talks on Zen I had with Kim On Wong back in Chicago and with Fred Katz on the road. I also read Gina Cerminara's books on reincarnation and books on Yoga; attended Manley P. Hall's lectures at the Philosophical Research Society; took a life reading with clairvoyant Betty McCain, which profoundly affected my outlook; and participated in lengthy, exciting discussions with the guys in my band.

In addition to wanting acceptance, and in addition to my budding spiritual interests, I was also doing everything I could to become a better musician. If fame and fortune resulted from improvement, then fine. But the main thing was to grow as a musician. That's why I formed my own groups. That's why I turned down thousands of dollars' worth of studio work and jeopardized my studio contacts to play twenty-dollar gigs at the Renaissance Club or Shelly's Mannehole. Musicianship, ambition, and spirituality were not yet balanced, but I was heading in directions that ultimately got me there.

"The Story of a Jazz Musician" touched upon my wife and children, and upon wine, women, and song. In 1959, Yvonne and I separated. She was pregnant with Robin, and our son Marlen was two years old. I lived only a few blocks away, always available for financial and emotional support. For ten years, between the ages of thirty and forty, I lived alone, never taking a live-in lover, keeping that space available for the kids to come over. My children were number one. Everything was finished with Yvonne, but I still wanted to experience fatherhood. We can never turn back the clock. If we miss our children when they are two, three, four, five years old, it's gone forever. I loved them and was there for them all the time.

Robin was born at the UCLA hospital on May 17, 1960. I was there but was disappointed that they didn't allow fathers to be in the delivery room.

I wanted to see him come into the world the way I had seen Marlen. Robin was just as precious to me as Marlen, and it was a great joy to have two sons.

Although Yvonne and I were separated, I lived nearby. If the kids wanted to call me, they called. If they wanted to drop over after school, they dropped over. They knew where the key was, and they let themselves in. They slept over whenever they felt like it, and I packed them lunch and sent them off to school the next day. It wasn't an awkward situation. Yvonne and I accepted the fact that we couldn't live together anymore. For all of us, the kids included, life was better and more peaceful this way.

During those years there was a lot of wine and many women. The rough and traumatic separation and final divorce from Yvonne took its toll. It hardened me. I was bitter for many years. I didn't see women as people, but as conquests. I'd see a pretty girl and want to go to bed with her, just to see if I could, and most of the time I could and did.

As a source of ego gratification, sex was like a drug—powerful, stimulating, and exciting. Ultimately, however, it became shallow because I didn't want a serious relationship. The few times I did fall in love, I wound up miserable.

Like a moth, I have always been attracted to flames. I found beautiful women irresistible. During these years, lots of beautiful, special, talented women matched the stereotyped Hollywood pinup beauty I fantasized about. And that's what I wanted—physical beauty, fantasy in the flesh.

Yvonne was a beautiful woman with a sweet nature. We had a strong physical attraction, but there was no mental or spiritual compatibility. There were too many gaps, and our physical attraction ultimately was not enough to keep us together.

I was out on the road a lot, and she was feeling lonely and neglected. As an impatient and somewhat overcontrolling man, I resented her complaints. Unfulfilled, we fought, taking our anger and frustration out on each other. Screaming and hollering one night, I looked down and saw Marlen listening to us. That made me sick with guilt. These bad vibes were not healthy for him. The next day I looked for my own place.

Beyond our physical attraction there was simply not enough mental or spiritual energy to inspire further growth. Yvonne and I were left staring at each other like strangers. However, if we had not gotten together, our two sons would not be on earth right now. Those children came through us.

They needed us in order to be born. To me, that is total justification for the marriage.

The other women were beautiful, too. But there were too many men involved in their lives, and that raised all of my insecurities. I dated gorgeous starlets and singers. In public places, other men looked at them like, "Wouldn't it be great to be with that chick." Well, I was with that chick, and it wasn't so great.

It was good in the beginning, of course, but sooner or later the time came when I didn't feel safe. I wasn't in control. I couldn't count on their feelings, and I felt insecure. I had to keep an eye out because tomorrow they might be off with some other guy. Inevitably, another man entered the picture, and I'd flare up in jealousy, and pretty soon the relationship self-destructed, leaving me with terrible hurts.

For a while, the highs were really high. When you're young, your emotional system is strong. You bounce back quickly. As you get older, your system becomes more fragile, less resilient to emotional trauma.

After ten years of ups and downs, I was fed up. Kris Kristofferson in one of his songs asks if the going up is worth the coming down. For me, the answer was no. I wanted to get past the confusion and pain. After an ecstatic, overwhelming affair with a particular Hollywood actress, everything in my inner life fell apart. Desperately needing to find serious and meaningful answers to my problems, I packed my bags and flew to India.

Someone once said that whenever you're in a relationship, you should hold on tightly, let go lightly. I never learned how to do that. I held on too long, giving the benefit of the doubt and hoping everything would be all right, even though I knew the relationship was wrong and I should leave it and let it end. Although I've not been able to follow that advice very well, it is good advice, and I do believe in it. When the time comes to let go, let go lightly.

BEYOND THE INTELLECTUAL TRAP

In the early sixties, I felt good about my career. Los Angeles was a jazz center, and great musicians came through town all the time. I was well known, making good money, and learning new things about music and life every day. I was recording my own music with top-flight musicians like vibists Emil Richards and Lynn Blessing, guitarist John Pisano, pianists Paul Moer and Mike Lang, bassists Jimmy Bond and Bill Plummer, drummers Billy Higgins and Bill Goodwin. Other musicians in town liked and respected me, and Miles Davis was my friend.

Nevertheless, I also found myself feeling restless and discontented. Something in my inner life was missing, something fundamental, and I couldn't figure out what it was.

When I moved from New York to Los Angeles in 1957, I quickly realized the East Coast was extremely conservative. California was wide open—an experimental, innovative, and exceptionally creative environment. People felt free to try new ideas, anything at all. If it was new and interesting, they went for it. This kind of atmosphere produces its share of kooks, weirdos, and psychotics, but it also produces brilliant concepts in science, art, business, education, and spiritual matters.

Californians were interested in Buddhism, Tantric Yoga, and reincarnation. Strange religions came up from Puerto Rico, Cuba, and Africa. Healers explored healing, and psychics gave life readings. Released from ties to Europe's conservative, rationalistic past, Californians delved into new dimensions. Where else could you find things like this in such abundance?

Today, of course, interests of this kind do not sound particularly odd. Shirley MacLaine, for example, writes best-selling books about reincarnation. However, in the late fifties and early sixties, you had to be careful; you couldn't talk to just anyone about these things. Nevertheless, quite a few people were interested in religion and philosophy and innovative ways of approaching spiritual development. There were exotic places in California, and new ideas to explore.

Whenever I felt a cold coming on, I went to a Puerto Rican fellow named Nilo. No last name, just Nilo. I hesitated to visit him at first, but friends of mine, bassist Joe Mondragon and vibist Emil Richards, assured me that he was okay. Before long, I too hung out once in a while. Nilo gave me a special herb tea—not cocaine or marijuana, no drugs—and my cold vanished. I don't know how it worked. It just worked. Nilo was also into African religious practices and healing powers, although not voodoo or black magic.

One day a fellow said to me, "You know, Paul, it's interesting to see you here, because you're an intellectual. It's unusual for an intellectual to be involved with these things." On both counts, he was right. But I was changing.

Reasons and logic are tools. On scientific, economic, and other practical levels, the intellect is invaluable. It is important to be able to analyze wholes into constituent parts and to synthesize parts into comprehensive wholes. It is important to be able to quantify external, material reality by means of numbers and words. Our entire Western civilization is founded upon the intellect's enormous capacities. When Descartes said, "I think, therefore I am," He identified human beings with the rational intellect, and that is how we Westerners see ourselves.

In no way did I want to give up my intellect, because it is valuable, but at the same time, I saw its limitations. The intellect can be a tremendous trap.

If I get too rational about certain things in life, I will never be able to know them. The intellect can easily block advancement on the spiritual path because the spiritual journey is internal and metaphysical. It cannot be rationally quantified or logically defined. When the intellect cannot grasp, understand, and contain something, it quite often condemns it as ridiculous or superstitious. I didn't want to be trapped by the intellect. I wanted to free myself from the purely Western framework that molded and formed me and to expose myself to psychological, emotional, and spiritual dimensions that are considered nonrational. I wanted to go beyond the intellect. I wanted to explore certain things that have nothing to do with reason, logic, or verbal understanding.

I had no intention of becoming one of Nilo's followers. Visiting him was simply an opportunity to try something new, to see what kind of experience I had, to see how I resisted or affirmed. Discontented, I wanted to leave the known and explore the unknown. My search began.

One day my friend Shorty Rogers, a well-known composer and jazz trumpet player, told me about *There Is a River*, a book about Edgar Cayce, by Thomas Sugrue. Shorty explained how Cayce was a famous clairvoyant, no longer living, who went into trances. Cayce was able to "see" into a person's body and analyze the physical condition. He also gave life readings, in which he talked about past lives and karma and the spiritual journey.

Known as the Miracle Worker, Cayce was a simple man, without much formal education. He was not a doctor, but in his physical readings, he used advanced technical medical language. He was an orthodox Christian, but in his life readings, he talked about reincarnation. When he came out of a trance, he had no recollection of what he had said. He recorded everything on tapes, and his secretary took notes. Over 50,000 of his readings are stored in the Association for Research and Enlightenment in Virginia Beach, Virginia.

I read *There Is a River*, and it blew my mind, especially the last chapter, which summarized Cayce's philosophy on creation, how we and the universe came to be. Each paragraph was so meaningful, I'd have to think about it a week before continuing. It took six months to read that chapter. Emil and Shorty and the guys in my band and I had terrific discussions about Cayce, reincarnation, creation, karma, clairvoyance, trance channeling, and related matters.

Of course, from a strictly rational viewpoint, many of these topics prove unsatisfying. However, if you are told that you did certain things in specific past lives and if those things ring a bell with you, then they are satisfying because you recognize elements from past lives that continue in your present life—and they help you in this life today.

A woman named Gina Cerminara researched Cayce's readings and wrote her Ph.D. dissertation in psychology on reincarnation and karma. She authored several books, the main one being *Many Mansions*, taken from the biblical phrase "my house has many mansions." We live many lives. For each life, the soul needs a body, a mansion. Hence, the soul has many mansions.

One day Shorty said, "You know, Gina Cerminara lives in Hollywood. I think she gives courses in her home."

We checked, and sure enough, Gina lived in Hollywood, right up the hill from Capitol Records. She gave a class once a week, based largely on the writings of Ouspensky and Gurdjieff. Emil and Shorty and I signed up.

Initially, I was disappointed. I thought Gina would talk about reincarnation and karma. Instead, she was giving a course on general semantics, the study of language and its pitfalls, things to watch out for, traps you fall into if you don't use language correctly.

"Why are we studying this?" I asked her.

"We are dealing with thoughts and words," she said. "Before you think and talk about things like reincarnation and karma, you should understand the mechanics of language. You must learn how to think as clearly as possible. You must understand how your thoughts are formed and how you interpret what you read. Semantics is a preliminary course, essential for understanding the subtleties of reincarnation and karma."

I took the course, and she was right. It was an amazing course, and Gina was a delightful woman. We invited her down to the club and came to know her personally. She said she was sorry she had not been able to meet Cayce or get a reading from him before he died, but she knew a woman named Betty McCain who gave life readings. In Gina's opinion, Betty came close to having the same abilities as Cayce. When Betty came to L.A., Gina set up an appointment for me.

TRANCE CHANNELING

In Sanskrit, the word "akashic" or "akasha" refers to the element of space. The Akashic Records are records "in space" of all events that have taken place on earth, from the very beginning. It is like a big book of the history of the world, of everyone who ever lived at any given time, of every action and event that ever occurred. All events have energy. Where does that energy go? It goes into the Akashic Records.

When knowledge of past lives is given to the psychic, it is given by an entity or spirit that has access to these records. Psychics are willing to give themselves up to the trance state, in which an individual spirit enters them and speaks through them, using the psychic as its channel.

I do not think Cayce and McCain were simply tapping into their personal, individual psyches and then projecting their own subconscious visions. I think they entered a state of trance and then surrendered their identities to an entity that used them as a vehicle, speaking through them, giving information about the soul-path from past to present and information about particular past lives, selecting from among thousands those that are relevant to the seeker's questions.

When you view past lives that relate to your present life and you explore unresolved conflicts from a greater distance and a larger perspective, you gain insight into some of the problems you're having now. We were not dealing with simple, superficial matters. We were dealing with deep wounds, deep frustrations, deep anger. If the information did not seem relevant, we could pass it off. If the information rang true, however, and we accepted it as deep and relevant knowledge, then maybe we could begin to unravel and resolve present problems in light of the new view.

Obviously, we cannot prove these things scientifically. But if they ring a bell, if they resonate as truth, then we can go with that resonance. It's an individual thing. It does not make any difference whether someone else believes it. The real questions are—Can I make use of this? Does it serve any constructive purpose? Does it offer any practical solutions? For me, it did.

Concerned about my wife and children and my spiritual discontent, I was eager to have this reading with Betty. Her price was reasonable, twenty-five dollars for two hours. You could bring your own tape recorder, which I did, and she later sent you a typewritten copy of what she said, transcribed from the tape she made for herself.

Betty was a sweet old lady, in her midseventies. She had gray hair and spoke in a quiet, charming, rather high-pitched voice. She welcomed me to the reading, which took place in a simple room at the Hollywood Franklin Hotel, in October 1961. She asked only for my name and for my date and place of birth. She did not ask what I did for a living, whether I was married, or whether I had any children.

She took off her shoes and loosened the belt of her dress. She lay down on the bed and closed her eyes. She started breathing heavily, fast and hard, in short, quick breaths, hyperventilating. I tried this myself later on and almost passed out. She breathed like this for about two minutes and stopped. The room was absolutely quiet. Then she did it again, very hard, very fast, and she stopped.

Suddenly, another voice came out of her—an eerie voice, much deeper, much lower, like a different person residing in her body.

"We now have contact with the psyche," said the voice. Throughout the reading, whenever the voice spoke of itself, it never said "I." It always said "we," the plural. I have no idea who that collective "we" was.

Before the reading, I had been told to prepare five general questions. Betty lay on her back on the bed, her eyes closed, never looking at me. The voice spoke again, loudly—"You will ask your questions now, please."

"What is the major purpose of this lifetime?" I said. "What latent talents do I have that I should be using? What is the karmic reason for my relationship with my wife, Yvonne Horn, age twenty-eight? How can I best help my son Marlen, age four? How can I best help my son Robin, age one and a half?"

I was amazed at the answers. In that deep, rapid, otherworldly voice, which rushed like a river, never pausing, she spoke for two hours. She— or the entity within her—began with, "You are a soul that has come forth in this present lifetime to learn many lessons, and you are learning them along your pathway. You also have brought forth with you a number of talents, specifically, music, music, music, music. And also you love color and you love beauty and you love rhythm."

In one life, she said, I was a sheepherder in Vienna in the 1600s. I loved the outdoors; I sang and played flute for the flock. In another life, I was more of a musician, still an amateur, who showed off for friends in the pubs, playing piano and singing. In Atlantis 15,000 years ago, I was involved with language and science and music; in Egypt, I was an interpreter and a painter; I was a female dancer in Africa, India, Spain, and China; a male folk dancer in Russia.

I was a monk in India—one of the statements I vividly recalled when I later visited India. She also said I was a Catholic nun in Italy and a nature worshiper in Phoenicia—all of which I found interesting because of my inner searchings and the spiritual directions I was beginning to explore.

She brought in past lives I had with Yvonne, pointing out that in order to grow together, it was essential that we resolve the problems, frustrations, and lack of fulfillment we experienced then, which we were also experiencing now. We still had things to work through.

Although I had told Betty nothing of my relationship with Yvonne, she put her finger on some of our problems. She said I was impatient and somewhat stern and that I was neglecting my wife. That was true. I have always been somewhat impatient, and I was out on the road a lot. In turn,

Yvonne felt neglected, lonely, unappreciated, and bored; she needed outlets for changes in her life. That was true, too.

McCain tied our present life in with one of our previous lives. In England during the 1400s, Yvonne's parents would not let us marry because I was a singer and a wanderer; as well, I needed to be alone and did not want someone clinging to me. Our relationship was unfulfilled then, just as it was unfulfilled now, except for our two sons. I later realized that our sons needed Yvonne and me to be together in order to be born. This was the reason and purpose for that marriage.

Betty McCain's entity gave some sterling advice about raising our boys. In past lives, my older son and I had been on opposite sides in several wars, and I had defeated him many times. I had to be sensitive to his feelings. From that reading on, whenever I played childhood games with Marlen, I could see how seriously he took it when he lost. Not all of the time, but some of the time, I purposely let him win, to help him develop confidence.

She asked if I hit my children. I said no, although when they got out of hand, I sometimes gave them little spankings. She said, "You should *never* do that. These are very sensitive souls. Have more patience. Reason with them. They have good minds, they are intelligent, and they will understand—provided you do not hit them." From that time on, I never raised my hand. I punished them when appropriate, but never physically.

All of the elements in this reading were important, but one part stands out especially vividly. "A complete new trend of music is coming forth," she said, "and you are going to find yourself in the midst of it. . . . The low systematic things on the earth-plane have to go. The vibrations have to be raised. . . . You are here to help in this way. You are here to help create because you do have within you the ability to be before people. You have a personality, and you can mix with people, and this draws you unto them. And thereby your whole life is filled with talent. . . . You are the individual who will be able to compose music to fit this new trend, and this will be of great beauty, and it will do away with the music which, with this rock and roll, disturbs the lower chakras and only creates the passions of the physical body of the young people.

"You will be the one who will feel the music pouring through you from the inspiration of your Soul-self, because you are an old soul on the earth-plane. This is what is needed now—a new beginning, a new beauty, not too slow, not too fast, and something which will raise the vibrations of mankind, something of beauty. . . .

"These things must be expressed to raise the vibrations of man, for this is a time of change on the earth-plane, when men must hearken and clear up within themselves, or find themselves destroyed in their own frustrations. Those with talent will find that they can take a great part in this awakening. . . . You must help humanity, and you will be one who will help to raise these vibrations.

"In England in the 1400s, you were in the male body, and your name was William Harris Abrams. You sang in that life, and you sang quite exquisitely, yes you did, and you always loved nature, and you have loved nature through many lifetimes. Thereby, this helps to intune you. It helps to keep you alive in your feelings. It helps to make all things of earth a part of you, and that's what you will do before this lifetime has extended itself. You will learn to be in tune with animals, to be in tune with nature, and to be in tune with your fellow-man, and to be in tune first with your own soul and God-self, which is the Spirit within the soul, pure wisdom. . . ."

She said new rhythms and different dances were coming, a reappearance of ancient musical forms that have not existed since Atlantis and early Egypt. I have certainly seen new rhythms and different dances come in, and New Age higher-consciousness music has been with us for more than twenty-five years, affecting many, many people, "raising the vibrations" of humankind in the process.

She blew me away, and as I look back now, I see the truth of her words. I recorded the first Jazz Mass, sacred music that appealed to mainstream audiences; I went to India, connected with my God-self, and recorded *Inside the Taj Mahal*, one of the first innovative New Age meditative albums; I recorded *Inside II*, using only my flutes and sounds from nature; in Canada, I played music for an ailing killer whale named Haida, attuning myself with this gentle giant, raising its life-affirming vibrations with music. And throughout my travels since Betty's reading, I have been increasingly interested in the beauty and transformative powers of spiritually uplifting music.

When the reading was over, Betty did more rapid breathing and came out of her trance. She had no recollection of what she'd said. Tears ran out of my eyes. I wasn't sobbing, but my cheeks were wet. I couldn't say I recalled the specific past lives and people she had talked about. Nevertheless, I felt it was true. "Yes," I said. All I could say was "Yes," and the tears wet my cheeks. What she said made sense to me. It felt real. It rang a bell.

I returned with Emil and Joe, and Betty gave us a reading about music. She got into odd time signatures, like 5/4 and 7/4, which are related to dances and rhythms of ancient cultures. Four-beat music is more modern, but by comparison it is rigid and boring, rather like a march. In India, Greece, Egypt, and elsewhere, odd time signatures are normal. I was just beginning to get into 5/4, 7/4, and 11/4 rhythms with my group, well before Don Ellis started doing similar things. After Betty gave our reading, these incredible time signatures developed very quickly, not only in our band, but in other bands as well.

More than ever before, my thinking expanded. If I lived in Atlantis 15,000 years ago, I've been around a long time. Life is not just these seventy or eighty years. It is much more than what most of us understand, much longer than we have conceived. Because of these readings, time became a different dimension for me. There is really no time, no beginning, no end. Clocks and calendars are pragmatically valuable, but they are illusions. Time is a device to measure eternity. At this point, I began thinking in eternal terms.

I did not try to convince myself to be a reincarnationist. It's just that the theory of reincarnation uplifted my spirits and gave me a wider vision of life, a deeper appreciation of my role in it, a new perspective of my evolving purpose, and a new sense of responsibility. I began thinking about it, wondering about resolving karmic situations and then blending back into life's harmonious Oneness of Being. Betty McCain opened my eyes. It was a new and incredible feeling.

I continued seeing Gina Cerminara as often as I could, on one occasion taking her to Tony Curtis and Janet Leigh's house for dinner. Gina was all excited. She got very girlish about going "up to Mount Olympus to see the stars." Gina left Hollywood when Betty McCain died and moved into Betty's northern California home. She did research, wrote books, and held seminars and classes. Then she toured the country giving lectures, after which she lived in Virginia Beach, where she had access to Cayce's readings. I saw her one more time, after I moved to Canada, and then she died.

ACTION AND REACTION

Some people believe there is no God and no afterlife; by extension, they also believe that reincarnation is superstition. These beliefs are highly personal, and I respect whatever anyone has to say about them. The belief in no God and no afterlife is as valid as any other. Personally, however, I do not find it satisfying.

I came from a Jewish family, and the Jewish tradition is part of my Western heritage. Nevertheless, I do not look at religions from a Jewish perspective, any more than I look at them from a Catholic or Islamic perspective. I view all religions the same way. There is a fundamental truth inherent in each, otherwise they would not exist. This underlying spiritual truth is what I want to know about.

There are many wonderful religions and philosophies in the West, and yet I was never particularly drawn to them. Zen Buddhism, however, rang a bell instantly. I immediately wanted to know more about it. The same with Yoga. There was no familial or cultural basis for me to be attracted to Eastern concepts, and yet I was definitely attracted to them, much more so than I was to Western ideologies.

To many Westerners, reincarnation and karma sound unusual. However, the entire Eastern world believes in them. For the majority of people on our planet—more than half of all peoples everywhere, including the entirety of India—reincarnation and karma have constituted a major part of the belief system since day one.

When I was exposed to the theory of reincarnation and karma, it too rang a bell instantly. It made sense to me. It appealed to my logical mind because reincarnation seems logical. What can I learn in seventy or eighty years? Very little. It does not seem logical to me that I was given this incredible human body and brain, just to have it vanish in the blink of a cosmic eye. This may be the case, of course, but it doesn't compute. It's not logical. My mind does not accept it.

Every action has an equal and opposite reaction. That is a physical law. Throw a tennis ball against a wall, and it comes back with equal force. The theory of karma is that same law, stated in metaphysical terms. For every action, there is a reaction. That is what karma is. Karma is not good or bad or right or wrong, it just is.

Death is an action, an event. Is there no reaction? Can you jump in the air without coming down? Do you stop in midair? That would be incomplete. The whole universe works according to the law of action and reaction. Logically speaking, you can't just say, "Well, death is the exception. You die, and that's the end of it."

Of all mysteries, death is by far the greatest. Sooner or later, every one of us thinks about it. What is death? What is on the other side of life? We don't know, but in the process of searching, we might discover things that will give our lives more purpose and meaning.

For example, what is my motivation for being good? It is just as easy to be bad. I want a lot of money. Why shouldn't I steal it? Why should I work so hard? Why not take the money from somebody else? Many people think this way. Crime is everywhere—in streets and in schools, with corruption in police departments, governments, and businesses. Obviously, moral principles and legal proclamations do not deter criminals.

It seems to me that the biggest deterrent would be a belief in the law of karma. We have free will and free choice. We are responsible for whatever we do. At the same time, every action has its reaction. If I steal money, some reaction will come back. It is not a question of being a good person or a bad person. Nor is it a question of legality. Stealing is neither right nor legal, but if I take responsibility for the act of stealing, I must also accept the reaction. Somewhere down the line, even if the police do not catch me, I must pay for that action—if not in this life, then in another.

Whether we are reincarnationists or not, all of us have experienced the karmic principle of action and reaction. Let's say you had a terrific day. Everything went right, everything worked, and everybody was nice. Or perhaps you had a lousy day—nothing went right, nothing worked, and nobody was nice. In both cases, you might stop and analyze yourself. How were you that day? What kind of vibrations did you send out? On the good day, were you relaxed and friendly to begin with? On the bad day, did you feel like a grouch as soon as you finished your morning orange juice? Whatever you send out comes back.

Physically or spiritually, the same law applies. Perhaps I have a materialistic philosophy. I believe there is no God, no afterlife, and that we live only once. As a result, there is no morality, no spiritual guideline, no reason for self-discipline or law or love or compassion. Get it while you can. If that is my philosophy, that is the way I will live. I live only once, so what do I care? Rip off as many people as possible, take the money, and run. Morality and ethics are irrelevant because I live only once. If I don't get it now, when can I? There is no tomorrow, live for today. Be greedy. Grab, grab, grab. Me, me, me, this is my chance.

I often hear people say these things. When you hear somebody talk like that, you know how he or she is likely to behave, because their philosophy sums up their attitude and vision of life.

Conversely, if I am a reincarnationist and believe in karma, then I also believe that whatever I sow, I shall reap. The bread I cast upon the waters will come back—if not in this life, in the next. Life is tricky, like being in water over your head. Before I take action, I want to watch what I say and do. I want to be a little more cautious, a little more careful—because it all comes back.

The materialistic philosophy offers no deterrent because it does not respect legality or morality. The reincarnationist philosophy is a deterrent against destructive behavior because it recognizes and respects the dynamic balance between action and reaction. It can be an inspiration for leading a life that is loving, supportive, creative, compassionate, and kind.

STUDIO LIFE

These were exciting years, and I was playing with some of the best musicians in the world. It was the kind of scene where you show up at nine in the morning to play in a fifty-piece orchestra at Universal Studios. No one's seen the music. You don't know what's happening. Then comes the downbeat, and everybody reads through it like they've been playing it for six months. You refine a few notes, smooth out a few rough spots. They say, "Okay, roll 'em." And you do a take.

Life was good. Tony Curtis was a friend of mine. Tony Bennett was a friend, too, and I toured with him several times. I was living in a city with musicians I had idolized since I was a kid. I loved guitarist Barney Kessell, bassist Red Mitchell, trombonist Frank Rosolino, drummer Shelly Manne, trumpeter Conte Candoli, all those guys—and now we were hanging out and sometimes playing gigs together, which was fun. They and other musicians were known in jazz as the cool school. Although I knew these guys, I never could crack into that clique as far as joining one of their groups on a permanent basis. Almost immediately after leaving Chico's group, I began studio work.

I performed on several of Frank Sinatra's records. Peggy Lee, George Shearing, Shorty Rogers, Ravi Shankar, Cal Tjader, and a lot of others asked me to play on their albums. Composers like Johnny Mandel, Lalo Schifrin, Dave Grusin, Pete Rugulo, and Quincy Jones asked me on their sessions.

Playing three hours a day on staff at NBC in 1959, I was earning $15,000 a year, a lot of money in those days. And I could still play my own jazz gigs, get free-lance studio dates, and accept calls to be the guest soloist on other people's albums.

Sometimes kids ask how to get started in studio work. All you have to do is get one or two dates and prove yourself. To do that, you've got to move to L.A. or some other recording center, like New York or Toronto. And you have to be willing to wait it out for a while—you don't know how long it might take. Obviously, you have to be able to play your instrument well, and you have to be familiar with many different styles of music. It's essential to be a good sight-reader, to be able to read anything they put in front of you. If you're a rock 'n' roll specialist, that's fine. But for overall studio work, you want to be called for anything that might come up. If you can do anything, rather than just one thing, your earning power increases.

For studio work, it's not only *what* you know, it's *who* you know. You have to connect with somebody who is already involved, like the contractors who line up musicians for recording sessions. Even then, you might have to wait. I once had two gigs on line, but saxophonist Bud Shank complained to the session contractor about giving the gigs to me instead of him, and I lost the jobs. The cliques were strong. After that incident, however, the contractor used me as often as possible.

On one recording session, which I remember vividly, Ravi Shankar showed up without any written score and developed the music right there in the studio. I had never heard of anything like that. In my experience, people came to the sessions thoroughly prepared, with the music clearly written out in parts. Ravi went to each musician individually and sang the notes of the part he wanted played. We grabbed our pencils, wrote his phrases down, and recorded *Portrait of Genius*.

The energy generated by this process was tremendous. We were creating and developing music in-the-moment, pressured by studio time, which costs a lot of money. Because of this situation, the creative energy felt intense and lively in a way that was different from anything I had known before. I later used this technique on a few albums of my own, including *Inside II*.

One of the peak experiences of my studio life came about as the result of a call I received, not from a composer, arranger, or contractor, but from Pat Willard, a free-lance writer for *down beat* and *Metronome* and numerous other jazz magazines. Pat was a good writer, and she was personal friends with nearly all of the major jazz musicians.

Pat phoned one day and said Duke Ellington was in town. He was going to be recording *Suite Thursday* that night, but Johnny Hodges, his lead alto player, was sick in the hospital with a bleeding ulcer. Pat told Duke about me. Was I interested in playing the date?

I couldn't believe it—a recording session with Duke Ellington!

On most dates, I arrived maybe five minutes early. When you know you can cut it, you get pretty blasé. This time, however, I arrived thirty minutes early, wanting to make sure I felt comfortable, that my reeds were properly wet, that my horns were in top condition.

Nobody was in the studio except the recording engineer, "Bones" Howe. I waited. A quarter to eight, no one there. Five to eight, no one there. Eight o'clock, no one there. Jesus Christ. Am I in the right studio? Maybe I blew it.

"Hey, Bones, is this where Duke's recording?"

"Yeah."

"Isn't it supposed to start at eight?"

"Yeah."

"Where is everybody?"

"I don't know."

About 8:20, baritone sax player Harry Carney wandered in—Harry Carney, one of the all-time greats, in the flesh. I was in awe of him, and there we were, in the same studio together. Pretty soon, a few others straggled in. These guys were legends in the most famous band in the world, many of them with Duke from the beginning.

They brought out what sheet music they had, which wasn't much. These guys had been in the band forever, and most of them had memorized everything. To memorize the melody of a song is easy, but if you are playing the fourth sax or the baritone part or the third trombone, you are playing harmony parts, which is not easy. These guys knew their parts by heart, and they seldom looked at the music.

Somebody put Hodges's lead alto part on my stand. It wasn't printed nicely in manuscript. It was almost illegible, written out by hand, in pencil, with no phrase markings. I didn't know whether to slur this phrase or tongue that phrase or how it was supposed to be interpreted—and yet my lead alto part was the most important part of the sax section.

By 8:45, all the members of the band had arrived. Duke still wasn't there. The guys were friendly toward me, which helped, because I was nervous. I had to play the lead part in a piece I didn't know. I was surrounded by famous people, and I was the only white guy in the band. But they were very helpful. They told me how to phrase it, and I made my own phrase markings with my own pencil so I could get a little bit of a head start.

At nine o'clock, Duke walked in, nonchalant, casual, smiling. He and the guys were all laid-back and relaxed, they way they were in clubs. After club intermissions, the band didn't get back on stage simultaneously. They came up one at a time, and when there were enough of them, they started the piece, and then the rest of them wandered up from the bar or the tables and joined in. Duke didn't crack a whip, and it was wonderful, real relaxed. Same way for this recording session.

Duke gave the downbeat. Without rehearsing, we started playing. Duke wasn't about to have a separate rehearsal just for me. Luckily, I take after my mother, who was a good sight-reader. In the conservatory, you practiced four months with the symphony orchestra before you performed a piece. Here, we ran it down once and then did a take.

Although I played the lead alto part, I didn't have any solos. The notes weren't difficult, and it was strictly section work. Also, the other players were so strong that they led me, which gave me the courage to play out as strong as they were. I knew I was being protected and looked after by the guys on both sides of me, and that made me feel good.

As I played, the music sounded really strange. My ear was not hearing "right notes," because Duke had a unique way of voicing the instruments. Usually, writers and orchestrators view each instrumental section as a minigroup of its own. They voice the chords within the sections. The lead alto has the melody in the sax section, for example, and the chord is voiced from top to bottom, from the alto down to the baritone sax. Same thing with the trumpets, the trombones, and so forth.

Duke didn't do that. He might voice the lead alto with the lead trumpet and the third alto. Or he'd voice the trombone with the tenor saxophone. He mixed it up, getting unique colors, like a painter mixing different colors to get a new color of his own.

As I played, I said to myself, "Good God, this sounds terrible." And yet when we finished and listened to the playback, it sounded terrific. As you stood at a distance and heard the full band, not just one section, the colors blended perfectly. The rhythm section cooked away, the band swung, and the level and quality of energy was great. It was a marvelous experience.

Paul Gonzalves, Duke's famous tenor sax player, sat next to me. He was a brilliant player, who had a big solo in *Suite Thursday*'s second movement, where the tempo is very fast. It started out with the band playing sixteen bars as a set-up for Paul. The sixteenth bar was silent. Paul had a pickup there, and then his solo began.

It was well known that Paul was a heavy heroin addict. Sitting next to me, he nodded out, like he was asleep, his head drooped down nearly to his chest, totally zonked. Meanwhile, the tempo burned, and it was almost time for Paul's solo.

I played, counting measures. No way was this guy going to make it for his solo. Should I nudge him? Unforgivably presumptuous. So I waited, counting 13–2-3-4, 14–2-3-4, 15–2-3-4. On the fourth beat of the fifteenth bar, he snapped out of his stupor, and, bam, right on the downbeat of the sixteenth bar, he blasted into his tenor pickup and played a tremendous solo. One take. That was it. He sat back down and nodded out again.

It was incredible to see how his mind worked. He knew he could relax and nod out. He had plenty of time, another second and a half. He didn't wet his reed, either—just boom, put the sax in his mouth, and he was off and flying. Gonzalves was beautiful, just beautiful.

We finished the whole side of that album in one hour and fifteen minutes—one take. Thank God I played my part well. And I was delighted that everyone complimented me.

Immediately after we finished recording *Suite Thursday*, Irving Townsend came over as I was packing up my horns. Irving was the head of A & R and vice president of Columbia Records on the West Coast. He produced this session with Duke.

"You sounded terrific tonight, Paul. You did a good job taking Johnny Hodges's place. By the way, Miles Davis has been saying nice things about you to me. How about let's have lunch next week."

The next week, we had lunch. It turned out that Miles had told Irving he should sign me up. There it was. I had a contract with Columbia Records.

After a few years, the romantic side of studio work wears down. Too many studio musicians measure everything in terms of money, and they rarely get to play top-flight music. While it lasted, studio work was great, but I was bored and drying up. On top of that, I couldn't break into the "cool school" jazz cliques and get my own music played. Their groups already had their players. The only way I was going to get to play my own music was to form my own band. That's exactly what I did. Miles played a major role in helping me evolve.

MILES DAVIS

I originally met Miles in 1957, on a tour I did with Chico. Three years later, my engineer friend Henry Lewy called. "Miles is gigging in town this week," he said. "He wants to know if we can come out for a swim in your pool." This was about 8:30 in the morning, which surprised me, but Miles is an early riser. "Well, sure, man, great," I said, and by nine o'clock, there stood Henry Lewy and Miles Davis, knocking at my door. Not only that— Miles remembered me from the tour three years before, even though we had not spoken. Today he didn't stand on formalities, and it was as if he'd known me all his life. We swam in the pool, cooked up some barbecue, and talked about my new album, *Impressions*, which he liked.

After that first get-together, Miles came over almost every day. Some of the other guys in his band started coming over too. Bassist Paul Chambers, drummer Jimmy Cobb, and pianist Wynton Kelly came over all the time, and Cannonball dropped in once in a while, and they brought their girl-friends. We ate and swam and had barbecue parties. Miles is a great cook. He did all the barbecuing. We had a heck of a good time, and Miles accepted me as his friend.

Sitting with me at my piano, Miles got into music, showing me different voicings. He taught me how to work with fourths and augmented fourths, strange-sounding chord intervals that enable a soloist to step outside of conventional harmonic frameworks. In this context, any note is right, and no note sounds wrong. McCoy Tyner later used these intervals playing with Coltrane. To me, this was a whole new concept. When Miles showed me these modal voicings, he became the first person to connect everything for me. I always wondered how Impressionist voicings and techniques like Ravel's could be incorporated into jazz. Well, Miles came along and did it.

He did more. In earlier days, Charlie Parker, Dizzy Gillespie, Miles, and the other beboppers played tunes with very fast tempos and nine million chord changes. To separate the men from the boys in jam sessions, they kicked off complex burners like "The Song Is You" and "Cherokee," very difficult, challenging pieces.

After exploring that type of music, Miles reversed himself and did just the opposite. He slowed the tempo down. He stopped moving chords all over the place. He hung out on one or two chords for eight or sixteen bars—or forever. He devised Impressionistic voicings on the piano and then played beautiful, spacious melodic lines over the top. Suddenly, there it was—Ravel with a rhythm section.

During this period, my most prolific, I felt incredibly creative. Tunes danced into my head a mile a minute, and it was hard to find time to write them down. One day at the piano, Miles said, "You ought to form a new band, man. Get Billy Higgins on drums. Go back into the Renaissance Club."

That sounded like a great idea, so I called drummer Billy Higgins, vibist Emil Richards, pianist Paul Moer, and bassist Jimmy Bond. We got involved with odd time signatures, like 5/4, 7/4, 11/4—and this was before Don Ellis and Dave Brubeck.

Our experimental quintet was new and exciting, and people loved it. We got a record out on Columbia, *The Sound of Paul Horn*, and our following grew larger and stronger. With the Paul Horn Quintet, I returned to the Renaissance Club.

I was on my own now, flying high. A lot of the tunes Miles inspired me to write appeared on my album, *Something Blue*, a title purposely and respectfully alluding to Miles's *Kind of Blue*.

I learned a lot from Miles about life and honesty. He's the most honest person I ever met, even to the point of brutality. Personally, I don't agree with his stance. I agree with Maharishi, who says, "Speak the truth, but sweet truth." Why hurt someone's feelings if you don't have to? Isn't there enough suffering in the world?

But Miles trusts his first reaction, and he is totally truthful. If he's introduced to someone and doesn't get the right feeling, he just abruptly walks away, not even shaking hands. If he likes you, however, then he's warm and affectionate. He gives you hugs and kisses and talks as if he's known you all his life.

After a while, Miles came to California less, and I didn't get back to New York very often. I went to India twice, recorded *Inside the Taj Mahal*, taught meditation, and moved to Canada. One night at a club in Vancouver where I was playing, Miles called and left a message for me to come over to the Holiday Inn, where he was staying.

Things change in every relationship, of course, and sooner or later people separate and lose contact. That has happened with Miles and me, and I've not seen him since that meeting at the Holiday Inn. He was a great inspiration, first through his music before I knew him, then through our friendship, which flourished three or four years.

On every level, he was one of my most important teachers. He opened new doors for me musically. He has no fear of dealing with people conversationally or physically. He has charisma and enormous strength. He never treated people nicely just because they might be important to his career. In every way, he is strong. I watched him interact with others, sometimes agreeing with how he handled things, sometimes disagreeing. In all instances, I learned about what I could and couldn't do in terms of my own development.

Perhaps above all, Miles taught me a certain kind of courage. He was never afraid to experiment. If you are a true jazz musician, you don't go to the gig like a classical musician, with everything rehearsed and practiced and planned out.

No, you take chances all the time. In a sense, you do your practicing on the gig, which means you will make mistakes. You'll go for a note, but it will crack; you try a double-time phrase, but you falter and can't carry it through. Maybe you miss a chord or botch a rhythm. If you're truly a jazz musician, you don't go on with the idea of playing a song perfectly. The idea is to stretch out as far as you can. You try new things. You test your courage and skills to the maximum.

And if you're a fan, you don't come to hear the perfect solo. You come to hear Miles or McCoy Tyner because you know they're going to try things. They'll experiment and shoot for the stars. You know you'll hear some weird music, and some of it might not please you, but somewhere along the line, an absolutely magical moment will happen, a moment worth it all.

That's jazz, experimenting in public every time, including big concerts where there are thousands of people watching you give your best, even when you miss. If you're a jazz musician you take chances, no matter where you are. Miles has taken chances all of his life. Our culture is immeasurably enriched because of him and his music. So am I. I love him very much.

GROUP LEADER

As the leader of three jazz groups during the late fifties and throughout the sixties, I learned a lot about music and even more about people. Instead of taking the authoritarian approach to leadership, I took the cooperative approach. A musician's ego is a fragile thing, and I never wanted to damage it. I learned how to be sensitive to musicians' needs, acknowledged their egos, and found ways to be kind and delicate when giving direction. Leadership is a challenge.

Bands are more than collections of individuals; they are much greater than the sum of their parts. I call this higher unity the X-factor. It's the X-factor that makes the magic in music. You're not just playing notes. You're relating to other members of the band, and that relationship carries over directly into the music.

Of course, if a musician does not play well enough to be in the group, the matter ends there. But if a guy does play well enough, then I ask myself several questions. How is he as a person? Is he a schmuck or a weirdo? Is he together, not only on his instrument, but in his head? Can he blend in with the rest of us? Are we going to have a good time together?

It is very important to me that we get along and like each other because that makes all the difference in how the music sounds. If I had to choose between two players, one of whom was the best in the world, the other very good, but not the best, I would look at who is going to be the most compatible. If the better musician is not compatible but the lesser is, I take the lesser, always.

When I was a sideman, I saw many leaders who never hung out with the guys, who traveled separately, who had their own social groups, who came together with the sidemen only onstage. I never wanted that. It was too lonely being that kind of leader, and I liked my musicians.

To me, Chico Hamilton was the ideal leader. There was no question that he was in charge, but we could also hang out and have fun and feel comfortable with him. When you want to bridge the gap between leader and sidemen, you have to walk a fine line. Chico did that, and he was my model.

Of course, Chico was about twelve years older than I, so it was easy to say "He's the leader." In my groups, however, we were all about the same age. How could I maintain the respect of the sidemen, enforcing certain things musically, and still be friends? Chico showed me how. The guys and I hung out together; we went with each other to various social events; sometimes our families got together. It was a nice combination of coworkers, friends, and family. Those feelings were reflected in the music, and that's what I wanted to bring out in my groups.

All musicians, perhaps especially the younger ones, have strong egos and a lot of pride. They are very protective of who and what they are. A good leader wants and respects these qualities, but he or she must also learn how to give musicians direction without offending them.

First, I got it clear in my mind what I wanted to hear. Then I let the musicians know that in no way did I want to infringe on their territory; in no way was I criticizing them; and in no way was I telling them how to play their instruments. Lastly, I gave them the concept of what I wanted to hear and then let them find their own way, respecting their ability to do so.

I also encouraged the players to speak out about their feelings, to talk to each other, to contribute, to feel a part of the group. I made it clear to them that the band was a cooperative effort, and *everyone* could feel inspired to utilize personal creativity, not just me.

In a way, I was instinctively doing what I saw Maharishi doing several years later. He incorporated all of us in his decision-making processes. He took the time to ask us what we thought and how we felt. He never said no. He always said yes. However, if the idea he received did not fit into his concept, he kept asking questions, gently leading us back to the path, incorporating those ideas of ours that did fit. He was sweet and gentle about it, considerate of each person. He wanted us to join in and feel a part of the family of meditators.

I had a family of musicians. I could have been authoritarian about it, and I still would have led a band, but it would have been a different kind of band and a different kind of music. I wanted our family to be a cooperative unit, happy with the music, happy with each other, happy with the creative process. And that's the way we were.

RECORDING ARTIST

To me, music has never been merely a job. It has always been an adventure. Music is stimulating and exciting. It creates energy. It helps me evolve as a human being. If it does not make me feel good inside, if it isn't fun, if I don't enjoy playing it, then I won't be involved with it.

During the nine years between 1957 and 1966, I recorded eleven jazz albums with a variety of instrumental combinations (see the Discography). On each album, I have tried to make a statement. The value of recording is that you create a sonic document of the person you were at that particular time. Each album is a kind of chapter in an ongoing book. Taken together, they add up to a lifetime.

Many musicians find a popular style and stay with it. I never wanted to do that. For me, the key words have always been "exploration," "creativity," and "evolution."

Right from the beginning, record companies went along with my rather innocent way of thinking. When Tom Mack of Dot Records offered me my first contract, he didn't say, "Look, our big star is Pat Boone, and we want you to give some of his hit songs a jazz flavor, like 'Down Town.'" He could have said that, and of course I would have said no. But I figured you want me to record an album. That means you have heard me play and you like what you heard. I'm not asking you; you're asking me. If you like my music, and you want me to record for you, then I will choose the music. And that is what happened.

For *House of Horn*, I brought in some of Chico Hamilton's Quintet. Chico couldn't use his name, because of his own recording contract. He is partly American Indian, and his middle name is Foresthorn, so on the record he is called Forest Thorn, but everybody knew it was Chico playing drums.

All of the music was written and arranged by me, Fred Katz, Allyn Ferguson, and Pete Rugulo, of Stan Kenton fame. Gerald Wiggins played piano; Larry Bunker played vibes; Red Mitchell played bass—an impressive lineup for my first time out.

House of Horn was pretty much a straight-ahead jazz album, a kind of stretched-out Chico Hamilton Quintet sound. I was especially proud of a pretty ballad called "To a Little Boy," which I composed and arranged utilizing a string quartet, in honor of my son Marlen, who had just been born.

At the intersection of Sunset Boulevard and the San Diego Freeway, a circular Holiday Inn was being constructed. For the cover photo, Dot perched me and my horns precariously among the crisscrossing orange rafters—the "House of Horn" theme—a fun album cover.

I was so proud when this record came out. Dot put a big display in the window of Music City, a giant music store on the corner of Sunset and Vine. The whole window was filled with copies of *House of Horn*, and I took endless pictures of it with my movie camera.

On *Plenty of Horn*, my second album, I retained musical direction and got a little more ambitious, using a big band. On side two, Allyn Ferguson arranged a suite in four movements called "Moods for Horn," featuring trumpets, French horn, trombone, tuba, bass, and drums. This time, Shelley Manne played drums, Larry Bunker played vibes, Mongo Santamaria played congas, and Fred Katz played cello. On tuba, we had Red Callender; on trombone, Milt Bernhart; on bass, Red Mitchell. Billy Bean played guitar—wonderful musicians all.

You have not suddenly become a new musician just because you're recording a new album. Transitions occur gradually. I think *Plenty of Horn* differed from the first album primarily in terms of the material and the big-band instrumentation. It was a fuller, more ambitious album, but not vastly different from *House of Horn* in terms of its concept—good, strong, multifaceted, upbeat jazz.

It also differed because I had grown another year as a player, influenced especially by Billy Bean, a wonderful jazz guitarist, incredibly gifted. He and I sat for hours in the evenings and played together, just the two of us. We repeatedly went over changes to difficult tunes, something I hadn't had the chance to do before. Although Billy was truly a great guitarist, one of the best of any era, he just faded away. I don't know where he is or what happened to him. I think *Plenty of Horn* reflected my musical development during this year with him.

I am especially attached to my fourth album, *Something Blue*, recorded around 1960 on a label called Hi Fi Jazz. It was done with the original Paul Horn Quintet and contains the music I composed when Miles and I hung out together. Musically, Miles opened big doors for me and everybody else. Personally, he inspired me to rise to new creative heights.

The quintet had been playing at the Renaissance Club many months, and our music was clean and crisp. Dave Axelrod, the record producer for Hi Fi Jazz, heard us live and signed us up. We had Emil Richards on vibes, Paul Moer on piano, Jimmy Bond on bass, and Billy Higgins on drums.

On the night of the recording, Dave called and said he wanted to talk about a couple of things before the session. He asked me to stop by his apartment. When I arrived, he lit up a joint, and we got high.

"I want you to feel as free tonight as you do when you're in the club," he said. "We'll get the sound worked out before you start recording. Once you start, you won't have to stop."

In a nightclub, you don't have take one, take two, take three. You play each song one time, continually moving forward, flaws and all. That's what jazz is all about. I wanted to do the same thing in the studio.

I told the engineer to set up his mikes. We would improvise on the blues for twenty minutes or so, during which time he would get his technical things together—levels, balances, E.Q.'s, and so on.

"When you're sure everything is correct, let me know, and we'll start playing. Everything is to be one-take tonight. I don't want to have to stop because of technical problems. By the way, turn out the lights."

In those days, no one ever thought about atmosphere. You walked into the studio, and the lights were harsh and bright—good for reading music, terrible for playing jazz. We wanted a nightclub atmosphere, so we turned off the overhead lights and used the small, indirect lights on the music stands. Dave Axelrod also turned out the lights in the recording booth. All you could see were amber reflections on his and the engineer's faces from the dim little lamp on top of the recording console. Not until the late sixties did studios begin taking atmosphere into consideration on a regular basis.

When everything was ready, we played. Normally, it requires several three-hour sessions to complete an album. We played everything in one take, just as I had wanted, and finished *Something Blue* in two hours. I had never recorded a jazz LP that way before. Because of the immediacy of the emotions, the intensity of the performances, and the music itself, which is especially close to my heart, I think *Something Blue* is one of the best albums I have ever done.

In 1965 my quintet consisted of Lynn Blessing on vibes, Bill Plummer on bass, Mike Lang on piano, and Larry Bunker or Bill Goodwin on drums. They played on the *Jazz Mass*, which included a full orchestra and a choir, and which won two Grammys.

That same year I recorded an innovative quintet album entitled *Cycle*, which was nominated for a Grammy along with the *Jazz Mass*. Different meters and extended compositional forms had become a part of our repertoire now. We all felt free and comfortable improvising in odd time signatures, and our playing had become much more relaxed and confident. What made *Cycle* truly unique, however, were the bagpipes.

I've always loved the sound of the pipes and looked for ways to do some songs with bagpipe players. I discovered a group of ten or twelve Scottish pipers who met once a week at an armory in Santa Monica, where they walked around in a circle, dressed in kilts, playing their bagpipes. When I suggested to the two instructors that they record with me, they felt a bit hesitant. "We don't play jazz," they said.

"I don't want you to play jazz," I assured them. "I just like the bagpipe sound. Your sense of time is real laid-back, the way I like it in jazz."

They said okay. I wrote one original, called "In the Bag," and did an arrangement of "Greensleeves" in 5/4 time. When we got to the recording studio and the pipes started to play, they were a half-tone off. I wrote the music in D minor, but because they were a half-tone flat, our improvisations had to be in D-flat minor, which makes quite a difference. There was no way we could adjust anything, so we had to transpose down a half-step.

Today, there is a lot of overdubbing in the studios. You walk in, put on a headset, play over whatever was recorded yesterday, and you never see the other musicians. Back in the early and midsixties, however, musicians still played together, surrounded by little three-foot-high baffle boards that separated the instruments. Each of us recorded on a different track, but we could look at one another and play together. I don't see how jazz can be played by overdubbing. You need eye contact. You need to see everyone's body language. You need personal and spontaneous interaction.

For *Cycle*, the recording engineer faced a real challenge because he couldn't isolate the bagpipes, and their sound spilled over into everyone else's microphone. That was okay for us, as long as principal players could rise above them, but it was hellish in the control room, where the bagpipes sounded incredibly loud and intense.

Because the pipers had some difficulty entering at the right place, we did several takes. By the time we finally completed one, the engineer and producer Al Schmitt were cross-eyed and holding their ears. They'd been driven out of their skulls, but the music sounded great.

I was pleased with the quintet as well. We had arrived at the point where we could go into a studio and get the same feeling we got in the club. Without philosophizing about it, we had all learned how to go inside ourselves and become one with the music. We could lose ourselves quickly and easily, and as soon as we did, any anxieties vanished.

When you play jazz, you are not reading music. You are bringing music out of yourself. In a studio, this is difficult, because no audience is present. It's almost like method acting. You create a state of mind that enables you to play as if you were in front of an audience, when in fact no audience exists. It is quite a challenge. The more you record, the easier it becomes.

With or without an audience, we simply attuned ourselves to each other. We were good friends, and we loved the music. When it came time to play, we did not rely on external help. We just tuned in, interacted, played our music, and had fun. *Cycle* was a good album—especially those bagpipes.

During this period, I also recorded a number of other albums, including a jazz version of the *Cleopatra* soundtrack, and a lovely ballad album with voices, called *Here's That Rainy Day*.

GROWTH, SUFFERING, AND CREATIVITY

The jazz years were vital years, essential for my ongoing spiritual evolution. And indeed, as I look back, I see steady growth and considerable variety—from straight-ahead jazz; to odd time signatures; to different sounds, such as small combos, big bands, orchestras, bagpipes, and voices; to different forms and structures that span the spectrum from pop tunes to classical music to free-form jazz improvisations. Maintaining emotional honesty, intellectual rigor, aesthetic awareness, and artistic integrity, I moved progressively toward the freedom and intimacy that characterize such albums as *Inside the Taj Mahal* and *Inside the Great Pyramid*. Today, I embrace all types and styles of music, feeling relaxed and natural and confident with each.

I never look back with regret at this or any other period. I feel good about what I have done. I don't cringe when I listen to older albums, thinking I could do better now, or this was a mistake, or I should have done something else. That was the best I could do at the time, and I respect what I did because I always played with good musicians and I was always a good musician myself. Of course I have grown over the years, and I can see the growth, which is natural and inevitable, the way it should be. Each album was a different experience, and I treasure each for what it is.

On another level, I should mention that during the years between 1957 and 1966 I was going through tremendous changes in my personal life.

There were heavy scenes in my marriage that were extremely destructive. I cannot say they did not affect the music. They must be a part of it, but they certainly did not destroy it. Retrospectively, I see that *any* kind of energy from *any* experience in life can be transformed into creative energy.

I will not take the stand, as some artists do, that grief, tension, and suffering are necessary in order to be creative. Many people have told me that anger, rage, and conflict stimulate their creative juices. That may be true. It may also be true that if they felt better, they might rise to considerably greater heights.

It seems to me that anything can push creative juices. The emotional energy of tension, strife, and suffering can emerge out of a state of happiness, contentment, and fulfillment as well. You have to be in touch with the whole of yourself, with *everything* you are, and then you are free to explore creatively *all* levels of your humanity, not just one or two, and you can do it in a healthy, constructive way. Instead of draining yourself as you produce music, you grow.

In any case, my emotions and thought processes during this nine-year period were in turmoil, and yet the music kept expanding. Conversely, after meditating in India and discovering my own source of inner peace, the music has continued developing and evolving in positive, uplifting ways. I do not believe that suffering is necessary for creativity.

SEVEN

THE JAZZ MASS

In terms of concept, recording, and live performance, the Jazz Mass was definitely a peak experience in my life. I recorded it for RCA in 1964. The original concept had nothing to do with religion; I just wanted to explore a larger musical form than is normally a part of jazz, and I wanted to involve an orchestra, my jazz quintet, and voices. The Mass seemed to be an ideal structure in which to do this. Although my original perspective was aesthetic, not religious, the recording session and a live performance of this music in Minneapolis dramatically altered and expanded my ideas about what music can do, what the purpose of music is, and the ways in which music can profoundly enhance our spiritual evolution.

I asked Lalo Schifrin if he might be interested in composing the music, and he said yes. In addition to the sections of the Mass normally set to music, called Kyrie, Gloria, Sanctus, and Agnus Dei, he added four additional musical sections—the Credo, Offertory, Prayer, and Interludium.

A week before the recording session, I heard on the news that the Ecumenical Council in Rome decided to allow the Mass to be sung in different languages. Until then, it was sung only in Latin, and Lalo was writing a Latin text. I quickly called him. "Did you hear the news tonight?" He hadn't. I told him about the council's edict. Lalo said, "Let's do it in English." That was my thought, too. He had only a week to alter the score, but he did it.

A year later, Duke Ellington recorded *Sacred Service*. Because of Duke's great fame, many people think he was the first to do a Mass outside the church. Indeed, *Sacred Service* was religious music, but it was not a Mass. Our Mass was the first written in any language other than Latin, and it was the first jazz Mass ever recorded.

For the instrumentation, we chose my quintet, which was vibes, bass, piano, drums, and myself; a brass choir consisting of trumpet, trombone, bass trombone, French horn, and tuba; and two harps, percussion, and voices. We used only eight singers, but they sounded like a full choir.

These sessions were magical moments. The music was difficult, and we felt we were doing something special. Lalo is a good composer, and this music was interesting and fun to play. The singers were great and able to sight-read anything; the brass choir, harpists, and percussionists were first-rate studio musicians; my band had been working together continuously for several years. As dedicated professional players, all of us were ready.

I vividly remember the Credo, which normally does not have music. This is the text of the Nicene Creed that affirms the believer's faith in Jesus Christ as the one Lord, and only begotten Son of God.

Lalo wrote no musical notes for this section. Instead, he gave the singers a kind of road map. He told them to create a mental image of being in purgatory, desperately wanting to get out.

The singers began reciting the text, paying no attention to the other vocalists. They progressed individually, at their own pace, one reading a little slower, another a little faster, beginning on the lowest note possible, chanting in a monotone. When a singer ran out of breath, he or she stopped and then continued on, singing the lines a half-step higher. The section began very softly and got louder and louder and louder. When the vocalists reached the point where they could sing no higher, they shouted and screamed.

I waited until things started and then came in playing solo alto sax, with no written music and no chord structure, freely improvising. At a certain point, Lalo cued the percussion in. With the choir ascending, the sax playing, the timpani drums rolling, we had one long crescendo that built to a powerful, intense, and crazy climax.

By the time the take was completed, half the singers had become hysterical. The women laughed and cried, some of the men, too. Nobody had seen the music before, and other people were in the studio, but the singers had lost themselves in the music. They got totally out there, which is what we wanted. Incredibly, we did it in one take. A second take would have burned us out. The vocalists and musicians gave their absolute all. It was extraordinary.

The next night we came back and recorded three more hours, expecting a third session, which was unnecessary. We completed the whole album in six hours, in itself amazing.

That year the Jazz Mass won two Grammys—one for best album cover and one for best jazz composition. Another album I did called *Cycle* got a nomination, too. All told, I received six Grammy nominations and two awards from two different albums released the same year. Later, in 1987, I got another Grammy nomination, for *Traveler*.

BEYOND ENTERTAINMENT

I had visions of performing the Jazz Mass live, and indeed we managed to do that on a few occasions, one of which enabled me to realize for the first time that music can be extremely powerful. It can penetrate much more deeply than conventional entertainment.

On the evening of this particular presentation, 5,000 people arrived at the huge Hennepin Avenue Methodist Church in Minneapolis. No one expected such a turnout. The main sanctuary quickly filled up. Thousands of other people sat in different rooms. They couldn't see us, but they could hear the music because speakers had been installed. Black people attended. White people attended. People of all ages and virtually all faiths attended.

I stood in the middle of the altar, up front, with the quintet around me. The choir was on one side, the orchestra on the other, the percussionists in back. The conductor stood in front to one side.

Whenever I played a solo, it was as if I were the minister, speaking through the music, expressing the vision Lalo and I had conceived back home. The Minneapolis Symphony Orchestra and the choir had rehearsed their parts well. Playing in a church like this with a full crowd inspired us.

The real magic began when the people took communion while we played the Offertory. This part of the performance affected me deeply and has stayed with me to this day. It altered the way I thought about music then, and it expanded the ways I've thought about music since.

Lalo began and ended the Offertory with a brief melody. In between, there was no music. The quintet improvised freely. Normally, the Offertory section ran three or four minutes. On this occasion, it lasted forty-five minutes. Dr. Pennington, the pastor, wanted to give everyone the opportunity to take communion, not just the 1,500 people in the main sanctuary. People in other rooms could participate as well.

I stood in front of the altar, right at the end of the center aisle. People walked down the aisle to take communion. Crippled people, blind people, and people in wheelchairs came down too. Some walked by themselves. Friends and relatives helped others. As people approached the altar and knelt to receive communion, I could see in their eyes how deeply moved they were by the music.

Although I am of the Jewish faith, I suddenly had an overwhelming urge to participate in the ritual, not just as a musician, but simply as a human being. I set aside my horn, walked down, knelt at the bar, took communion, walked back up, and continued playing.

During this performance, I realized that music has another dimension. Originally, as I said, my motivation had nothing to do with religion. I thought of the Mass as an expanded musical form. Now, however, I too was deeply moved—so many people, so many different faiths, so many walks of life—all of us together, inspired and united by the music.

Most of us think of music as a pleasant distraction for riding to work; as a way to nostalgically visit our yesterdays; as something to use for weekend dancing. Indeed, music can do these things. It is wonderful that way. However, as I watched people taking communion, I also saw for the first time how music can transcend entertainment, how it can transform and uplift the spirit, how it can move listeners deeply, how it can heal our mind, body, and soul. I was directly experiencing the beauty and potency of music's spiritual dimension.

I wasn't just thinking or reading about it. I could *see* these people walking down the aisle, some with tears of joy in their eyes. I could *feel* what the music was doing to them and to me, to the other musicians, and to the thousands of people in the audience. This occasion was a turning point. No previous event had moved me this way. These were experiential seeds that greatly influenced my future development. The whole evening was extraordinarily powerful.

Since then, I have consistently thought of music in spiritual terms. Wherever I play—concerts, clubs, studios—the spiritual value of music is always present in my consciousness.

Today's better New Age musicians share this awareness. They are not necessarily religious people; they don't always belong to an organized church. However, they are spiritual people. They realize and understand the deeper, more meaningful values of life. They appreciate life itself; they stand in awe of this unbelievable gift; they know it is a miracle to be alive and a part of creation.

They are also aware that music can be an integral part of spiritual realization because music is sound; sound is vibration; and the whole universe, including human beings, is made up of vibrations. Our material bodies are made of sound, which is why people respond so quickly and easily to music. This is also why music is a universal language and why it has the capacity to interconnect us with each other immediately. It touches our deepest psychological foundations. It expansively fuels our highest spiritual aspirations. Today's finer New Age musicians transcend artificiality in music, awakening in us a sense of our own divinity. I think these values have permeated music, particularly high-level New Age music, since the mid-sixties.

My jazz years continue, of course, because I love jazz and will always play it, but how fulfilling it is to play quiet, introspective music as well. Without those jazz experiences, I may never have realized my youthful ambition for fame, acceptance, and praise and may never have evolved beyond it; I may never have visited India; I may never have grown discontented with the superficial values of Hollywood's industrial music machine. As it is, I met and liked and loved some wonderful and beautiful people. And I got to play a lot of incredible music. By the time I moved to Canada, I was teaching meditation and had rediscovered the innocence I knew as a child. The music expanded to embrace the joy of inner quietude. Victoria is the perfect place for me to live and work. Not once have I regretted moving here. What a beautiful, peaceful place.

PART III

THE TRANSITION

EIGHT

THE DONOVAN TOUR

When I returned from India the first time, I got back into studio work a little, but most of it was run-of-the-mill jingles and tedious TV background music. I took fewer gigs, sometimes stood in unemployment lines, went to the beach, played occasionally for myself. I loved meditating and teaching meditation. But music seemed shallow, and the Hollywood studio scene felt unbearably boring.

Then Donovan called.

He and I played together in India at the ashram, and now he had an extensive North American tour coming up. He wanted me to join him—just the two of us, his voice and guitar, my alto flute, no backup band. Real simple. I liked that.

We turned money matters over to our managers. They agreed I'd play forty concerts, at $2,000 a night—more than I'd ever made on tour as a jazz musician. That made $80,000—good bucks.

Donovan could pay good money because in 1969 he stood at the peak of his career, a bona fide superstar, as popular as the Beatles. We played "Mellow Yellow," "Jennifer Juniper," and "Atlantis" to sold-out coliseums that seated more than 18,000 people. Some, like Madison Square Garden, seated 25,000.

Donovan sat cross-legged on a carpet by himself. He sang and played guitar for about twenty minutes, then brought me out. I sat cross-legged beside him, accompanying him on flute for a half-dozen songs, occasionally improvising solos. After intermission, we began the second half together. Then he cued me. I took a bow and left. And he finished the concert.

We opened in Los Angeles, at the Hollywood Bowl, a very special concert for me. We put a nice Persian carpet on a little riser at center stage, flowers all around, and the two of us sat there and played. Simple, quiet, powerful.

Before, I was snobbish about pop music. I was trained in conservatories. I intellectually appreciated the complexities of music's higher art forms. Donovan's music was neither complex nor challenging, and it was not high art. It was simple music, but it communicated deeply. It made one's heart open and unfold like a flower. Listening to him and watching his music touch the people, I began reevaluating my ideas about music's purpose.

Does music exist just to satisfy intellectuals and academicians? Maybe music's real purpose is to *communicate* with people, not just intellectually, but on all levels. And Donovan communicated. I took his music as a challenge—could I satisfy myself and others who appreciate music's intellectual aspects and still make it simple and direct and powerful? I felt I could.

One beautiful moonlit Hollywood summer night, Donovan and I played quiet music in front of 20,000 people, creating a gentle, potent, uplifting experience. It was a meaningful night. I presented myself in a new context and did not receive criticism from my peers. I learned how to appreciate music from a new perspective and felt comfortable with Donovan and the context.

On the road, we were treated like royalty. Playing jazz, I never had such luxuries—a private Hunza jet, bigger than a Lear; our own pilot and co-pilot; a limousine that drove us out on the tarmac, right to the waiting plane; a private stewardess serving fabulous meals; a limousine waiting at the next airport. Inside the limo, we were given keys to our rooms. First-class hotels, already checked in, bags taken care of, room service for everything we wanted, all wishes fulfilled instantly, road managers who took care of details, and women—lots of them. We were pampered and spoiled. I loved it.

Each night, our road managers walked through the audience and picked out the prettiest girls. Would you like to come backstage afterward and meet Donovan and Paul Horn, maybe drop over to the hotel? The answer was always yes. Heaven.

Donovan was a hero among the flower children of the late sixties. As a result, he never gave encores. If he did, he'd be mobbed to death. After the last number, he took his bows, ran offstage, and both of us rushed to the car waiting backstage. Don Murfet, our roadie and driver, kept the doors open, the motor running. We hopped in. Don stepped on the gas. With two police motorcycles leading the way, we roared out of the coliseum and back to the hotel while the audience was still clapping.

Madison Square Garden was a difficult concert. It was theater in the round, with a stage in the middle and the audience around us. To enter, we had to walk from the back, down a long aisle, through the people, into the arena, out to the stage. The houselights went down. A spotlight came on. We surrounded ourselves with police and huddled in the middle, moving down the aisle as fast as we could. The kids knew what was happening. Out of the dark, hands reached over the policemen, grabbing anything they could—shirts, hair, pants. Someone ripped a beautiful Indian shawl off Donovan. Somebody else tore my sleeve. An unbelievable situation.

And how were we to leave? We ran up the aisles as fast as we could, giving the impression we'd be back for an encore. We ran to the limo, of course, and split back to the hotel—a more exciting departure than anything I'd known before.

Donovan was completely relaxed and leisurely. Onstage, he came out, sat down, sipped a little tea, looked out, asked everybody how they were. He was the same person onstage as off. He told little stories about what happened that day, creating a feeling of one-on-one intimacy, talking and singing and playing in such a casual, easy way. In press interviews, he was just as natural and relaxed as he was onstage or in the plane.

Pretty soon, I said to myself, "Why can't I be this way? I don't have to put on a mask. I can just be me." On my gigs after the tour, I started doing that. It worked, and it was fun. I told stories and made nice connections with the people, presenting myself in a natural, non–show-biz way, communicating with my voice as well as the music.

The kids knew Donovan had been with Maharishi. Wherever we went, meditators came to see us, invited us to the meditation centers, fixed us dinner. Donovan handled adulation well. He was polite, a gentleman, a nice man.

Donovan perfectly reflected the times. It was a period in which people wanted peace, and Donovan was a gentle man who played gentle music. Police at the concerts carried guns and clubs. Violence defeats itself when people are strong enough to be nonviolent. When the cops threatened with clubs and guns, the kids responded with flowers and hugs and kisses. Nonviolence can't be beat.

Donovan was younger than I, but he was an unusual young man and a great teacher. There was a clearness in his eyes. He was an evolved person who immediately understood meditation. Maharishi liked him too. Donovan knew I had spent considerable time with Maharishi, and he felt free to ask questions. We had wonderful philosophical discussions, and he was receptive to metaphysical concepts.

We traveled all over the United States, briefly into Canada—that's when I saw Vancouver for the first time—and then the tour ended. I returned to L.A., totally charged up by my new experiences.

NINE

LEAVING THE HOLLYWOOD NEST

Having just completed a Canadian tour that took me to Vancouver and Victoria, British Columbia, I remember coming in for a landing at LAX. Looking down at all that greenish-yellowish smog I said to myself, "That's it. I've had it! I'm going to move to Victoria where the air and water are clean and life is more peaceful."

Fed up with Hollywood, the music business, and even with music itself, I just wanted out. I took care of financial affairs and dealt with Canadian immigration to get Landed Immigrant status, which allowed me to live and work in Canada. After flying to Victoria and renting a $250-a-month house near the beach—on Paul's Terrace, coincidentally—a major question suddenly dawned on me: what about the kids?

I had assumed they would come with me. They were living with Yvonne, but she had a serious drinking problem. In later years, she attended AA and recovered. At this time, however, she was not as responsible as I thought she should be; I was concerned about how her condition affected the kids. Could I assume she would let them go? No. I told Yvonne about my plans and asked if I could take the kids. She said yes. We signed a piece of paper that made things legal, and I could bring Marlen and Robin to Canada.

It was hard work putting things together, but I eagerly looked forward to the move and to a new era in my life. I must have been out of my mind, because not once did I stop to think about finances. When it got down to the nitty-gritty, I'd saved almost nothing.

But I didn't care. I wanted out of the music business. I could take a nine-to-five job, something normal for a change—a cab driver, a sheepherder, a filing clerk. It didn't matter. If I was moving to Canada, I had to take full responsibility. Nobody was going to drop out of the sky and provide anything for us. I would do it all.

But who was going to take care of Marlen and Robin while I worked? Was I going to get a job, cook the meals, do the washing and cleaning and parenting all by myself? I thought about the women in my life. By far, Tryntje was the most important.

TRYNTJE

I wasn't seeking marriage, but Tryntje and I had romance and physical love, and she was the only woman I knew who demanded nothing at all from me and who never bugged me. She gave me total freedom, and she was always happy to see me. She was a disciplined, creative person. The more I thought about her, the more I appreciated her strengths and character.

Tryntje—pronounced "Train-ja"—was a famous fashion designer, first for Du Pont, then for Catalina. Her companies manufactured fabrics by the millions of yards. Tryntje designed the fabrics and worked with weavers in the mills. Then she developed a line—knitwear, sportswear, and children's clothes. Her Catalina designs took off, and the company made millions. By the time I met her, she was earning $42,000 a year, with living and travel expenses paid, which was big money in those days. She maintained one place in New York, another in L.A., both paid for by the company, and she traveled back and forth with her two basset hounds, all expenses paid. In Hollywood, they put her up at the Chateau Marmont, a famous hotel and apartment building on Sunset Strip. She checked in for a week and stayed seven years.

I met her at a checking session at the meditation society. She was with another man, on a date. She and I struck up a casual conversation, and that was it. I had no thoughts of going out with her.

A couple of weeks later, I was on a Columbia recording session for vocalist Pamela Poland, who brought Tryntje with her. During the breaks, listening to playbacks, Tryntje and I talked. I asked her for her number. Perhaps I could come over and have tea. Sure, she said, and she left the studio. That night after the session, I drove to the Chateau Marmont at about 2:30 A.M. From the lobby I called and said, "How about that cup of tea?" I stayed until 6:30, when, with no sleep, Tryntje left for work.

Tryntje is an exuberant woman, with great enthusiasm for life. She has an incredible amount of energy, like a power plant, and she's almost always upbeat. She sparkles with positive energy, and she's intelligent and physically attractive.

Born in Holland, she couldn't attend regular school because the Second World War raged all around her and Holland was occupied by the Germans. She went to a trade school and studied sewing. For fun, she rollerskated, becoming Holland's figure skating champion for many years. At twenty-one, not knowing a word of English, she came to America with twenty dollars in her pocket, sponsored by someone in the United States. Talk about guts—no English, no money, traveling all the way across the ocean to a new, strange country, where she began a new life.

At first, she worked as a maid and a carhop. She'd take an order, not knowing what it was, and run back and tell the cooks what it sounded like phonetically—"Pleese for me, a meelk shake and an ahm-boorger."

Eventually, she met a man who owned his own sportswear company in New York and saw and appreciated her creative abilities. He encouraged her and channeled her into serious designing, showing her what to do and how to do it, teaching her patience, and developing her potential.

Unlike the starlets I dated, she didn't come on like a groupie. In fact, she was not aware of my fame. I gave her a copy of *Inside the Taj Mahal*, which she played over and over again, but I didn't talk about my career very much, and she didn't know about my thirteen other albums. As far as she knew, I was just a nice young meditator who happened to play sax and flute in the studios. I liked her, she liked me, and we dated for about a year and a half.

Artistically, she is amazing. Tryntje can envision things in every detail. Once she sets her mind to it, she has the determination, energy, discipline, and ability to create it. Whether it be a painting, a wall hanging, a dress, a jacket, a flower arrangement, a garden, a sculpture, a house, anything artistic—if she sees it in her mind, she can create it. She has enormous talent.

In stronger and stronger ways, I saw that she was a terrific woman, a marvelous companion and lover, and that she would be a wonderful mate to help raise my children. She owned a 1966 convertible Mustang; I had a 1965 Dodge van. She had two basset hounds; I had one cat. When it came time to leave Hollywood, my father dropped over to say good-bye and wave us off. We piled Marlen and Robin, the dogs, the cat, and the instruments into the cars, hopped in, and followed each other up Highway 101 to start our new life in Canada.

ON THE ROAD AGAIN

All kids want to drive, of course, and I used to let Robin sit next to me and steer, while I stepped on the gas. On Highway 101, he asked if he could step on the gas himself. I pulled him up on my lap and let him drive.

As we cruised along, I thought about Hollywood, realizing that nothing pulled me back. Except for my father, I couldn't think of anyone I would miss. After Mother died, Dad remained a bachelor for many years. When Marlen was born in 1957, I said to my father, "Why stay in D.C.? Come out and live with us." He did, eventually meeting and marrying a nice woman, who stayed with him for twenty years until he died. I knew I'd miss Dad.

Robin pressed harder on the gas. We were going about seventy, then seventy-five, faster than I normally drove this van, but traffic was sparse, and he was having a good time.

If I didn't miss anyone after nearly fifteen years in L.A., if I felt no strong tugs, not for my close friend Emil Richards, not for the guys in my band, not for other people I knew, then how meaningful were those relationships? Maybe it was just a matter of my own changes. The relationships were meaningful, but now I was detached from them and thinking in different terms. Before, I was a jazz musician, tied in with the industry. Now, I was a meditator, a free spirit on the move, and. . . .

Suddenly I saw smoke spewing from the engine. Robin had us up to eighty miles an hour. Something was burning. I waved to Tryntje to pull off the road. The hood for the van's motor was between the passenger and driver's seat. When I lifted it, smoke erupted into the cab, and I saw flames. The van was on fire. I couldn't believe it. A man stopped and helped us put out the fire, and a tow truck hauled us to Salinas.

We spent that first night of our great trip to Canada depressed as hell, sitting around a dreary motel room in Salinas with two dogs, a cat, two boys, Tryntje and myself, watching TV. When the repair shop opened on Tuesday, they took two days to fix the van. Four days after arriving in Salinas, we got back on the road.

VISITING WITH MAHARISHI

In Arcata, a northern California town a few miles north of Eureka, Maharishi was giving a monthlong meditation course to more than a thousand people at Humboldt College. We arrived, parked in a trailer camp, slept in the van, and spent a couple of days visiting.

When I was alone with Maharishi, he seemed surprised and puzzled by my decision. Why was I moving to Canada? I told him about my changes and that I was no longer interested in music. What was I going to do? I didn't know. I had no plans and no job. Perhaps I could become a full-time meditation teacher. Until then, full-time teachers received no money; now, the movement generated enough to pay them.

Maharishi said no. I could bring awareness of meditation to people just by virtue of the fact that I was an established musician. I could best serve by continuing to play, maybe 60 percent playing and 40 percent teaching TM. I was not entirely happy with his answer, but I accepted it. He planted a seed, the first indication that I would probably continue with music in Canada.

It was lovely to see Maharishi and attend his lectures. He gave Tryntje and me some advanced meditation techniques, and personally initiated

Marlen. Robin was not old enough at ten to be initiated, which brought tears to his eyes. Maharishi said Robin should not worry. When he dropped the zero, he would be eligible. When Robin "dropped the zero" by turning eleven, I initiated him and taught him how to meditate.

We felt marvelous on the road after spending time with Maharishi. We arrived in Canda on the evening of August 29, 1970, feeling in great spirits, having taken a ferryboat over from Port Angeles, Washington, arriving in Victoria around sundown—at 8:29 to be exact, an interesting "coincidence." We drove to our new house, but the furniture had not yet arrived, so we slept on the floor. The next day, the moving van pulled up and unloaded, and we began our new life.

PART IV

NEW LIFE IN CANADA

TEN

VICTORIA

Tryntje and I are both high-powered individuals. We don't feel good just sitting around doing nothing. Our creative minds seek ways to fulfill themselves, and indeed the old cliché is true—necessity *is* the mother of invention.

I had just come from a city in which I was consumed by my career for nearly fifteen years. Now, all my old activities had stopped. How was I going to keep busy?

Spiritually speaking, this living moment is our only true reality. Obviously, concepts of past and future are pragmatically valuable. Metaphysically, however, they are illusory mind-games that only keep us locked into regrets about the past and anxieties about the future. I refused to weep or worry. I did not fear the newness of life in Victoria. I relished the challenges and creatively plunged into daily life. I trusted the moment, took the first steps, created work, and watched as everything evolved. Instead of being uptight, I had fun.

First, I set up a concert in Victoria and brought my quintet up from Los Angeles. I booked, produced, promoted, advertised, and performed it. The newspapers interviewed me and Tryntje, and suddenly we were known all over Victoria. At the TM center, I gave introductory lectures and initiated people into meditation. I booked nearby Shawnigan Inn for two weeks, brought my quintet up from L.A., and held a two-week symposium, combining the subjects of music and philosophy. While the quintet was here, we recorded two live albums at Gassy Jack's Club in Vancouver—*July 9th and 10th* and a double LP called *A Special Edition*. I soloed with the Victoria Symphony Orchestra, playing Bach's famous B-minor suite for flute and orchestra, a Cimerosa concerto, and a piece called "Night Soliloquy." I wrote to colleges, booked jazz concerts, and played all over Canada.

With Robin and Marlen as our two best men, Tryntje and I got married. Then, with money I earned from a second tour with Donovan, we bought land overlooking the ocean. Quite unexpectedly, a New York entertainment lawyer landed a recording contract for me with CBS. I recorded *Inside II*, and with the advance paid for most of a 4,000-square-foot house, which Tryntje designed herself and we built together. Additional money for the house came from an eighteen-week, half-hour, prime-time CTV network TV series called "The Paul Horn Show."

That house is Tryntje's masterpiece. Although she had never before designed a house, she paced the premises, selected a site, and drew up a design. On top of a ping-pong table, she built a large scale model of the new house out of apple boxes, complete with little pieces of furniture, also made to scale. When satisfied, she hired a draftsman who drew up the blueprints. Tryntje and I got out with the workers, pitching in whenever necessary. During one two-week period, Tryntje hauled 600 pounds of plaster, bucket by bucket, and built the fireplace herself.

The completed house is magnificent—4,000 square feet; two large wings, each with an upstairs and downstairs; four bedrooms, two bathrooms, a full-sized music room; two big balconies; French doors; a front window with a 180-degree view of the ocean; a post-and-beam interior; beamed cedar ceilings; hemlock floors, with arched doorways and windows; inner walls of white plaster. Tryntje decorated with Persian rugs, Indian baskets, Japanese woodcuts, plants, flowers, paintings, and art objects she made herself. The outer walls are covered with over 20,000 oyster shells, and the foundation rests on solid bedrock. "If we have an earthquake," said Tryntje, "this will be the only house on the island that stays up."

Outside in front, overlooking the ocean, Tryntje created her gardens—a beautiful multitude of flowers, vegetables, and fruit trees. In the back, she built a corral for her five goats and two sheep. At the moment, we also have four dogs, two cats, and one pet chicken.

When I was in L.A., pushing hard, I was intense. Here in Victoria, I had a smile on my face, I felt good inside, and everything was fine. I focused on teaching meditation and took no money for it. Personal concerns sat on the back burner. I was not seeking fame or fortune. I was just trying to be a good person, selflessly serving others in a loving way, and that's when all these wonderful things happened. Nature supports, and God rewards.

GROWING UP

Marlen and Robin are both musically gifted—Marlen on piano, Robin on drums—but in other respects they walked separate paths.

Marlen was easygoing and socially adept. He was well liked, had no social problems, made friends easily, was a bright and capable student, and excelled at baseball, basketball, and golf. In L.A. during the summers, he participated in playground track meets and came home loaded with ribbons (which, alas, the maid threw out one day while cleaning).

Robin was an individualist, headstrong and independent. He found it difficult to master basic subjects like arithmetic or writing but easily grasped abstract philosophical concepts. He had his own ideas and occasionally got in trouble. He was one of the first boys in L.A. to have long hair, for example, and his teachers bugged him about "looking like a girl." One day he came home crying because of that. I went to the principal and righteously complained, telling him they were behind the times and should let him alone.

Robin was a totally different entity than Marlen—different personality, different physical structure and appearance, different everything. Once again I was reminded how unique every human being is, coming from the same parents and yet so different; two distinctly individual souls choosing Yvonne and me to be their parents in this lifetime. How fantastic.

Robin was a funny kid. He made me laugh all the time. Even as a baby, he had great coordination and balance. He used to walk on narrow ledges but never fell off. His exceptional coordination is part of what led him to the drums in later years. He had his own way of dressing and picked out unique styles and colors of clothing. He changed names each day and would respond only to that name. "I'm not Robin. I'm Bruce." "Okay, Bruce, get your ass into bed. It's late."

Across the narrow street in front of his house was the porch of a friend's house. Every Sunday, a dozen or so people got together and dropped acid for their weekly "religious" experience. I came to pick him up in midafternoon. He was about four years old. As he was getting into my car, he stopped, looked at the people who were pretty stoned by then, and shouted, "You're wrong up there." They all cracked up and yelled back, "Oh, no, we're not." And he kept saying, "Oh, yes, you are. You're wrong up there."

I had a chance to observe and be a part of their sibling rivalry—for about twenty years. I thought it would never end, but it did. Marlen and Robin are very close friends now. Miracles do happen.

Both boys somewhat resented being taken from L.A. to a new, strange environment, and both resented being told what to do by a woman who was not their mother. Sometimes I got caught in the middle, which made things difficult, especially if I agreed and sided with the kids against Tryntje. At times, I had to walk a tightrope.

They spent summers in L.A. with their mother, who was much more lenient. They could go out at night, do what they wanted on the streets, come back late. When they returned to Canada, Tryntje and I had to be disciplinarians, and it took at least two months to get things back on track.

When Marlen was about sixteen, he grew moody and sullen. We didn't get along well. No matter what we said, Marlen resisted. I started feeling annoyed and began losing patience. Marlen stayed in his room, depressed and unhappy. Eventually, he decided to return to L.A. permanently, where he attended Hollywood High.

Meanwhile, Robin got along well with adults, but not with his peers. He found it difficult to make friends and got into fights. A sensitive boy, he was devastated by criticism. Fed up with the amount of work and discipline we demanded of him, he too left Canada and spent the better part of two years in L.A., where he got involved with marijuana, even a little cocaine. We finally enrolled him in a private school. When he was fifteen, he decided he wanted to come back and live with us again. We said okay but insisted he stay until he finish school and that he abide by our rules. "No problem," he said. "I want you to be hard on me." I'll never forget that. He *asked* for discipline.

From that time on, things were better. He did his homework, came home at night, avoided drugs, called when he knew he was going to be late, and kept the loving connection with Tryntje and me.

When Marlen was about twenty and Robin eighteen, I visited them in L.A. and suggested we spend an evening together. We sat by the fireplace in Marlen's house and had a long talk about what happened in our lives, why I came to Canada, why they were taken from their mother. By this time, they were old enough to see Tryntje's position as well, the difficulties she must have had, and the positive, constructive things she brought to their lives. I was glad we had that talk. We healed wounds and built bridges.

After Marlen left Canada, he studied music in college in L.A. for two years, then got a job one summer with a friend's father in the wholesale clothing business. He presented good ideas and contributed to the growth of the company and soon became a full partner. They're now also in the manufacturing business and Marlen designs as well. I am proud of his impressive success, and I am especially proud that he has remained a good human being. He married a woman named Robin—now we have two Robins in the family—and they have a daughter, Brittany Horn, my first grandchild. I look forward to visiting whenever I'm in L.A.

Robin attended DeAnza College in northern California for two years and studied music. He then briefly attended the University of Toronto, but a strict classical conservatory was not for him. Robin wanted to be a drummer and a player, not an academician. He left school and took private lessons with Jim Blackley. He also studied piano and arranging with Ted Moses and then returned to L.A., where he became a professional musician and married Beth Teller, a fine jazz flutist. He's an excellent drummer and a marvelous human being. I am very proud of him and often include him as a member of my band, not because he's my son, but because he's a first-rate drummer and musician.

Parenting was one of the great teaching and learning experiences of my life. Through the children, I learned about patience, understanding, reason, and love. I got to see how human beings develop in various stages of their lives and came to realize the profound responsibility of parenthood.

We do not "own" children. They are not "ours." They are just on loan to us. They emerge into the world as individuals, and they deserve our respect. As open, innocent, receptive, vulnerable people, they can be great teachers for us. Never should we try to make them into whatever we want them to be. We should treasure their individuality and do everything possible to help them discover and fulfill their unique, personal destinies.

ELEVEN

THE SYMPOSIUM OF MUSIC AND LIFE

Music is not an isolated subject, disconnected from daily life. It is a reflection of life; it is life itself, and it is interrelated with everything we do. Our lives spill over into music, and the things we learn through music spill over into our lives. I wanted to combine music, philosophy, and current events into an integrated whole and present them to anybody who was interested, especially to young musicians. I drove up to Shawnigan Lake, booked the Shawnigan Inn for two weeks in the summer of 1971, and brought my band up from L.A. to have a symposium—The Symposium of Music and Life.

A woman named Frankie Nemko had helped jazz guitarist Howard Roberts set up guitar seminars, so I brought her up from L.A. to help with our symposium. We planned two separate weeks. Students could sign up for one or the other, or both. People from America and Canada attended— twenty the first week, thirty the second, ranging in ages from early teens to sixty and seventy, with most in their twenties. Several teachers attended, as did one nonmusician woman, seventy years old.

We devoted our mornings to practice and private lessons. Art Johnson taught guitar; Dave Parlato taught bass; Bart Hall taught drums; Lynn

Blessing taught vibes; and I taught woodwinds. After lunch, Lynn taught a theory class—how music is structured, and what is involved with improvisation. Immediately after his talk, we broke into small combos according to performers' abilities and applied what he had just discussed.

Shawnigan Inn has a cozy, country ski-lodge atmosphere, with a big stone fireplace and comfortable chairs. After dinner, we gathered in the main room by the fireplace. Our band gave a little concert so the students could see what professional groups do. We used material developed in the classes, along with standard jazz tunes, and in between songs we left space for questions, analysis, and comments.

After our miniconcert, we opened the floor to discussions of larger issues. It wasn't just a lecture by me. We talked about the dangers of drugs, for instance, at a time when drugs were accepted. We talked about the concept of meditation, the importance of it in one's life, and how it helps the music. We talked about creativity and the intricate, important relationship between music and the way we feel about ourselves.

Two disc jockeys drove up from Victoria and rapped about music and radio. They thought their rock 'n' roll was hip. The kids felt the DJs should include other forms of music, especially jazz. I was surprised by the intensity of this discussion and rather enjoyed watching the kids back these guys into a corner. The DJs were sweating by the end of the evening and left feeling less than successful in their presentation.

At the end of each week, we had a graduation ceremony. Individual groups either composed an original piece or worked on a song they knew and performed it for the whole class, applying what they had learned in their lessons. It was such a joy. When each week ended, there were tears in everyone's eyes. We had become a family.

I fondly remember many individuals who attended, one in particular. Joey was an eleven-year-old boy whose older brother took the course. They lived with their parents near Shawnigan Lake. Every evening, Joey came to hear the concerts and lectures and discussions. After the talk on meditation, he introduced himself to me and said he wanted to learn how to meditate. But he was very young, and his parents were not meditators, so I said no. I put him off, not taking him too seriously, and told him to think about it. He came back the next night and asked again. After the week was over, he called long distance several times, persisting, until I finally said, "Okay, Joey, bring your parents to the meditation center and let's talk."

I told the parents that meditation is not a weird cult, that Maharishi is not a fraud, that meditation is not a religion but a process. I assured them I normally do not initiate children whose parents do not meditate; otherwise, too many divisive misunderstandings might arise. The parents said if Joey had a strong desire to meditate, it was okay with them.

I initiated Joey, and pretty soon the parents called. Joey loved to meditate; his problems in school had straightened out; he was thoroughly enjoying his life. Before long, the parents themselves took the initiation and began meditating. In most instances, parents are teachers of their children, but in this case, Joey became the teacher, leading himself and his parents to the spiritual path.

CREATIVITY

Several of our most interesting symposium discussions revolved around the concept of creativity, not only in the arts but in daily life as well. Most of us associate creativity solely with the arts, but that is a rather narrow conception because all human beings are creative, so I will speak of creativity in two ways.

In the arts, creativity involves talent—the natural inclination and innate ability to play music, paint pictures, write words, and so forth. We often call that talent "God given." That is, God lives within us. We are God's messengers, his hands. We often think we do things, but it is really God-within-us who does them.

Creativity also includes acquired traits, particularly knowledge of one's craft, and discipline. Understanding parents and a good home life are as important as good teachers, because young artists, like all children, are at the mercy of the people who mold them.

A healthy ego is important, which again comes back to parents and teachers. Young artists should have a strong sense of identity and personal worth, especially if they are performing artists. Without self-esteem—a strong ego—how can an artist appear before the public and communicate?

The whole idea is to get in touch with the source of creativity itself, which lies deep within, like a well of limitless and unbounded creative intelligence. When we touch that unlimited reservoir, creativity flows through us to the extent that we are open to it. If we are closed—because of anxiety, stress, illness, or physical disability—we cannot receive the full flow. Once we tap into the reservoir, anxiety diminishes, trust expands, the creative flow increases, and we gradually evolve to higher levels.

The technique for leading us to the direct experience of the creative reservoir within ourselves is meditation. I am not saying Transcendental Meditation is the only way, because there are many ways to meditate and many techniques. But meditation of one kind or another is imperative because creativity is not intellectual. You can't reach it intellectually. If the process is not intellectual, what is it? It is meditation. Through meditation, creativity can fulfill its potential.

In workshops and seminars at places like Esalen, on California's Big Sur coast, I quite often combine the interrelated subjects of music and meditation. Many, many people feel a lack of self-worth. They think they are "not creative." They come from many walks of life, usually businesspeople and homemakers of all ages, and they regret not having pursued music.

The object of my course is to give them a feeling of self-worth by showing them they can play music. I set up situations where they improvise, without knowing anything technical about music. I bring in little percussion instruments, wooden flutes, mallets, cymbals, gongs, and drums and encourage them to use their voices. I talk about how to listen, how to wait, how to leave space, how to trust. If they feel like singing or playing a note, they should do it. Don't worry about right or wrong, just do it.

As we improvise together, they begin to experience the reality of communication. They hear the musical conversation we create. Just as in other conversations, there is a time to speak, a time to listen, and you can't do both at the same time. Pretty soon, they are enjoying themselves, playing music, conversing through sound. They are being creative—and they love it. Their self-esteem increases tenfold. This changes their feelings about themselves, and they extend that feeling beyond music, into daily life.

BEYOND MUSIC

What does it mean to live a creative life? Most of the time, we are occupied with mundane things. But when we take the time to be still, to touch our inner Selves, we open our minds, reexperience the value of life, and live each day to the fullest. We live creative lives when we appreciate and value the unbelievable miracle of life itself and perform our daily tasks with joy.

Throughout the seventies and eighties, holistic conferences increased by leaps and bounds, attracting growing numbers of New Age people—people who are changing their values. Organizers bring in qualified speakers who talk about a host of topics in fresh, new ways—creativity and self-worth, physical health, mental health, nondenominational spiritual values, vitamins, health foods, acupuncture, meditation. I've heard speakers such as Rusty Schweickart, former astronaut on the moon; Mother Theresa; the Dalai Lama; Peter Caddy, founder of Findhorn in Scotland; author John Lily—wonderful people with brilliant minds and impeccable credentials.

No one tries to convert anyone to a particular religion. They simply speak of the God-force within us all and discuss principles of unity in diversity. New Age values and perspectives have become popular because they address personal, spiritual, and environmental issues in ways that make sense. Old ways of thinking, which are based upon competition, acquisition, and power, have led us to the brink of global suicide. New Age values affirm the sanctity of individual creativity in a context of cooperative, interdependent world unity.

Even among politicians, New Age views have made inroads. Barbara Marx Hubbard, an astute person with a brilliant mind, was a nominee for Democratic vice president. Jerry Brown was the governor of California. I have even seen retired military generals attend these conferences. The exterior of people, or their past or present vocation, does not necessarily reveal their thinking. New Age values cut across all categories.

From my own experience, I know that the Whole Life Expo in Los Angeles annually draws 30,000 people, further physical evidence that this new way of thinking is increasing. Conferences help people form networks and support groups. Many times, individuals start thinking differently, but their relatives and friends believe they are crazy. When such a person attends a conference that has 30,000 people, he or she feels more confidence—"Maybe I'm not crazy after all." People exchange addresses and keep in touch, helping each other learn more about self-esteem, global unity, and personal creativity.

At this time, New Age people remain in the minority—some 10 percent of the population, perhaps 25 million people—but they are growing to a more sizable minority all the time, and, as I point out in chapter 16, about the USSR, this ongoing evolutionary process keeps me optimistic about the future of our planet.

TWELVE

HAIDA THE WHALE

A year or so after our arrival in Canada, Dr. Paul Spong called and asked if I would bring my flute down to Sealand of the Pacific in Victoria and play for two Orca whales, Haida and Chimo. Spong, a marine biologist living in Vancouver, had been conducting a series of experiments on so-called killer whales in an effort to measure their intelligence, which he considered high. Researchers such as John Lily had worked with dolphins, but Spong was one of the first to work with whales.

He had played recorded music for them through hydrophones, which carry sound underwater. The whales definitely reacted in discriminating ways, favoring classical music and jazz, but not rock 'n' roll. Would I play for his whales in person?

I stood on the feeding platform the first day and felt uncomfortable. The whales were very big, with large mouths and sharp teeth. People watched as I played for a couple of hours, and the whales bobbed up and down, approaching me in curiosity, moving away—nothing conclusive.

The second day I played again, still feeling uncomfortable. Paul Spong said, "It's natural that you feel a bit fearful. Sometimes I do, too. But the less fearful I feel, the better I communicate with them." Paul reached out and touched Haida, petting him, and then literally put his head in the whale's open mouth—and Haida did not bite it off.

I immediately felt more relaxed, and on the third day Haida and Chimo vocalized back to me. Paul had told me not to play all the time. Just play a little and then, if they swim away, stop playing. In this fashion, they learn to swim toward you if they want to hear more music. Sure enough, they followed this pattern.

A cute thing happened when I brought my Nikon camera to the aquarium. The lens cap fell into the pool. Haida dove down and picked it up and brought it back to me on top of his nose. When you picture how big a whale is and how small a lens cap is, you can imagine how amazed I was. Just like everybody else who works with whales, I fell in love with them.

Paul said he loved them, too. He thought about them day and night, even when he went to bed. Other people who worked at Sealand felt the same way. Whales are intelligent, emotionally developed mammals. They have their moods, just like people. Some days, they felt full of energy and spunk, exuberant and cheerful; on other days, they felt down, moody, a little grumpy. Each day the employees asked, "How are Haida and Chimo? Performing their tricks? Eating well? Feeling good?"

Paul was a total fanatic. He even breathed like whales—and didn't know it. He took big gulps of air, held his breath for a long time, then made an exploding sound when he exhaled. I'd be talking to him, and every once in a while he breathed like that. When he saw my look, he'd catch himself and laugh.

After a week of playing a few hours each morning, I felt completely comfortable. I could see their interest and feel the communication between us. They paid attention to the music, playfully bobbed up and down, vocalized, and did little dances in the water for me. Paul was quite pleased with our progress.

I went on tour and came back to sad news. Chimo had died in the pool quite suddenly, and Haida felt despondent over her loss. He lay motionless in the corner on the surface of the water, refusing to eat and refusing to perform his tricks for the show. Depressed whales sometimes carry this behavior to extremes. Humans can fast for sixty to sixty-five days before dying. Whales are the same way. They can go without food for a maximum of sixty days, and then they die.

Haida had taken no food for three or four weeks. Hardly breathing, he lay on the surface without submerging, drying out. He developed big cracks in his blow hole, like severely chapped lips. The trainers rubbed Vaseline on the cracks, but they didn't know what else to do. Physically, there was nothing wrong with Haida, no infections or injuries. He was deeply depressed, heartbroken over the death of his loved one.

I walked over to his corner and leaned over the rail. Haida lay in the water, with people looking at him. No movement, no motion at all. I played. No response. I continued playing for forty-five minutes. No reaction. Nothing. For the next two days I played again, each time for forty-five minutes, but still no response. I started feeling depressed myself and wondered if I should bother returning.

One of the women trainers said, "You might want to try a more positive approach."

"What do you mean?"

"Well, when humans suffer a loss, you can deal with them in either of two ways. You can cater to their suffering and let them indulge their misery, or you can provide positive energy and make an effort to bring them out of their depression. I get the feeling you are playing rather sad music, reflecting his unhappiness. Maybe you should try the positive approach."

All right. I leaned over the rail and spoke to Haida directly. "Look, Haida, I've been coming here for three days now, and you have totally ignored me. I get no response from you, and I'm getting bugged.

"We know you have suffered a great loss, and you are deeply saddened, and we sympathize with you. But tens of thousands of people come here to see you—families, children, teenagers, old folks. They love and respect and admire you, but you are letting them down. Not only that, you are letting yourself down and you are letting life itself down.

"Well, life is a very precious thing, Haida, so get your act together and snap out of it. I will come back one more time. If you don't respond tomorrow, then I won't come back again."

The next day I started playing, and right away he moved his head, the first movement he had made in a month. I walked down the side of the pool. He slowly drifted away from his corner, floating listlessly—but floating. I walked all the way around the pool, playing my flute, and he followed me. We were encouraged and excited by Haida's breakthrough.

For the next couple of days the same thing happened. I played and walked. He followed. Toward the end of the week, I dangled a herring in front of him. He reluctantly took it in his mouth, and that started his eating process. By the end of the week he ate regularly. He came out of his depression and went on to perform his shows.

This was the first dramatic example I had seen of using music to bring a nonhuman, intelligent life-form out of a state of depression. Many people use music for relaxation. It helps remove tension. Yoga teachers use quiet music for classes. Others use it for meditation. I played healing music for Haida.

All music comes from God, the Creative Source. The more we connect with that Source and open ourselves to it, the more we become clear channels for music that can heal. When music springs from high awareness and a deep appreciation of life, it definitely has healing powers.

Haida perked up, and his health returned. Meanwhile, Greenpeace and other ecological organizations asked me to talk and perform at their meetings. Television crews came down and did stories on us. Writers interviewed me for newspapers and magazines. On tour, people always asked about Haida's health. Was he okay? Had he recovered? How was he performing?

Sometimes I felt guilty when I went to see him, because TV film crews were there taping another show. "I'm sorry, Haida," I said. "I'm not here only because the cameras are rolling. They're here, and I feel bad about it, but I want you to know I came today just to play for you."

One day, Haida pulled an amazing stunt. I stood off to the side of the pool, out of his line of vision, talking with Bob Wright, the aquarium's owner, and with Tryntje and two or three trainers. In the middle of our talk, I suddenly walked away, not even realizing what I was doing. It is not my nature to leave a conversation abruptly without saying, "Excuse me," or "I have to go to the bathroom." I just split and walked to the other end of the pool, where Haida floated on the surface. As soon as I came into view, he quickly swam across the pool, right to where I stood. He carried a piece of seaweed in his mouth, and he gave it to me.

It was a game he often played. He brought seaweed up from the bottom. I took it and threw it back, and he retrieved it, like a dog retrieving a stick. Evidently he knew I was in the building, even though he could not see me, and he wanted to play his game. Through the power of his mind, he called me. His message cut through the conversation and all of my upbringing and normal social behavior. He got me to leave in the middle of the conversation and walk directly to him. He knew I would come, and he waited, ready to play, the seaweed already in his mouth.

Sealand brought Haida a new girlfriend, whose name I don't recall. After she had been there a week, I went down to play for them, looking forward to meeting the new whale.

I stood and played on the feeding platform as usual, but Haida didn't come around. He circled the pool, passing me by each time. He just looked and kept on swimming. I couldn't get him to stop and be still.

His girlfriend was interested. Clearly curious, she hung around as I played, as if asking, "Who is this? What is this nice sound I'm hearing?" Haida kept making passes around the pool.

Then Haida submerged. I didn't see him for a long time. Suddenly, about twenty-five feet away, he leaped out of the water at great speed, flew up in the air, and smacked back down on the water as hard as he could. I saw it coming, but it happened so startlingly fast that I didn't even have a chance to move my fingers off the flute. A huge wave of water whooshed into the air and poured down all over me.

It seemed clear that he was either jealous of me or annoyed that his girlfriend was more interested in the flute than she was in him. I was a possible rival, and he didn't like it. Whatever the reason, he was pissed off and got me soaking wet.

I went on the road again. Several weeks passed before I returned, this time for a television show. It turned out to be the last time I saw Haida.

He swam underwater to the other end of the pool and surfaced. When he spotted me, he swam over and stood himself up in a vertical position. Whales can't see straight ahead. They have to turn their heads from side to side, and it's easier for them to look when they stand vertically in the water.

Haida stood up, moving his head back and forth, looking at me as I played. He didn't swim away even once, and he let me touch and pet him. Normally, he didn't like me to touch his dorsal fins, but today I could do anything. I touched him, and he rolled over on his back. I scratched his belly like a dog, and he made sounds, then again stood up vertically as I continued playing.

Usually, Haida stayed five or ten minutes and then took a breath, swam around the pool, and came back when he wanted to hear more music. On this occasion, he didn't take a single break. He stayed for a full forty minutes and would have stayed longer if I had not left.

His attention span was amazing. I've played for dogs, cats, sheep, and goats but never got anywhere near the reactions I got from Haida. A whale's consciousness is more highly evolved. I was not Haida's trainer. He didn't associate me with food. When I played for him, there was no reward other than the music. If he wanted to hang around, he did so at his own choosing.

I always felt warm inside after playing for Haida. I don't know what to call it except interspecies communication. I felt real contact, with strong feelings. It was quite an experience.

The word about Haida got around, and the people at Marine World, south of San Francisco, asked me to play for their whales too, which I did. This was when I got a wonderful reaction that was widely shown on televison. A whale jumped out of the water and kissed me on the cheek. The whole time I was there, she swam over to me, then swam out into the pool and danced in the water, really enjoying herself. There was so much interaction between us that the trainers themselves were amazed.

Back in Victoria, Haida eventually died, a very sad event. He was fourteen years old and had a massive heart attack. Whales are known to live up to seventy years in the ocean. In captivity, they rarely live more than fourteen or fifteen years. I was quite saddened by his death. Sealand has other whales now, but I don't go there any more. It was a joy playing for Haida. He gave me memories I will always cherish.

THIRTEEN

BUSINESS AND MUSIC MERGE

Although I continued developing the "Inside" series after *Inside the Taj Mahal*, I never wanted to repeat myself because my primary motivation was music, not money. Throughout my life, different kinds of music have manifested themselves through me, and I have done my best to serve them. As I grew and changed over the years, so did my music. With *Inside the Taj Mahal*, I discovered new directions and followed them, developing and expanding as I went along.

Epic Records renegotiated my contract in 1972, requesting another solo flute album. There was no way I could duplicate the innocence of *Inside the Taj Mahal*, nor was I interested in trying. However, the solo-flute concept itself was fascinating, and studio technology offered interesting possibilities.

With *Inside II*, I did a variety of things, such as playing multiple flute parts, stacking them up on top of each other (a process called overdubbing). I included a number of Bach chorales, playing all parts myself, and performed one of Palestrina's fifteenth-century works, "Mass—Kyrie," which had six different melodic lines, each of which I performed. And I composed a long suite called "The Mahabhutas," based upon the five elements—earth, air, fire, water, and space. There were many different things on that album.

I love to play my flute outside, in the forest or by bodies of water. At first, I thought I'd record *Inside II* in nature, but quality sound-control proved impossible. So I used recorded sounds of nature and, employing techniques I learned from Ravi Shankar in Hollywood, created compositions in the studio, improvising over different backgrounds, such as surf, rain, thunder, sea gulls, children playing, and whales singing. Without exception, all of the sounds on this album came from my flute or from nature. No electronic sound-sources were used anywhere.

Inside II was an adventurous recording, and I was quite proud of it. When I submitted it to Don Ellis (not the trumpet player, but the man who replaced Kapralik as Epic's head of A & R), he said it was brilliant, a masterpiece. Clearly, through myself and a few others, a growing awareness of alternative musical styles had begun to emerge.

Inside II got great reviews, and the people who heard it loved it. Unfortunately, the record company did nothing in terms of promotion and airplay, which frustrated me to no end. But my listeners were loyal, and when word of mouth spread the news that this was a good album, they bought it. Interestingly enough, *Inside II* became my second-best seller, over 300,000, topped only by *Inside The Taj Mahal*.

Epic picked up my option, and I did *Visions*, a fusion album with Tom Scott and the L.A. Express, interpreting famous songs by well-known artists in an attempt to cross over into the pop field and reach more people. The only other time I did this was on *Monday, Monday*, arranged by Oliver Nelson for RCA. *Visions* showcased tunes by Joni Mitchell, Stevie Wonder, Joan Baez, and Crosby, Stills, and Nash.

Once again, disappointment followed. The company did not support *Visions*, which baffled me. Joni Mitchell participated on one track, and she was a superstar. Tom Scott and his L.A. Express were hot. I was well known. The tunes were popular, and our arrangements were first class. You would think Epic would have launched a major promotional campaign. Instead, they did nothing. Once again, I hated the situation. The money one gets from record companies is nice, but the continual frustrations and disappointments are just not worth it.

In 1975 I shifted gears again, merging my Western point of view with musics from other cultures. In the late forties and early fifties, the idea that American music could be combined with influences from other cultures was already coming in. I liked that idea right from the beginning and welcomed the challenge of doing it myself. How could I bring various cultural influences into music I already understood? How could I assimilate and integrate them in logical and musically intelligent ways?

There are many ways of doing that, of course, one of which is rhythm. If you dig down deep enough, rhythm is common ground—as human beings, we *all* relate to rhythm. Rhythm is ancient. In fact, rhythm is the first thing—primitive people, dancing in the jungle to the beat of the drums. Just as rhythm is basic, so is melody. These are the fundamental ingredients of music in general. Harmony came much later. For *Paul Horn & Nexus*, I played melody on woodwinds while Nexus, a group of fiery percussionists from Toronto, played African, Indian, American, and South American rhythms on a variety of drums.

We played good, upbeat, multicultural jazz on this album, and it holds up well over the years. Eckart Rahn, president of Celestial Harmonies and Kuckuck, reissued it on compact disc, along with another album I did for Epic, called *The Altitude of the Sun.*

Brazilian guitarist Egberto Gismonti had no recordings available in North America, and nobody had heard of him. One day a friend of mine brought me a tape of Egberto's music. When I heard it, I flipped out. He was great.

My producer, Teo Macero (who was also Miles Davis's producer at CBS), contacted Egberto, and he flew to New York. Egberto brought with him a drummer named Roberto Silva. We got Ron Carter on bass and two other Brazilian percussionists. Egberto played guitar, piano, and synthesizer and wrote all arrangements. The basic session—the heart of it, the live part of it—was the percussion section, the bass, myself, and Egberto playing piano or guitar, and I was happy to introduce Egberto to North American and European audiences.

Once again, I encountered problems with the company. Figuring *Altitude of the Sun* was "South American" music, which suggests the carnival in Rio, they decided to put a devil's head on the cover—complete with red horns, a black face, green, bloodshot eyes, and vampire teeth. I was furious. In no way did this picture reflect the positive, uplifting energy of our music. Thankfully, this was my final album for Epic.

As time went on, my "Inside" solo flute albums became a series. In 1976, I traveled to Egypt and recorded *Inside the Great Pyramid*. I went to China in 1978 and did some recording inside Peking's Temple of Heaven as part of an album called *China*. I visited Scotland in 1981 and recorded *Inside the Magic of Findhorn*. Then *Inside the Cathedral* was recorded in Lithuania on a 1983 tour of the Soviet Union. I returned to India in 1989 and recorded a second album inside the Taj Mahal.

In a sense, music has always led me, and I have followed wherever it has taken me. I've never wanted to be locked into one commercial category or limited to one musical style. Whatever the style or category—jazz, classical, New Age, pop, fusion, whatever—I have followed my musical inclinations, merging and blending influences whenever it seemed adventurous and appropriate.

GOLDEN FLUTE RECORDS

I kept hoping that a change of consciousness would happen in the recording business, but it didn't, and I don't think it ever will. With their continuous takeovers, acquisitions, and amalgamations, record companies just get bigger and bigger, like huge monsters, and the musicians receive almost no personal attention.

The music business is strictly big money, and that means pop records, which is the only music the big companies are interested in. Anything else sneaks through by accident, and the companies do little or nothing to promote it. It may be musically fulfilling, and people may love it, and it might even get nominated for a Grammy—and yet the companies refuse to support it.

I looked around and saw that Windham Hill, Steven Halpern, Georgia Kelly, and numerous others were doing well as independents, and they didn't have the experience, the reputation, or the numbers of albums I had.

Figuring I'd give it a shot myself, I formed my own label, Golden Flute Records, and set myself up in Canada and the States.

I learned the other side of the record business, such as album covers, photographs, designs, layouts, graphics, four-color separations, liner notes, LP, CD, and cassette formats, manufacturing, and packaging. For all of these things, I learned the process in detail—and spent money.

Alas, the sales weren't there. Looking for new avenues, I signed on with New Age alternative network distributors. According to the feedback I got, the people involved were a lot more honest than in the normal record business. That is, distributors paid you.

Well, this went along fine for a while, then the New Age distributors became old age. They didn't pay for their orders. They didn't deny they owed money, and they didn't make excuses. They just didn't pay. I could sue and win, but so what? You spend more in court costs than the distributors owe, and all you get is a legal piece of paper saying they owe you money—which you knew in the first place. The courts don't collect the money for you. That's a whole other ball game.

It's a horrendous process, totally negative, and the bottom line is you still don't get your money. At one time, distributors owed me $30,000. Ultimately, with a lawyer's help, I collected about half. When all was said and done, Golden Flute Records maybe broke even overall—and I considered myself lucky.

On the positive side, I produced and owned the masters for eight of my own recordings, including *China, Inside the Magic of Findhorn, Jupiter 8*, and two albums from my USSR tour (see Discography). I went for quality pressings and quality covers. I could spend my own money any way I wanted, and I wasn't stingy. I also had fun designing graphics and setting up album jackets.

CHANGES

Around 1982 I met Eckart Rahn, who owned the Kuckuck label in Germany and set up his distribution in America under the name of Celestial Harmonies, which eventually became a first-class recording company in its own right. Eckart specializes in classical music, jazz, and what we call New Age music. He has excellent taste in music, graphics, artwork, and printing. His pressings and manufacturing are top-flight. He wanted to reissue *Inside the Taj Mahal, China, Inside the Great Pyramid,* and *Inside Russia* (retitled *Inside the Cathedral*). I said okay. With my eight Golden Flute albums and the four that Eckart reissued, I had twelve recordings on the market.

By the mid-1980s, it took too much for me to run Golden Flute, so I called Eckart again and asked him if he would like to take over my entire catalogue. He liked the "Inside" things but didn't care for some of the other albums. I said I'd think about it.

During the interim, Will Ackerman of Windham Hill approached me for a one-album deal with his subsidiary label, Lost Lake Arts. He wanted to make up a compilation album, the best of my Golden Flute series. I said okay, and we released *Sketches* on Lost Lake Arts.

I passed on Eckart's offer and connected with Global Pacific, a New Age label about to sign a distribution deal with CBS. Global took my whole catalogue and said they would promote it.

Eckart was upset with me. Who is Global Pacific? What do these kids know about the record business? I've been established twenty-five years.

Tryntje agreed. Eckart had proven himself and done well. He understood my music, packaged albums beautifully, had excellent distribution, paid honestly and on time. Why was I going with Global? I just had a feeling. I should have known better.

With synthesist Christopher Hedge, I recorded *Traveler* in 1987 and leased it to Global Pacific. The multicultural instrumentation and musical styles reflected external travels from many countries and sonic travels through historical time, from the present to the distant past. Through the meditative pieces, it also reflected my inner travels, the journeys within, the ongoing spiritual odyssey that we all share. *Traveler* seemed like a nice title to sum it all up. Happily, it was nominated for a Grammy.

When Global Pacific began having money problems, I called Eckart Rahn again to see if he might be interested in developing a more comprehensive agreement. This time, he said he wanted to take over my entire catalogue, not just part of it, and he would reissue virtually everything. In exchange, he only wanted control over the graphics, and if I did any "Best of" albums, he wanted to select the material. He offered a long-term contract—ten years.

I thought about his offer. As a businessman, he can't be beat; his covers are often stunningly beautiful, and he uses only the very best manufacturers and pressing plants. He has a deep appreciation of music, signs good artists, and releases music he loves. He is knowledgeable about jazz, classical, and New Age music, and he has two labels I can work with—Kuckuck for my meditative musics, Black Sun for my jazz recordings. I liked that.

When we talked again, he said, "What would it take for you to live like a country gentleman?"

We agreed on $1 million—$100,000 a year, guaranteed, for ten years. If my records earn more, I get more. I can live off that quite comfortably and be secure in the music business until I'm almost seventy. In return, I record one new album every eighteen months. I feel quite pleased with our relationship.

PART V

THE TRAVELER

FOURTEEN

INSIDE THE GREAT PYRAMID

As head of Epic's A & R department, David Kapralik saw the potential of *Inside the Taj Mahal* when nobody else did and released it. Now, eight years later, in a casual conversation, he planted another seed. "Lately, Paul, I've been thinking about something. It seems to me you ought to go to Egypt and record in the Great Pyramid. It's the logical successor to *Inside the Taj Mahal*." About a year after that, his idea became a reality. In early 1976, I packed my bags, brought recording engineer David Greene and photographer Roger Smeeth with me, and flew to Egypt.

Before leaving, I read a number of books on the pyramids, including *Secrets of the Great Pyramid*, by Peter Tompkins; *The Secret Power of Pyramids*, by Bill Schul and Ed Pettit; and *A Search in Secret Egypt*, by Paul Brunton. Reading these books, I found myself fascinated with the unbelievable dimensions of the Great Pyramid and with the mystery left to us from that ancient civilization. There are many theories, but no one knows exactly when, why, or how this pyramid was built. The Great Pyramid is the tallest, so huge it staggers the imagination. We could build thirty Empire State buildings from its stones. Its dimensions are perfect, and it is the only one

193

that has chambers within the structure itself. Supposedly it is a tomb built for Cheops and his family, but no bodies have ever been found.

The books talked about people who had various experiences inside the pyramid, some of which were frightening. When author Paul Brunton came out, he was terrified. When Napoleon conquered Egypt, he visited the Great Pyramid and asked to be left alone in the King's Chamber while his soldiers waited outside. When he emerged from the pyramid, all of the color had drained from his face. He was ashen and looked absolutely shaken. People asked what happened, but he refused to talk about it and ordered that he never be asked again. On his deathbed someone remembered this incident and said to him, "Do you remember the time you spent in the King's Chamber and wouldn't speak of it? What happened?" Even on his deathbed, Napoleon refused to discuss the matter. These things fascinated me.

Some of the books talked about pyramid power, a special energy that exists within the pyramid's perfect geometrical structure. If someone builds a small replica of the pyramid, keeping the dimensions exactly in proportion and aligning the model with true north, certain very interesting things happen.

For instance, you can place a piece of fruit inside the replica, and it will not rot for one month or more. You can easily test it by putting one apple inside, one outside. In a few days, the apple outside decays, while the apple inside does not. Razor blades placed inside remain sharp for weeks when used, whereas ordinary blades left outside become dull after three or four shaves. Plants watered with water left inside the pyramid flourish better than plants watered with regular water. Such experiments were easy to set up and verify. These and many other things intrigued me.

Before leaving, I received a call from a man named Ben Pietsch from Santa Rosa, California. He introduced himself by saying he was a pyramidologist. He had lectured and written many articles on the Great Pyramid, including an unpublished book, *Voices in Stone*, which he later sent me—a fascinating work. He had heard via the grapevine that I was going to Egypt to play my flute inside the Great Pyramid. He loved the idea and said that sonic vibrations constituted an integral part of the structure. In fact, he said, every room has a basic vibration to it; if we found it and identified with it, we would become attuned to that particular space. I had never heard that theory before, but it made sense to me.

The King's Chamber is the main chamber in the Great Pyramid. Within this chamber is a hollow, lidless coffer made of solid granite. Pietsch said that if I struck this coffer, it would give off a tone. I should tune up to this tone in order to be at one with it, thereby attuned with the chamber. "And by the way," he said, "you'll find that note to be A-438." In the West, our established A-note vibrates at 440 vibrations per second. He was saying that the A-note of the coffer was two vibrations lower than ours, which would make their A-note slightly flat, only a shade lower in pitch, but different nevertheless. Although he had not personally visited the Great Pyramid, he seemed to know this quite definitely.

In the weeks to follow, I located a battery-operated device called a Korg Tuning Trainer, which registers on a meter the exact pitch of any tone. "What the heck," I thought. "Just in case."

The Great Pyramid of Giza is the largest, heaviest, oldest, and most perfect building ever created by human hands. Eagerly, we bounded up stairs carved in rock to the entrance 20 feet up, a forced entrance, created in A.D. 820 by a young caliph named Abdullah Al-Mamun. At that time, the original secret entrance, 49 feet above the ground, had not been discovered. I had seen diagrams of the inner passages and chambers, so I knew that once inside we would soon arrive at what is called the Ascending Passage, a low, narrow passage 129 feet long, 3' 5" wide, 3' 11" high, and quite steep.

Handrails had been placed on either side of the passage, and wooden slats covered the slick granite floor. The passage was well lit, but still a difficult climb for anyone but a midget. At the end, we entered an utterly amazing passage called the Grand Gallery, 157 feet long, ascending at the same steep angle. It is some 7 feet wide and 28 feet high; its sides are made from huge monolithic slabs of polished limestone, which weigh up to seventy tons each.

At this point, instead of continuing upward, one can follow a very low horizontal passage for 127 feet, ending in a bare room approximately 18 feet square with a gabled ceiling 20'5" at its highest point. This room became known as the Queen's Chamber, because the Arabs entombed their deceased women in rooms with gabled ceilings.

Deciding to visit this room later, David and Roger and I continued on to the top of the Grand Gallery. Again, the handrails and wooden slats assisted our climb, which culminated when we mounted a huge rock 3 feet high, 6 feet wide, and 8 feet deep, called the Great Step. By this time, panting, dripping with perspiration, we stopped to get our breath. Looking down, we saw almost to the end of the 300-foot stretch we had just climbed.

Going ahead, we had to stoop down and pass through a horizontal passage about 28 feet long, called the Antechamber, before entering the most famous and mysterious room of the Great Pyramid—the King's Chamber—which is 34 feet long, 17 feet wide, 19 feet high. Its walls and ceiling are made of red polished granite; nine slabs compose the ceiling, each a seventy-ton monolith. The lidless coffer, or sarcophagus, carved out of a single huge block of granite, stands at one end of the room, one of its corners chipped away by souvenir hunters. Behind it, to one side, rests a big slab, the purpose of which is unknown, and against the north wall stands another rock, about 3 feet high, also a mystery. It appeared to me to be an altar. Two vent-holes on the north and south sides emit fresh air and keep the room an even sixty-eight degrees throughout the year.

Deep silence permeates the environment. We sat on the floor and relaxed, propping our backs against the wall. I meditated for a while. Gradually we stopped perspiring and soon felt comfortable.

We spent the better part of an hour there and began our descent, exploring the Queen's Chamber on the way, after which we felt tired from all of our stooping and climbing, so we returned to the hotel.

RECORDING IN THE GREAT PYRAMID

At the very last minute, just before Frank, our Egyptian guide, picked us up, I thought it would be a good idea to bring candles along. We rushed around the hotel but couldn't find any new ones. A busboy grabbed a bunch of used candles, half-burned from the night before, scraping them off the tables. I also brought along a picture of Maharishi and some incense and a couple of flashlights, just in case.

Frank picked us up right on time, and we were on our way through rush-hour traffic, which, for lack of a more precise description, I'll characterize as utterly insane—bumper-to-bumper, everybody uptight after working all day, horns squawking, drivers shouting and waving their fists, nobody obeying any laws whatsoever.

On the way, Frank filled us in on the details of his meetings. He had managed to get permission from the minister of antiquities, the main authority at the Cairo Museum. Two of us could spend three hours alone in the Great Pyramid, beginning at 6:00 P.M. We were to deliver our official permits to the authorities at the plateau. At 9:00 P.M. sharp, we were to be out.

In half an hour, we arrived at the Giza plateau. A few officials waited for us in another car. Frank got out and talked with them. We then walked over to a nearby police hut, showed our permits, and everything was set. A guard got the keys and joined Frank and Dave Greene and me; the four of us walked to the pyramid. It was so much more peaceful here at this time of day. No tourists, no street hustlers, no cars or camels or horses. Just a warm gentle breeze in the air, with a red-orange sun setting over the vast surrounding desert, a magical beginning to a magical evening.

The guard opened the great iron gate at the entrance and threw a switch, turning on all the lights. We told him we'd like him to turn the lights out once we were settled in the King's Chamber, estimating it would take about twenty minutes to get there. Frank left us, saying he'd pick us up afterward. The guard waited below to throw the switch, after which he, too, would leave, locking us in for the designated time.

Dave and I began the long climb, which was more difficult this time because we had a lot to carry and didn't want to make two trips. In one shoulder bag, I carried my flutes; in another, blank tapes. Dave carried his tape recorder, the mike, and all the cables. It was hard going, especially in the Ascending Passage, which had a very low ceiling. We stopped and caught our breath for a few minutes at the bottom of the Grand Gallery before continuing. By the time we reached the King's Chamber, we were both dripping wet and out of breath. I lit some candles and placed them at several points in the chamber and began unpacking my flutes.

While Dave set up his equipment in the Antechamber, the lights suddenly went out. What a difference! The humming from the fluorescent tubes disappeared, and for the first time we felt the pyramid's absolute still-ness . . . so quiet, so peaceful. Fantastic.

We hurried to finish our preparations. I then lit some incense and per-formed a short ceremony called a puja on the large stone by the north wall, which I felt had been an altar at one time. I had not planned this ceremony; it happened spontaneously. Feeling a strong spiritual force, an intense, eternal energy permeating the atmosphere, I simply responded to it.

I subscribe to the theory that the Great Pyramid was a temple of learn-ing; that the priests held very advanced, specific knowledge; and that this chamber was a temple of initiation for people ready to receive that knowledge.

Written in Sanskrit, the puja is the integral part of teaching someone meditation. I learned it at the ashram in India. Its purpose is to eliminate the teacher's ego. The teacher-initiator is just a link in a long chain of priv-ileged individuals who have been assigned the responsibility of perpetu-ating the pure knowledge of how to experience the Self directly. Once the puja has been performed, the technique of meditation can be passed on in a pure state from the nonegoistic teacher to the receptive student.

The puja was also a way of expressing my gratitude for the privilege of being there and of expressing my respect for the sanctity of the King's Chamber, acknowledging the spiritual value of whatever purposes this chamber had served in the past. As well, I thanked God for the gift and blessing of life, not only for myself, but for all sentient beings everywhere.

After the ceremony, I sat cross-legged in front of the coffer and medi-tated. David also sat quietly and closed his eyes. In that deep, deep still-ness, I heard what seemed like chanting voices far away, very clear and very real, but so distant I couldn't make out a specific melody. They sounded like whispered chants from thousands of years ago, or like strings inside a piano sympathetically resonating quietly after you finish playing a note on the flute. They were beautiful tones and seemed to envelop me and the whole room. There was nothing spooky about this. I felt warm and com-fortable. It was as if the chamber accepted me, welcoming my presence, and I felt quite happy and secure.

After ten minutes or so, I opened my eyes. David looked comfortable, peaceful, and relaxed. At first, I wasn't going to say anything about the voices, but the sound seemed so real. "You know, as I was sitting here,

Dave, I thought I heard voices, like angels softly chanting from far, far away." Immediately, I felt self-conscious and wished I hadn't spoken—it sounded weird. David simply looked at me and said, "So did I." Both of us had heard the same thing.

I thought of Ben Pietsch from Santa Rosa, and his suggestion that I strike the coffer. I leaned over and hit the inside with the side of my fist, producing a beautiful round tone. What resonance! I remembered Ben's saying, "When you hear that tone, you will be immersed in living history." I picked up the electronic tuning device I'd brought and struck the coffer again. There it was, A-438, just as Ben had predicted.

Ben's concept of living history is interesting. Everything that has ever happened on the face of this earth since the beginning of time is still in existence somewhere. An action, a spoken word, even a thought has energy, and this energy endures. Although it diminishes, it is still there and can never be not-there. History *is* alive.

In a confined space like the King's Chamber, the events and peoples of the past are still present; their energies continue to exist. If you are quiet enough, as I was in my meditation, you can sense them. I believe those distant voices were the voices of people who sang inside this temple many centuries ago.

I felt comfortable in the room, with no fear in my heart—regardless of Napoleon's and Paul Brunton's frightening experiences; and my receptivity opened me to the comforting and protective spirits that were still there. I was immersed in living history, and I felt its presence in the deep silence of my meditation. When I played, I opened myself to these vibrations; their presence came through me, into the music, out into the air.

The moment had arrived. I adjusted my flute to the A-438 pitch Ben had predicted and attuned myself with the room, an important part of this process. Each room has its own sound. Its vibration is the essence of the room's walls and ceiling and floor. It is dependent upon the shape and size of the room, the materials used to build it, its function, and whatever presence or presences still exist within it from the past. If the people who used the room were peaceful and loving, the vibrations of the room are also peaceful and loving.

The King's Chamber had its own vibration, made up of all events that had taken place there. David Greene and I were in the heart of the power center, enclosed within a huge mass of solid rock, bathed in the tremendous energy that came through because of the structural perfection of its geometric dimensions and its exact true-north alignment. Our own vibrations mingled with the vibrations of the room, increasing the intensity of our feelings.

Sitting on the floor in front of the coffer, with the stereo mike in the center of the room, I began playing alto flute. The echo sounded wonderful, lasting about eight seconds. I waited for the echo to decay and then played again. Groups of notes suspended in air and came back together as a chord. Sometimes certain notes stood out more than others, always changing. I listened and responded, as if I were playing with another musician.

This recording was not as innocent as the Taj Mahal album because I came to the pyramids with the intention of recording a commercial product. I had thought about the pyramids and prepared myself emotionally for this evening's music. The Taj Mahal experience could never be repeated, and I knew that.

Nevertheless, I still felt a certain kind of innocence. I hadn't written anything specific to play. A precomposed work written back in the States would be totally inappropriate here—this was a different place, a different mood, a different atmosphere, and certainly a different time. Clock time had no meaning here. Within these chambers lived the spirits of kings and queens and their servants, people who had walked and talked upon the earth thousands of years ago. I wanted to be in touch with them, not with my personal self. So, although my intention was not as innocent, I still kept the music pure through improvisation, which is the true expression of the living moment.

My job was to open myself as much as possible to the vibratory influences permeating these rooms and to respond to them as intuitively and deeply and honestly as I possibly could. By transcending preconceptions and personal ego trips and then improvising music in response to the environment, I could bring to the album an experience that would be psychologically clean and spiritually innocent.

I became totally absorbed in the music. I gave myself up to the eons of vibrations and ghostly choirs present in the chamber, letting the music flow through me with a life of its own. About one minute before each twenty-two-minute reel ended, David signaled to me, at which time I brought the solos to a close.

I switched to the C flute, but for this room the alto flute seemed more appropriate, so I switched back. I've never sung on record before, but here for some reason, I felt like trying. My voice had a different resonance than the flutes, and the act of singing turned out to be one of the most personal musical experiences I've ever had. Now I myself was the resonating instrument, not the flutes, and it felt great.

Human bodies contain seven energy centers, known as *chakras*, which range along the spine from the base of the spine to the top of the head. If the *chakras* are open, life-energy flows freely within the body. If they are closed, the flow is restricted. Most of these centers are closed to us because of stress. As we expand our consciousness, our nervous system becomes more purified, the *chakras* open, and the energy flows freely.

Specific sounds can open the *chakras*. I think the music that evening was pure enough to open those of receptive listeners. I did not play with that intention, but I was so open that the music which came through seems to have the power to awaken those centers.

Many people have told me over the years that this pyramid music is especially meaningful for them, even more so than *Inside the Taj Mahal*. Some people felt they experienced through the music the essence of the pyramids, without having been there. Others said the music brought back recollections of past Egyptian lives.

It seemed a magical time. The best thing I could have done was perform the puja, which aligned me with the inner spirit of the place, got rid of whatever ego I had, and helped me return to my natural innocence. I could be wide open, a clear channel for whatever came through my flute in addition to the notes that were played.

Two hours flew by. With only one hour of precious time remaining, I suggested to Dave that we move on to the Grand Gallery and the Queen's Chamber. David had acquired a new friend, a flat-nosed mouse who seemed more interested in the cables than in David—it probably thought the cables were something new to eat. Its flat nose looked funny, and we laughed. Perhaps the mouse was descended from an ancient species, but Dave and I figured he'd bumped into too many walls in the dark. We said farewell to the mouse and moved on.

I stood at the top of the Grand Gallery and played a few notes, which I eagerly looked forward to hearing. In *Secrets of the Great Pyramid*, author Peter Tompkins repeatedly mentioned "the unusual echo" of that room, and I wanted to hear it. Much to my surprise, there was *no echo*. In fact, the notes sounded dead, and the echoless passage was literally as quiet as a tomb, appropriately so, of course, but nevertheless surprising and somewhat disappointing.

Time was running out, so we moved on quickly to the Queen's Chamber. I felt more inclined toward the higher flutes here and played the piccolo as well as the C flute. Although this room doesn't have the acoustic qualities of the King's Chamber, it has a special feeling of its own, reflected in the improvisations.

When David signaled the end of the tape, our watches said 8:55 P.M. We started packing up. At *exactly* 9:00 P.M., the lights suddenly flashed back on. The guards kept precise tabs on us. We hastily gathered our gear and hurried down to the main entrance. I didn't want to take advantage of the people who had been kind enough to give us this marvelous opportunity.

Outside, Dave and I strolled across the sand to the road a hundred yards away and sat down on the curb to wait for Frank. The night air was cool, and the skies were clear and dark, with all the stars shining brightly up in the heavens. We sat in silence, looking at the pyramid. We had done so much talking and planning, and we had traveled so far, not knowing whether we were going to be able to do this. Now we were here, sitting quietly on the curb beneath the starry skies, looking at the pyramid, reflecting upon our adventure. Our dream had fulfilled itself. Now it was a thing of the past. Dave put his arm around my shoulder and said, "You did it, man." I looked at him and smiled. That Thursday evening, May 6, 1976, gave us an unforgettable experience.

PUSHING OUR LUCK

The next day at the hotel I asked Frank about a thought that had been jostling my mind all morning. "What are the chances of entering the other pyramids after hours?" I had played music in the Great Pyramid, but not in Kephren or Mycerinus. I expected Frank to tell us it was impossible, but instead he said, "The big one was the hardest. The others should be easy. I'll see what I can do."

While Frank checked things out, Roger Smeeth and I spent several hours photographing the Great Pyramid inside and out, which I enjoyed. Until now, I had been too busy to take pictures. Later that evening, Frank informed us everything was set for tomorrow night, Saturday. He managed to get the same arrangement, three hours, from six to nine in the evening, and he would pick us up at five. I couldn't believe our good fortune.

The next afternoon, we were on our way to Giza once again, but this time the skies were not blue, and we could hardly see the sun. A sandstorm had sprung up. It was beginning to get nasty. "Very unusual for this time of year," said Frank. The storm was so strong our driver could hardly see the car in front of him. For once, traffic moved along at a sane pace. By the time we arrived at the plateau, the storm had become fierce.

In the blowing wind and whistling, stinging sand, we handed our official permits to the police authorities, then drove on past the Great Pyramid to Kephren's entrance, about a half-mile away. Since we had three hours in which to cover two pyramids, we asked our driver to come back please in ninety minutes to take us to the Mycerinus pyramid, another half-mile or so away.

We entered a long, low, descending passage that led to the burial chamber of Kephren's Pyramid. This chamber was supposedly the resting place of Kephren, brother of Cheops. It was larger than the Cheops King's Chamber (46½' long; 16½' wide), with a gabled ceiling 22½' high. An open granite sarcophagus stood at one end, its lid placed behind it. Graffiti marred the walls, but the sound was quite good, with a quality somewhere between the King's and Queen's chambers. The feeling here was different, rather heavy and oppressive. Dave and I both felt it.

I lit some incense, gave a puja, meditated, and tuned my flute to the room. This time, I struck the lid of the sarcophagus, and the tone turned out to be G. I played all the flutes and chanted again, improvising freely.

Time sailed by much too quickly, making us a little late for our 7:30 appointment with the driver. When we got outside, the sandstorm's intensity had increased. Our driver had become apprehensive. He wanted to drive back to town, but we urged him to take us over to Mycerinus, the third pyramid, letting him know we had only one hour remaining. Grudgingly, he said okay.

Once again we entered, loaded down with equipment, bending over in the long, low, descending passage. This pyramid has two subterranean chambers. One has an arched roof and is smaller than the Queen's Chamber of Cheops. It contains a sarcophagus. The second room is adjacent to the first and is even smaller, with a low, flat ceiling. It contains six separate indented chambers and is known as the Children's Burial Chamber. Supposedly, it was for the children of Mycerinus, whose burial place is next door.

I played most of the music, not in the children's chamber, but in Mycerinus's chamber. For atmosphere and attunement, Dave and I again performed the ritual of incense and candles, puja and meditation. I did not tune the flutes to the room, however, because the coffer did not produce a distinct tone.

This pyramid felt cozy and comfortable, but because of the smaller dimensions and lower ceiling, there was relatively no echo. Nevertheless, the vibrations and general atmosphere of the room are contained in the improvisations. Because there is no echo, the tones of the flutes do not sound unique, but the feelings were special and reflect the moment of creation.

Running out of time, I had recorded only one selection in the Children's Chamber before a loud knock on the iron door above suddenly resounded throughout the passages, startling us. It had the ring of urgency about it, clearly indicating that the guards meant business. We packed up quickly and hurried up the narrow passageway, out into the sandstorm.

Our driver had panicked, almost leaving without us. The storm had grown more severe, and his car had been taking a terrible lashing. With the wind wailing and the sand whipping our faces, we heaved our equipment into the cab and jumped in, slamming the doors behind us. The driver felt much better when the wind subsided as we reached the edge of town.

At the hotel, Dave and I gave hugs and farewells and good wishes to Frank, our trusty and effective guide. What a beautiful person. As we said good-bye, I realized that the primary instrument in the pyramids had not been my flute—but Frank. Without him and his successful efforts with the officials, we could never have accomplished our mission. God bless him.

FIFTEEN

INSIDE CHINA

We had been in China only a few days when the realization struck us: The vision of China we held in our minds was based upon our readings, nearly all of which dealt with China's past. But the China we encountered in the late seventies had nothing to do with the China of 1,000 years ago. It was not an *inner* society at all. Buddhist monasteries were no longer active, and the energy of China was distinctly *outer*. There seemed to be an underlying direction and purpose to this modern society—they were winning their battle for survival.

We quickly appreciated the fact that China is the most heavily populated country in the world. About 25 percent of all people live there. America is multiracial and multicultural, but in China, the people are predominantly of one race. Everywhere we looked, we saw only Chinese people, and nearly all of them wore Mao suits—the men in blue, with little caps; the soldiers in green.

Almost a billion people lived in China when we visited for three weeks between December 19, 1978, and January 7, 1979. Today, the population is *over* a billion people. In America, we never think of the logistics involved with feeding a billion people every day and handling waste and trash. China was doing it and doing it well.

Under their system of government, they are surviving, and like Russia, they have certain freedoms—freedom from the fear of being robbed on the streets or in the house; freedom from the fear of unemployment; freedom from the fear of being unable to pay medical bills; freedom from the fear of not having enough money to educate their children. These are not written in America's book of freedoms, but they are freedoms nevertheless.

Two generations had been born and raised under a system that emphasized the collective, not the individual. And from a Western point of view, they have few material comforts. They do not enjoy the personal or social wealth that we have.

Instead of feeling unhappy about it, there was a lightness to the people, lots of smiles and laughter, which was contagious. Nearly all of us commented about how we smiled and laughed much more here than we did back home. We were on vacation, of course, but nevertheless the lightness of the people affected us directly.

Chinese people work hard. They do not build roads using giant supermachines. Men and women alike cleared stones from the roads by hand and carried heavy buckets of clay on their shoulders. It was hard, physical work—but at least everyone was working.

They do not have to endure the terrible psychological impact of collecting unemployment. They don't have to get up in the morning full of energy and vitality only to face a day in which there is nothing to do. In America, unemployment is an awful thing, not only in terms of the pocketbook, but also in terms of mental health. In China, everybody has the opportunity to work, to participate, to contribute—one of the major reasons the general mood of Chinese society was so upbeat.

MY FIRST TRIP TO CHINA

Many years ago, Norman Bethune, a famous Canadian doctor, volunteered to take care of people injured on the front lines during the revolutionary war that brought Mao to power. The Chinese regarded Bethune as a great hero of the revolution. When Mao erected the Bamboo Curtain, he severed relations with America but kept the door open with Canada, largely because of China's respect for Norman Bethune.

In 1977, Bob Wright, a friend and owner of Sealand of the Pacific, had teamed up with a tourist group sponsored by the Chinese-Canadian Friendship Association and traveled to China with his wife. When Bob suggested in 1978 that Tryntje and I join him and his wife and twenty other people on an organized three-week tour of China, I jumped at the chance. Just two weeks before we left, Nixon made his historic China visit, and for the first time in thirty years the Bamboo Curtain parted. As a result, our group of Westerners was one of the first to visit China under the new policy of openness, China's version of *glasnost*.

The first city we visited was Peking, the name of which has since been changed to Beijing. It was December, and snow and ice covered everything. The hotels were not prepared for tourists, and by Western standards they were not very comfortable. Tryntje and I did not mind. Although we almost froze in our rooms, the hotels were quite charming, left over from the British occupation of many years ago.

Amost immediately, we noticed people's honesty. The first night in our hotel, a man said, "Oh, God, I left my bags at the airport." The next day, his luggage arrived safely. The hotels had no door locks. We wondered what to do with our valuables while touring, but our guide assured us that we need not worry. "Nobody takes anything here," he said, and that was true. You could leave money and jewels on the dresser. When you came back eight hours later, everything was still there. For the most part, it is a very honest society.

I had hoped to make a film of our journey and to record within a temple. I brought with me a recording engineer named Rob Mingay and a husband-and-wife film-making team from Toronto, Fran and Peter Mellen. Before leaving, we requested permission to record in the Temple of Heaven and in Mao's mausoleum. Chinese officials said no to Mao's mausoleum, but they left open the question of recording inside the Temple of Heaven.

Peter and Fran wanted to bring 16-mm equipment with them, but that kind of equipment is considered professional, and it would have taken a year to get permission for it. Peter decided to bring Super-8 cameras and film, which he blew up to 16 mm back home.

With two translators, a man and woman in their early twenties, we wandered about on our own, shooting whatever we could, getting general background material. Originally, we envisioned Buddhist monasteries and meditation music. But as I said, the China of today is not an inner society. It is an outer society, dedicated to survival. As soon as we realized this, we changed our concept.

PLAYING FOR THE CHINESE

We had hoped to set up a concert, but that did not happen. How could I play music for the people? Someone suggested I take my flute out on the streets. I had to think about that. I had never done it before. If I didn't play on the streets back home, how could I do it here? In China, being Western is like being from Mars. Most of the Chinese people had never seen a white face their whole lives. I mulled it over and decided to go ahead.

The next afternoon, the film team and the interpreter and I went out on the street, and I began playing. I soon realized what the term "population explosion" means.

Most of the cars and trucks in China are government vehicles. Bicycles are the people's primary means of transportation. Over there, bicycles cost about as much as cars in proportion to their incomes, a tremendous outlay. In China's larger cities, hardly any stoplights exist. There are so many people moving all the time, that if they had to stop for thirty seconds or a minute, the result would be terrible congestion. Instead of stopping at intersections, people just fed their way through—amazingly, it worked. No matter how wide the sidewalks were, they were not big enough to contain the numbers of people using them. Thousands of people walked everywhere, spilling over from the sidewalks into the streets. Between the pedestrians and the cars and trucks and bicycles, there was a lot of traffic.

I started playing my flute on the street, and within five minutes throngs of pedestrians started backing up. The crowd grew larger and larger by the second. Playing my flute on the sidewalk, I was like a dam holding back floodwaters. It was frightening, and our interpreter was panicking. What were we supposed to do?

We looked for a policeman, but China has very few policemen or military personnel watching people or directing traffic. People just act on their own, in an orderly, harmonious fashion, as long as traffic is allowed to flow in its normal way. Well, I was stopping the flow.

Within a few minutes, some 2,000 people had backed up, and the crowd kept growing. The interpreter rushed up to me and said, "We have to stop. We must leave."

As soon as I had started playing, Peter took his camera out and got some excellent footage of this scene for our half-hour documentary. From then on, I did not play in the streets, but in parks and schools and other places where people could gather without stopping traffic and causing problems.

Through our interpreters, we got permission to record inside the Temple of Heaven, a beautiful all-wood circular temple several hundred years old, used by the emperors of past dynasties as a private place of worship. But the officials would not let me in after closing time. If I wanted to come in when there were relatively few people present, I had to arrive at seven in the morning.

It was a bitterly cold morning, below freezing, in the twenties, with all the windows and doors open, and no heat in the place. A few people were there, but the officials held them back, which I appreciated. I said it would be all right with me if they looked in from the windows and doorways.

Rob Mingay set up his recording equipment. Fran and Peter rolled the film, and I played for an hour. For the most part, I improvised, but I also played a Chinese piece I had worked on for many months, in case I had an opportunity to perform a concert. It was very difficult playing Chinese style on my Western flute.

I was amazed I could play at all. My fingers were almost frozen. I couldn't feel them. The flute was so cold that I worried about my lips sticking to the metal. But when you really want to do something, the power of the mind pushes through seemingly insurmountable physical obstacles. We were successful in our recording and very happy with it. Later, back home, I recorded additional pieces in the studio with several musicians, including David M. Y. Liang, and released *China* on my own label, Golden Flute.

Guilin, a southern city, is the most famous place in China that has dragon-toothed mountains. Along the Lei River, the hills rise sharply to pointed peaks and slope quickly down again, one after another, like drag-on's teeth. It is one of the most beautiful and unusual places in the world.

Whereas life in the north, close to Peking, seemed more rigid, life in the south felt more relaxed. In the north, for example, if men and women displayed physical contact in public, like holding hands, they were socially ostracized. In the south, this was not so. Young lovers held hands in public, although it was forbidden to kiss, even casually. Clothes were drab and standardized in the north. In the south, they were more expressive. Not all of the men wore Mao suits, and the women wore colorful skirts, dresses, and sweaters. In general, the south felt more lively and vital.

Seeking places to perform, we visited several communes, which had schools for all levels. In one preschool, cute little kids with sweet little doll-like faces sat there all bundled up. The schools were not heated, so the kids wore five layers of clothes. When they stood up, they sort of rolled instead of walking. I played flute for them, and then, like the Pied Piper, walked out into the yard and played and danced. They followed along behind me, dancing and laughing, their eyes bright and happy.

I teamed up with a teacher, who played accordion, and one of his pupils, who played Chinese flute quite well. They played, and I improvised along with them, fooling around. They thought I had memorized what I was doing, because they did not understand improvisation.

In another southern city, I played in a cultural park, where different groups from nearby communities entertained. The people had no television, and they were poor, so they did not go to movies. They entertained themselves in different ways.

Every little town and commune had a dance company, a theater, and an orchestra made up of Chinese instruments. Towns sent different groups to this cultural park, which formed a variety show. One troupe danced in costumes. Somebody else came up and sang, followed by a musical group. About 5,000 people attended.

I said to my interpreter, "Go back and find out who's in charge here. See if I can play."

He returned running, out of breath, and said, "You're on next."

There I was—"You're on, Paul." What was I supposed to do by myself, with 5,000 people out front? Thank God I'm a jazz musician and can improvise. So I went out and played solo flute, which was very well received. It was a wonderful experience and added to our film.

The Canton Song and Dance Company, a fine troupe of dancers, singers, and musicians, was touring the southern provinces. They performed traditional Chinese dances in traditional dress, with an orchestra composed of traditional Chinese instruments. They invited our group to attend one of their performances. This was a big production in a large theater. Again, there was no heat, so everyone sat in overcoats, listening to the music with smiles on their faces, not complaining, enjoying themselves. The building was old and run down, and the stage was somewhat splintered, but the inner light of the people was bright indeed, wonderful to see.

I thoroughly enjoyed the show and afterward went backstage and met the conductor. The flutists in the orchestra very much wanted to meet me. They did not know me by name, but here I was, a Western flutist, and they were interested. The musicians had their instruments out. A flutist said to me, "Let's play together."

"Why don't we improvise something?" I suggested.

He sort of looked at me, and I could see this might not set well with him. I didn't know what was going to happen. When we started playing, he began floundering. He didn't know what to do.

I did not want to embarrass him, especially in front of his peers, so right away I stopped and said, "I'll tell you what. I have a better idea. I would enjoy it very much if you played a piece that you know, and let me see what I can do." He gave a big sigh of relief.

He played a simple melody, easy to follow. I stayed in the background, weaving in and out of his music. By watching his body language, I could tell when the piece was coming to an end, and we ended together. Well, everyone thought that was magic, like Doug Henning the magician was here. Good God, how does he do this?

We retired to another room, along with the orchestra director, a couple of musicians, and my interpreter. They served tea, which was most welcome, because we were freezing. We sat around a table, drinking hot tea and talking.

Along the way, I asked the director what he thought of jazz. Through the interpreter, he said, "Jazz is self-intoxication."

"Whoa," I thought. "That's a heck of a statement."

I wondered to myself if he knew about jazz. Had he ever heard any? Did he know what I was talking about, or was he associating it with rock 'n' roll?

"Jazz is the art of improvisation," I said. "You bring all of your experiences to it, and all you know about music, and express yourself spontaneously instead of through a written piece of music. Many musicians do it only for themselves, and I'll grant you that some jazz can be self-intoxicating."

Before this, I had never thought of jazz that way, but he opened up the possibility in my mind, and he wasn't all wrong. At the same time, I was thinking of jazz in terms of what I had come to know through my spiritual pilgrimage. If your ego is out of the way, then jazz is not self-intoxication.

These thoughts would have been a bit detailed for him, so I put it in different terms. "Imagine a young person brought up in your society, accepting the social and political values he is taught by his parents and schools. He is totally Chinese. He is not self-centered but dedicated to the collective welfare. He has studied music, and he understands the language of music. Now he picks up his instrument and plays spontaneously. Wouldn't his personal, individual music be an extension of his social, political, and cultural background? In such a case, how could spontaneous music be self-intoxication?"

As the interpreter relayed my words, I could see the director begin to smile. Getting the point, he beamed. "Yes," he said. "You are right. I never thought of it that way."

This was a valuable moment. It was probably the first time that anyone had talked knowledgeably about jazz or tried to formulate and express in words the essential element of jazz to him. Unfortunately, we did not get this conversation on film.

Before I went backstage, Tryntje said she wanted to return to the hotel. I said fine, I wanted to go back and talk with the musicians. I gave her a little kiss good-bye. The people near us almost had heart failure. Kissing is not done in public. It is scandalous for a man to kiss a woman, even if it isn't a passionate embrace.

As I looked at the people staring at us, I realized once again what a different part of the world this is, how vastly different Chinese society is from ours. It felt wonderful to be here. What a precious opportunity for learning about other people and their ways. I was not here strictly as a musician. I was also here as a person, just a human being fortunate enough to see these things.

Wherever we went—on the streets, in department stores, anywhere at all—people stared at us. They had never seen Westerners before. They did not stare at us with hostility, but with childlike warmth. They stared with wide-open eyes and totally innocent curiosity. In no way did it make us feel self-conscious.

They had a tender way of greeting us. We walked down the street and all of a sudden heard clapping. When we turned around to see what was happening, we saw people applauding us. That is how they greeted us, with applause. We applauded them in return. When our tour group returned home, they felt like public celebrities. Nobody had ever walked the streets before and received applause. They applauded. We applauded. And there were smiles all around.

CHINESE *YAGYA*

The communes don't exist anymore, but they did then, and they were huge, like cities. Sometimes as many as 60,000 people or more lived in one commune. Chinese society is so big that they had to break it down into segments, setting up systems of self-government within each commune. In some places, it was even broken down into city blocks, with one person in charge for that block. When a problem arose, it was reported to that person, who reported it to someone above him. This was the system they used to interconnect a billion people.

They had a policy of self-criticism within each commune. Any time a problem arose or someone did something wrong, they were told to go back and think about it critically and then return the next day to talk about it. In a conflict between a boss and a worker, they self-criticized before anyone decided who was right or wrong. I thought this policy was wise and humane.

There are no formal places of worship in China and no formal religions. They don't speak in terms of God, nor do they speak in philosophical terms. And yet, paradoxical as it may sound, China is one of the most spiritual countries I have ever visited. I saw a selflessness in the people that I do not see back home.

The spiritual path teaches us to look at life in a selfless way, to perform acts for the sake of the action, not for the sake of personal reward. In Sanskrit, the word "yagya" means action for the sake of the action, not for the fruit of the action. It is a privilege to be alive and able to do something positive. Positive work is beneficial, not only to you and to your family, but to society at large. You work because it is a joy to do something meaningful, contributing to the whole, even if it is sweeping the streets.

In China, there is a lot of trash, and the streets need to be swept. The people who do this job are not made to feel like lowly street sweepers, because everyone is doing whatever is necessary in order to move forward and survive as a whole. Whether they are street sweepers or managers of great buildings, there is mutual respect for human life and each other. These people were not so involved with themselves and their personal considerations that they could not think of the collective good.

In terms that I consider spiritual, they worked for the sake of work, not for the fruit of the action. In our society, those on the spiritual path work hard to attain this level of selflessness. China, by virtue of its political system and the reality of overpopulation, has already attained it. On a concrete daily basis, selflessness manifests itself in Chinese society. I was cognizant of this and appreciative of it.

In the West, we see things differently. We believe the individual is the most important element. Individual free choice is the basis of our value system. We look at social selflessness as the suppression of human individuality.

This is a difficult and complex concept, impossible to understand unless we are exposed to the reality of cooperative Chinese living and unless we are willing and able to see it from their point of view. The concept is complicated further by the fact that so much has happened since 1978, including the 1989 student massacre in Tiananmen Square, in which the ugly part of totalitarianism revealed itself for all to see.

Back in 1978, I was not viewing it that way. I saw people who were happy and gratified to be on a winning team. They were winning the battle for daily life. Before the revolution of the 1940s, when Mao came to power, they had a chaotic society. A few rich landlords owned virtually everything, and millions of people suffered in poverty. When I visited, the Chinese people looked back at prerevolution times and felt good about what they had accomplished during their thirty years of hard work. Compared to the West, they were still poor, but now, after Mao's economic reforms, their poverty was not ugly and dirty and hopeless. They had pride and purpose. Each individual played a role in helping the whole society lift itself up by its bootstraps.

We have been conditioned to believe that individuality is most important. And yet, in our society, if an individual shows talent for music or sports, he or she is rarely given the proper support to develop those abilities. In China, a talented musician or athlete receives support. The country believes that if society develops the talent of individuals, then all of society will benefit—and they are right. This is something that we in the West could learn.

We have the freedom to choose whatever we want in the West—but what do we want? What are we supposed to choose? The only time I ever saw my father sad was when he said, "I never found out what I really should do in life." Many, many people never find that out; or they want to be a musician or an athlete, but they don't have the talent. What good is freedom of choice for them?

The real problem comes when a person has the talent and desire but doesn't have the money to pursue his or her natural direction. Athletes have to rely on donations before they can compete in the Olympics. Most musicians have to work day gigs to support themselves. China does not have these problems. They encourage and develop talent wherever they find it—all of which helps their total society grow and improve.

This is not a black-and-white issue. I have not been able to think in black-and-white terms for many years. Every system has its good and bad parts. In dealing with its enormous population, China has evolved a system of non-Russian Communism that has enabled its people to survive. To me, it is more humane and evolutionary to think in terms of all of us, rather than in terms of self-interest alone. I am sure they do not consciously say to themselves, "We live by spiritual values," but through necessity—overpopulation, in particular—they have devised a system of selfless cooperation that, in essence, is deeply spiritual.

We can intellectualize and rationalize all we want. My analytical mind says they are living spiritual lives. Their probably nonanalytical mind would deny it. Recognizing and honoring it intellectually is beside the point. The point of the spiritual life is to incorporate spiritual values into daily life, feeling happier and more purposeful because of it. The China I saw in 1978 was doing this.

When you embark upon the spiritual path, you may begin as an intellectual who has a million questions. But as you venture deeply within yourself, exploring your psyche and your soul, you come out the other end of the tunnel an aware person. It is an entirely nonintellectual process. You are changed, and your daily thoughts and actions reflect this change. You have left the intellectual orientation behind. You are back like a child again—innocent, pure, open to life, taking each moment as it comes. You have shed intellectual complexities, and life is simple once more. Such a person is in a state of cosmic consciousness or enlightenment. An enlightened person is a simple person.

In China, these people had not gone through the process. In this sense, they were not enlightened. And they were living the lives they had been taught to live since birth. In this sense, they were not conscious. But as an observer, I saw them as truly spiritual people. They were innocent. They had a lightness of being. They had few material comforts, and no material values, and yet they felt fulfilled in life through their interactions with each other. They worked hard every day and felt satisfied and happy with the work itself and with the purpose of the work—which was to help society as a whole. We don't usually talk about spiritual matters in these terms, but China gave me an opportunity to think about these things in new and different ways.

We completed a thirty-minute documentary entitled "Paul Horn in China." It was coproduced by me and Fran and Peter Mellen and shown on the CBC network in Canada, and on PBS in the United States. It was an honest and factual documentary, with no compromises, showing the wonderful connection that took place through the universal language of music.

MY SECOND TRIP TO CHINA

It was exciting to return to China in 1982, not as part of a tour group, but as part of a $1.5 million television special, the first coproduction between American and Chinese television companies.

The special was called "Cycling through China." The American producers were from Portland, Oregon, and the premise was both fascinating and appealing. We would bicycle around the Guangdong province in the south, near Guangzhou (formerly called Canton), shooting footage of the land, the towns, and the people.

The Chinese wanted to know about us, and we wanted to know about them, but the language barrier was too much. The producers believed the barrier could be transcended through the creative arts and athletics. So they selected several stars, including Kate Jackson, Ben Vereen, Lorne Greene, Joe Cunningham (formerly one of the Harlem Globetrotters), a magician, and a pantomimist. I played flute. My son Robin brought his drums. As singers, dancers, actors, magicians, athletes, and musicians, we would communicate with the people through our various performances, winding up with a big concert at the Sun Yat Sen Memorial outdoor park in Canton.

The producers drew up schedules showing where we should be, how far each village was from the next, and for three weeks we bicycled from town to town, sometimes fifty miles or more. If people wanted to ride fifty miles, that was fine. But those of us who weren't quite in shape for a ride like that piled our bikes into a truck. We rode a bus part of the way, then stopped twenty miles outside of town, took our bikes off the truck, and pedaled the remaining distance.

You could easily separate the film people from ordinary Chinese because we all had beautiful ten-speed bicycles, with red saddlebags on the sides. You saw us coming a mile away. Individual bikes had our names on them and were given to us to keep. No one in China has a ten-speed bicycle with gears to shift. Instead, they have no-speed bicycles, requiring just hard, steady pedaling.

Whenever we wanted, we stopped in little village cafés and sat down and enjoyed a beer or a soft drink. Or we stopped by the side of the road and talked to farmers plowing their fields. We exchanged cigarettes with them or gave them a postcard or some other gift from America that we carried for such occasions. Our Polaroid cameras were the biggest hit because we could take pictures and give them to the people right there. These experiences were usually for our own pleasure, not always part of the film.

Sometimes, through advance scouting, the director knew of a picturesque place ahead. He'd say, "When you get to the bridge about ten miles up the road, stop and wait. We are setting up cameras, and we want to film you from a distance going over it."

The southern provinces are beautiful, just like in the paintings, with tall mountains rising up between hazy layers of clouds and bonsai trees. We saw pagodas and temples and gazebos and lovely lakes and hills. Between the scenery and contacts with the people, we made a wonderful film.

We experienced many nice things in our visits to communes, especially in one containing 60,000 people. We had a lot of fun that day because we played a basketball game.

It was set up as a game between China and the United States. Former Globetrotter Joe Cunningham went over to the Chinese side. He is 6'7" tall. All he had to do was stand under the net and stick up his hand, and the ball went in every time. The people loved that.

I had fun when the game started, because I had to jump against Joe, who is a full foot taller. Of course, we did a big comedy act, where he held the ball up as far as he could, his right arm stretched high, and I jumped up and down like a little kid. No way in the world was I going to touch that ball. It was cute and fun. Kate Jackson, Ben Vereen, Robin, and all of the other film people played, too.

After the game, we gathered around in a little dirt area, and I played flute for the people. We had a little Cassio keyboard piano, almost a toy, but it worked well, and we improvised. Robin brought his brushes and played on pots and pans, keeping the rhythm going. The situation did not demand highly technical equipment, and in no way did the primitive conditions prevent us from enjoying ourselves. The whole purpose of this journey was to make contact with the people. We wanted to be friends, to show them that there are good people and good things in the West, even as they showed us there are good people and good things in the East.

The last full feature I scored was our one-hour special called "Cycling through China." I was also one of the featured performers on camera, along with Ben, Kate, and Lorne.

Scoring music for films opened a lot of doors. When I began to get calls to score films, I had to learn how to time things out with click-tracks. Fred Katz helped me, and so did the music editors on the various films. In 1958 I scored three animated cartoon series for TV, with fifty-two episodes each. They were "Clutch Cargo," "Moon Mullins," and "The New Three Stooges."

Next came a full-length feature film called *Ballad of a Bad Man*. Allyn Ferguson and I split the writing chores. I did some commercials for Carnation Milk and Diet-Rite Cola, a Father's Day spot, a half-hour Oregon coastline promotional film for Air West, and several series for Wolper Productions, including my own half-hour special documentary *Story of a Jazz Musician*.

The most creative times were scoring some films with my quintet, totally improvised. The writing continued when I moved to Canada, with several films for the National Film Board of Canada and a documentary promotional film for the British Columbia government, called "Island Eden," about Vancouver Island, where I live. It won the Cindy Award for best film music in that category. I also wrote a full-length feature for a movie called *Hard Feelings*, produced in Montreal, directed by Daryl Duke.

CHANGES IN CHINA

A lot of changes had taken place in China during the four years since my previous visit. Mao was still the hero in 1978, but by 1982 his presence was hardly felt. The giant forty-foot blow-up photographs of him in Beijing's Tiananmen Square had been taken down. Mao was no longer deified, and with the inevitability of change, his era had passed and a new system had been installed.

Unfortunately, newspapers, radio, and television ignored the positive elements of the new society and presented to the West only its suppressive aspects. It feels quite different when you are actually there, able to experience the culture and the people for yourself.

We live in a free enterprise system and think it's great. Does that mean everybody should live in a free enterprise system? Does that mean anyone who does not live in a free enterprise system is either a bad guy or a failure?

In my opinion, whatever system works best for people in any given area at any given time must be right for them. Instead of condemning China or any other country for doing things that are contrary to Western thinking, we should grow in our consciousness that we live in a world society, not just a Western society. At least we might acknowledge the right of people to live under systems different from ours as long as it does not threaten us. Can we do it? That is the big question.

I don't see how free enterprise can flourish in China. How can one billion people who have no money start a free enterprise system? Nevertheless, they are trying, at least to a degree, and great problems have already arisen. They've opened Pandora's box.

Coca Cola arrived. So did Sony Walkman. Television antennas decorated the rooftops. People wore colorful clothes. Citizens had become aware of material things, and they wanted them. To get them, they needed more money. Because people needed money, the government expanded its role.

They created a modest form of free enterprise, still under government control. During the week, you sold vegetables or shoes for the state, but on weekends you worked and could keep the money yourself. In this way, people who were more ambitious could make more money in socially and politically approved ways.

What about people who are not so ambitious? How do they acquire money enough for a new color TV? They need jobs. If everything is not controlled by the government, then one billion people compete for jobs, which creates unemployment. When people want things, but they don't have money or jobs, they steal. Indeed, by 1982, China's crime rate had increased significantly. They experienced Pandora's box.

Television itself created problems. Hong Kong imported and aired many American shows, and Chinese people now had TV sets to receive them. As a result, they watched the violence, robberies, drugs, sadism, degradation, sleaze, and brutality that we in America so dearly love. People in China began to see how crime earns a lot of money, which provides luxuries. A flood of violent images was unleashed upon an innocent society that was unable to understand its implications. Television was changing them. The government quickly perceived this and became more selective in what it allowed people to see.

Once again, this is totally contrary to our way of thinking. We take offense if anyone tries to control what we watch. And yet, if we consider what China's needs and goals are as a society, it makes perfect sense. It is not so horrible when their government prohibits certain socially destructive programs. What *is* horrible is allowing that hideous violence in too quickly. It is dangerous because people can't handle it; everyone goes crazy, and social cohesion, which they need, begins to disintegrate. In 1982 this was happening—TV had arrived, and the government was learning how to cope with it.

The main difference I saw in China during this second trip was the tremendous growth that had taken place, particularly in Guangzhou-Canton, the most liberal city in China, only an hour away from Hong Kong, a world trade center still owned by the British in 1982. Hong Kong did a tremendous volume of business, and its dense population easily spilled over into Canton, influencing everything.

In an effort to accommodate the tremendous number of people visiting China, many of whom wanted to establish businesses there, Canton had become a hustling, bustling city. Huge hotels were under construction, and consumer goods appeared in the marketplace—Coca Cola, more stylish clothes, appliances, TV, and so forth. Energetic excitement permeated the air. Something new was happening—growth, expansion, luxury. The government and the people hoped they could handle it well. I could see they were having difficulty dealing with what little had come in already. Hope and confusion teetered in precarious balance.

It's true that China has problems. They must feed, house, clothe, and clean up after a billion people every day. We can't look at this casually and say, "Give these people freedom." As I pointed out above, they already have many freedoms that we don't have, and Communism works for these people. Just surviving from day to day, moving this huge population along, is an enormous accomplishment. They found a way to do it, and that way is through their interpretation of the Communist system, which is communal living, emphasizing collective values over individuality. When we broadly and casually say, "We have freedom and they don't," we are making a gross and ridiculously immature overstatement. Their system is significantly different from ours because their needs are different, and yet we judge them for it. We cannot continue doing that.

The world is changing so rapidly that every political system on the face of the earth is obsolete. The only way we can grow into the next evolutionary stage is to think in global terms—eradicate borders; establish one standardized currency; develop free trade in a world economy; deal cooperatively with environmental problems, space exploration, poverty, hunger, and AIDS; set up an interlinking, one-world government, perhaps by turning the United Nations into an effective organization that is inclusive rather than exclusive.

These and many other things are not impossible. America began as a group of separate states. It became the *United* States. Europe is in the process of doing the same thing, of becoming the *United* States of Europe. Throughout industrialized countries, especially in America and Europe, the concept of world unity and world cooperation is gaining momentum by leaps and bounds.

Whether we are American, Russian, Chinese, or any other nationality, we cannot continue passing judgment on each other, condemning other countries because they don't do what we do. For the world's survival, we *must* learn how to think in global terms. This means the sacrifice of old, outmoded, and obviously destructive ways of thinking. We have to let go of nationalistic attachments and learn to think of ourselves as global citizens. World survival depends upon it.

COMING TOGETHER WITH THE CHINESE

Before Mao came to power in the late 1940s, a fellow named Sun Yat Sen was one of China's heroes. In Guangzhou, the Sun Yat Sen Memorial Park was named after him. Within the park there was a huge building with a blue tile roof, designed in the Chinese style, of course. Outdoors in front of the building, they set up a stage for our final performance. The park could easily hold thousands of people.

It was a cloudy day, overcast and drizzling. What were we to do? If it rained, our performance would have to be canceled. The show was too big to be held elsewhere on such short notice.

We had to bring in extra generators for this production. We needed enormous outputs of electricity. We had a sixteen-track recording board and hundreds of lights for filming and stage effects. Fuses blew out continually. So did our electric pianos and synthesizers. The rain threatened for several hours—and then came down in torrents. Our whole film led up to this production. For the first time in many generations, a major Western concert was going to be performed for the Chinese people—and now it looked like the concert would be rained out and our film would lack its grand finale.

Producer Charles Jennings came to me backstage. Like the rest of us, he felt depressed. "My God, what can we do?" he said.

"All we can do is surrender, Charles. It's in the hands of the Almighty, completely out of our control. We don't know if the rain will stop in time for the performance, so why don't we just be quiet. Let's meditate a while and hope for the best."

We could postpone the show until 2:30 that afternoon, but if we had to wait longer, we wouldn't be able to get everything in. Lo and behold, the rain stopped at two o'clock. Each one of us grabbed a mop or a towel and cleaned up the stage, getting it dry. At 2:30 we went out and began our performances.

We did not charge admission. People could come in free. Chinese officials were reluctant to have a free show, afraid so many people would attend—perhaps 20,000—that it would be impossible to control them. The rain drove many people away. By 2:30, perhaps 7,000 remained, still a lot of people, but the officials relaxed. The show could go on. That rain was a blessing in disguise.

Chinese and American performers entertained each other. The Chinese featured balancing acts, musicians, acrobats, and jugglers, and they did a big dance with a dragon and a lion. Then Ben Vereen danced and sang. I came out and played flute. The pantomimist did an ad lib bit with the audience, which was cute and fun. The magician did his tricks. Lorne Greene was the emcee.

It was a wonderful performance, and it came out well on film. It showed once again how two countries with totally different ideologies and life-styles can come together easily and effectively through art and entertainment.

We hoped that a two-hour special would be picked up by one of the three major networks. For whatever reasons—which nobody can fathom —this did not happen. A one-hour version was sold and shown on the Disney channel. This was primarily an entertainment version. The two-hour version contained many segments of personal on-camera interviews of us speaking about the many positive experiences and observations we were having. Perhaps it was not yet time for the American public to see and accept this.

If you let people alone, they are wonderful. Everywhere in the world, we have so much in common. All of us want to be happy in life. All of us want to protect our families. All of us want to avoid war. We want to live in peace. We want to laugh rather than cry, to be happy rather than sad. We want proper food and shelter. We want to avoid the hurts and enjoy our pleasures. These and many other things are common to people in every country, state, city, and town.

When people from different countries are given the chance to meet each other, they want to. They are curious about each other. They want to know how life is in China or India or Russia or America. As human beings, we want to share the ways we see things, the ways we live and love and work.

As performing artists, we felt we could overcome any and all barriers, and we did. The Chinese people related to every one of us. They loved Ben Vereen's singing and dancing. They loved my flute playing. They loved Joe Cunningham and his athletic tricks, juggling the ball around, doing crazy and wonderful and funny things with it. They loved the pantomimist and the magician. We brought to China a universal language on many levels, and the communication we experienced was so meaningful and deep that it brought tears to our eyes many times.

It was almost as if it had been too much to bear our separation for so long. The differences between us have been built up and perpetuated to the point of fear. And yet, when people get together, not as political representatives with vested interests, but simply as living, breathing human beings, there is so much joy and fun, so much childlike play and curiosity, that you cry for the sadness of what has been happening on this pain-racked planet of ours. Political bullshit—and that's exactly what it is—stands in complete contradiction to natural human tendencies and needs and desires.

We all felt this in our own way. Joe Cunningham wrote a fine poem, beautifully expressing the sentiments just described. Ben Vereen was visibly moved when Joe read it, as were Kate Jackson and Lorne Greene. All of us felt deeply touched.

In 1978 and again in 1982, I saw China at a time when it was still relatively innocent. It retained evidence of the culture they had been experimenting and living with for thirty years. On both trips, wherever we went, it seemed to me that a real sense of fulfillment and accomplishment showed on people's faces. They were part of a team that was winning the battle for survival. They were making headway, and they were rightfully proud of what they had accomplished.

SIXTEEN

INSIDE RUSSIA

I've made four trips to the USSR, and as I look back, I see a country very different from ours. From a Western viewpoint, we see things there that are impossible to agree with. On the other hand, if we remain open-minded, we will see much that is good. The relationship between our two countries is not a black-and-white matter of the "Evil Empire" versus the "Good Guys." A rational mind would never perceive the situation so simplistically. The USSR is a complex country. It is constructive for us to focus on the elements we share in common.

Time will tell whether or not Gorbachev will be able to bring about change. However, as the saying goes, "When the student is ready, the master appears." Russia is now ready. And there is Gorbachev. I don't think he could or would have come to power ten or fifteen years ago. The country was just not ready. Now let's see if he can survive.

Back in 1983, our country wasn't ready either. When I returned that year from the USSR, I had hopes of appearing on a lot of talk shows. In the past, I had been on Johnny Carson's "Tonight Show," "Good Morning, America," and "The Today Show." I figured they would want to talk with me about my Russian experiences, and I thought *Time* and *People* magazine would be interested, too.

This was not just an ego trip or a career move on my part. I saw a lot of things over there that were different from what I had read about and unlike what we already knew. I wanted to talk about some of them and let people know what was going on over there.

However, just as I returned, the Soviets shot down the Korean jetliner. Now nobody wanted to hear *anything* good about Russia. That incident blew it all. Needless to say, I was frustrated and disappointed.

Instead of signing me up for the talk shows, the networks had Ronald Reagan out there saying, "Evil Empire, Evil Empire. How could they do such a thing? See how inhuman they are? They shot down a plane that carried civilians. We're dealing with a monster."

With all of that crap stirred up again, the public was certainly not ready to hear me come back and say, "Well, the Russians aren't *all* bad. I was just over there. I think we can utilize music as a universal language to help us get together."

People would have loved to hear me talk about policies and situations I did not agree with. I could have done that, but I wanted to say a few nice things, too. I wanted to raise people's consciousness a bit, to see if I could help our countries heal a few wounds. But I didn't get a chance to do that.

When I took my first two trips to the Soviet Union—originally in 1976 with Tryntje and my two sons, then in 1983 with a band—I saw a lot that was fundamentally wrong. If those things had continued without changing, Russia would have come to the point of revolution. The younger generation simply would not have continued to buy the government's line, and they would have rebelled. Witness the current proof of this prophecy in the Baltic states and Armenia.

However, by the time I took my third trip, in 1987, and my fourth trip, in 1988, Gorbachev had appeared on the scene. Russia and the times were ready for a man with liberal and progressive ideas. He appeared. And now Russia is moving forward. On an international political level, Gorbachev seems to be the one who offers hope for us all.

America and the Soviet Union can't go on calling each other names. Perhaps we will eventually grow up and learn how to treat each other with mutual respect. All of us are human beings. All of us have to share this planet. Both countries have enough nuclear power to blow the world up a hundred times over. You don't have to be very smart to see that we *must* treat each other with respect.

We have to shift our attitudes and perspectives. We must sit down and reason together. Both countries have to be willing to tolerate and accept our different systems of government. If their system is different from ours, so what? I would hope that we could reach the point in both of our countries where we can pick out the good and strong points of each system and make a serious and responsible effort to create a system that includes the best of both worlds.

In America, we insist that the Russian goal is to take over the world. Well, that may be in their manifesto, but in no way is it a reality. Everything the world over is in flux. Just as America is becoming more socialized, so Russia is becoming more democratic.

FIRST IMPRESSIONS

When my wife and two sons and I spent two days in Leningrad in 1976, our first impressions were not very good. "Boy, I never want to go back there," Tryntje said later. "That is one country that does not appeal to me."

From Helsinki, we took an overnight boat trip up the Baltic Sea to Leningrad. As soon as we docked in Leningrad, the captain announced that the boat was now in Soviet territory and under the control of Soviet personnel. Even though the boat was docked and going nowhere, a new Russian captain and a whole new Russian crew came on board and took over.

They made a big deal out of this, with lots of formality. They marched in step, looking very austere in their uniforms, telling us not to take photographs, supervising our every move.

We walked down a gangplank to get on a bus that would take us on a sight-seeing tour of Leningrad. A Soviet soldier stood at the bottom of the plank collecting everyone's passport. If you tried to venture out on your own and were stopped, you would have no identification. Another soldier looked down on us with binoculars from a nearby rooftop.

All day long on the tour bus, a young woman pointed out the sights, giving endless monologues on the Great Cultural Revolution, the history of Russia, with all kinds of statistics about the average worker, how great things are in the USSR, and how happy everybody is—total propaganda.

Everything in Leningrad seemed austere and drab, with very little color. No curtains were in the windows, there were hardly any flowers, and nobody wore colorful clothes. Public parks were unkempt, with a few trees and benches, sporadic grass, dirt all over the place, brown weeds— a dreary and ugly environment. We were closely supervised every step of the way.

When I returned in 1983, arriving in Moscow with my band, my initial impressions were not much better. We were shocked to see that the Soviet Union for the most part is like a Third World country. You would never think this country is a superpower. We even made jokes. "They haven't sent any rockets up into space. That's all propaganda. How can they have the technology to do that when they can't even fix a broken mike cable and the whole country is as run-down as India?"

Russia is poor. The buildings are crumbling. Even new buildings start falling apart after five years because of inferior workmanship and inferior materials. Everything is in disrepair. The roads are bumpy, with potholes all over the place. Equipment in theaters and everywhere else is antiquated. The lightbulbs don't have enough watts to light up a room properly.

The airports are dingy and dirty, even in Moscow. It's a long haul to Russia. You fly some twenty-four hours. You arrive. You're tired. You get out. You stand in line at immigration—and it takes forever.

The inspector takes a minimum of five or ten minutes to check each person. If you're on a 747, that is a lot of people and a lot of time. A Russian soldier sits behind the glass of a booth. He's in full uniform, very stiff, with his hat on.

You slip your passport under the glass. He opens it up and looks at your picture very intently. Then he raises his eyes, just his eyes, not moving his head, and looks you straight in the eye. He stares at you for maybe twenty seconds. Then he looks down at the picture again, then back up at you for another fifteen or twenty seconds.

This goes on four or five times, and pretty soon you're feeling paranoid. You haven't done anything, but you feel as if you *must* have done something because of the way he scrutinizes you, with never any smile, never any courtesy.

Once he's satisfied that you are who you say you are, then he looks through several books. Are you a criminal? Are you a spy? Finally, after all of this, you can go on.

This happens to each person, and you haven't even gone through customs yet. All they've done is check your passport. Once you get past immigration, you go into customs, where, thank God, your interpreters meet you and help you. What a way to enter a country for the first time. When you leave, it's the same thing.

The hotels weren't bad. We stayed in the Rossia Hotel, the largest hotel in the world, with over 6,000 rooms. You can get lost in it and literally spend hours walking around trying to figure out where you are. You can't ask anybody because nobody speaks English.

The government does not want people to congregate anywhere. There are very few restaurants to hang out in, and the few that do exist are usually for foreigners. The hotels have no comfortable lobbies, and guards stand at the doors. You have to show your room key to get in, and if you expect a guest, you have to come down and greet that guest personally. "It's okay," you tell the guard. "This person is with me. Here is my key." Then the person can come in.

Both Moscow and Leningrad are dreary and colorless and drab. Other than potatoes, many foods are difficult to get. Fresh vegetables and fruit are very scarce. The meat is unappetizing. In the few existing restaurants, service takes forever, and when you do manage to get a waiter, he's unsmiling, unfriendly, gruff, sullen, and sometimes hostile. Cab drivers are paid by the state, so why should they pick you up? If you want to go where they want to go, then maybe you'll get a ride. Otherwise, it's "See the guy behind me."

They don't have supermarkets over there, but they do have a few stores where you can buy several things under one roof, like bread, meat, and dairy products. However, instead of putting all of your things in a basket and checking out in one line, you have to stand in a long line just for the bread. You stand in line for fifteen minutes, get the bread, pay for it, then stand in another long line to get your meat. When you finish with that line, you stand in still another long line to get your dairy products. On and on and on. It's crazy. Everyone spends hours each day just standing in line. In the winter, it's cold, so sometimes you're freezing your butt off while you stand in line to get inside the store—where you stand in more lines to get your food.

Everything is set up and monitored in such a way that the Russian people don't really enjoy their lives very much. The environment is disintegrating, the people are suppressed, and there is little or no motivation because everybody is paid by the state.

I couldn't really figure it out, but it seemed that the government did not *want* things to be too comfortable for the people. Poor organization and public suppression may have been intentional so the government could maintain control. If people had a little more, then they might want still more. After a while, it might escalate to the point where we are in America, dominated and motivated by the sickness of greed. Just make life hard; don't make it too easy—that seemed to be the government's position.

As a result, everything was falling apart, and the system simply was not working. In fact, the system was its own worst enemy. Even in 1983, we could sense that change was inevitable—and it was. Only six years later, in 1989, six Eastern European countries dramatically abandoned the Communist system—Poland, Hungary, Bulgaria, East Germany, Czechoslovakia, and Romania. All along, Gorbachev realized that reform was absolutely necessary for survival, and in early 1990, against the fierce resistance of his own country's hard-line conservatives, he called upon the Communist party to yield its monopoly on power. He asked for multiparty political pluralism and free-market economics—radical departures from the Marxist-Leninist stance—and he succeeded in getting them. If he can remain in power, his spectacular reforms will continue to alter political and economic relationships throughout the world.

MY FIRST TOUR OF RUSSIA

When the band and I went over to Russia in 1983, none of us realized that we had embarked upon a historic journey. In the recent past, jazz musicians had to function underground. The Soviets were afraid of jazz because jazz represents the epitome of individual expression, something alien to the Soviet system. However, the tide of the underground was rising, and people who wanted to play jazz and those who wanted to listen to it in public were growing in numbers. Apparently the government figured, "Well, it's not worth having a revolution over jazz. Let's give in on this point and still keep control."

John Cripton, a concert promoter and agent in Ottowa, Canada, had gained the respect and trust of the Soviets because he handled all of the ballet companies, symphony orchestras, circuses, and other Russian entertainers who came through Canada. Now, for the first time, the Russians asked Cripton to send some Canadian groups over to the Soviet Union.

That's how we came into the picture. We were the first group Cripton booked. Although we were handled through Canada, all of us had American passports and considered ourselves to be an American group.

Our 1983 visit opened the crack that we today call *glasnost*, or openness. That crack has widened immeasurably since then. Soviet jazz musicologist Vladimir Feyertag told me it had been fifty-six years since an American small jazz group had gone onstage and played for a public Soviet audience in Moscow and Leningrad. Nobody had done it since Sidney Bechet in 1927.

Other groups had in fact gone over through the State Department's cultural exchange program, but the tragedy of it—and a little-known fact to the American people—is that those groups for the most part never played for the Russian public. At the U.S. taxpayers' expense, they went over and played for maybe five hundred people, which included employees and their families of the American embassy. The audiences were Americans, and the concerts took place in the American embassy. The Russian *people* never got to hear a note. The same situation existed in the Canadian embassy.

In this band, John Stowell played guitar. David Friesen was on bass. My son Robin played drums. We did eighteen concerts in four different cities—Moscow and Leningrad, and then Vilnius and Kaunas, in Lithuania (once a part of Poland). These were not one-nighters. Instead, we played eight nights in a row in the State Concert Theater in Moscow, six nights in a row in Leningrad, and two nights apiece in Vilnius and Kaunas. We didn't have to pack up, tear down, travel, and set up all the time. Beautiful.

All the halls we played filled up every night. Jazz was so fresh and new that people turned out in droves. Here's a jazz group playing a 3,000-seat hall eight nights in a row, selling out every night. That doesn't happen in the States, not for Miles Davis or anybody else. There might have been a few jazz fans, but certainly not 24,000. When we looked out into the audiences, we saw a true cross section—young, old, and middle-aged. Most of them had never heard a jazz concert, and they really went for it.

As I did with Sauter-Finegan and Chico Hamilton and with all of my own groups, we played a wide variety of material, everything from classical music to jazz, ranging from standards like "Summertime" to blues and original compositions, and from up-tempo tunes to ballads.

John Stowell is a unique guitarist, and I love the way he plays. David Friesen, a wonderful bassist, is unique too. They both approach their instruments differently than anybody else, something I appreciate because I greatly respect uniqueness and individuality. I watched my twenty-three-year-old son Robin with detached admiration. I expected him to play well, and he did.

I've tried to put myself in Robin's place—playing with experienced, mature musicians who were twice as old. I'm in another country on the other side of the world, a strange country, Russia, and we are one of the first groups to play there in public in two generations. There are 3,000 people out there, and this kid's playing well. I've got a lot of respect for that. It takes guts. I myself couldn't have done it. When I was his age, I could not have come up to that kind of test. I was twenty-six when I went with Chico. The guys were a little closer to my age, and I had had a little more experience than Robin. My situation was not nearly as extreme as his. As the concert tour went on, I watched him grow stronger and stronger. That was really nice to see, and I am proud of him.

The Soviets are more reserved as an audience than Westerners. Instead of yelling and whistling, they clapped in unison, the equivalent of our standing ovation. When they do that, it sets up a thunderous vibration that makes you think the walls will topple down.

Many people bring flowers to the concerts. If they like what you're doing, they give them to you. If they don't like what they hear, they take the flowers home and put them in a vase. They don't wait until the end of the concert before they give the flowers to you. After any number, if they liked it, or if they liked a particular soloist, people come right up onstage and present the flowers to individual members of the group. Sometimes that takes five minutes. When that happens, you know they really liked the last number you played.

I remember how strange it was to see a beautiful young lady emerge as if from another world out of the spotlight shining in my face, to see her present me with a lovely bouquet, give me a kiss, and then disappear back into the spotlight. Was I dreaming? If at the end of the concert the stage looked like a flower shop, you knew it had been one hell of a performance.

Even as we played, people brought old albums of mine right up onstage and asked me to autograph them. Where they obtained those recordings remains a mystery to me.

And that's the way it was most nights for us. That kind of warmth was overwhelming. It also stood in stark contrast to some of the extremely restrictive aspects of their society. That whole tour was a real eye-opener.

For example, when people wanted to come backstage and talk, nobody would let them through. So I purposely walked out onstage after the concert, in case some people wanted to talk. The ushers quickly broke up any kind of gathering.

Vladimir Feyertag traveled with us. Every night before we played, he talked for five minutes, giving some background and information about jazz and improvisation and me. Each night during a certain part of his monologue, the audience applauded when he spoke about my trip to India and my involvement with meditation. That was a mindblower!

Also, many of the kids who came down to the front of the stage after the performance greeted me in Indian fashion. They put their hands together in front, made a little bow, and said, "Namasté," which means "My soul and your soul are one," each hand representing one soul touching the other as one. Where they found out about this, I don't know.

One night, a group of kids was asking me about India and meditation, among them, a woman violinist who wanted to study jazz in America. She wanted to know if I could recommend any teachers. Immediately, an usher came on with, "No, no—you must go now." Everybody had to leave. One girl said to me as she was going, "Stay free and be happy."

I thought that was an incredible statement because she put those particular two things together—stay free, and be happy with your freedom. In America, we have many freedoms that so many other parts of this world do not have—freedom of the press, freedom to express ourselves, freedom of choice. However, we are not necessarily happy with our freedoms. As a matter of fact, I see a lot of unhappiness—psychotic crime, broken homes, the desperate need for psychiatric treatment, the frantic race for riches. The list goes on, and it shouldn't. Why, in spite of all we have, are we so unhappy?

Material acquisition does not automatically bring happiness, that's why. The only thing that brings happiness is spiritual awareness. We are finally beginning to realize this, and we are finally beginning to grow in that direction.

In the USSR that idea became clear to me when the girl said, "Stay free and be happy." She did not just say, "Stay free," which would have been a political remark. She said, "Stay free—and be happy." Everybody in the band remembered that one.

An interpreter of ours was interested in meditation. As we walked around town or rode the buses or the trains, she asked questions, and I explained things to her. After a while, she said, "Can you teach me?" I said I could, and I initiated her in a Leningrad hotel room—she became the first and only person I taught in Russia. If she's still doing it, there is at least one meditator in Russia.

Quite often, Russian people said to me, "Why are you trying to annihilate us?"

I replied, "When you say 'you,' are you talking about me? I don't want to annihilate you. I think I'm fairly representative of average Americans, and they don't want to come over and annihilate you, either.

"If you want to know the truth, I don't think either of our governments is leveling with us. I didn't come over here to convince anyone about my system of government. I came over just to play some music and meet you. I'm enjoying what I am seeing. I'm enjoying playing the music. And I'm enjoying meeting you."

That satisfied their questions, and from then on we were just human beings, sharing the planet together, drinking a little vodka, eating some dinner, laughing a lot, playing some music, having a good time people-to-people. Simple.

We in America have not built up a fair image of Russia, any more than they have built up a fair image of us. It's really been criminal deceit on the part of both governments. These people in powerful positions walk around in three-piece suits, very dignified, and we say, "Yes, sir," and think they are our noble leaders. *That* is frightening.

I get very emotional when it comes to this, because these leaders are criminals—high criminals. They incite the human race to fight against itself. They cause fear. They cause hate. Just for their own self-interest and political power, they place us on the brink of complete and total destruction. This sort of thing is the highest, most heinous crime I can imagine.

But when you meet the people face-to-face, you find out that the realities are vastly different. We were blown away by that tour. It really opened our eyes. We had great receptions and great experiences in each town, and we heard a lot of Russian musicians.

One example comes immediately to mind. There's a wonderful musician in Leningrad named David Goloshchenkin. He plays violin and flugelhorn and several other instruments, all of them well. His wife sings—just like Ella Fitzgerald—and her name happens to be Ella. They go out as a team and play concerts.

Russia had just begun to allow musicians to play jazz for a living. Their job is to be full-time jazz musicians, and they are paid by the state. They don't have to look for a day gig. All they have to do is play jazz, and they are guaranteed a living. From an American musician's point of view, that is a hell of a good deal.

As Dave and Ella explained it, the government can demand that you perform up to eighteen concerts a month. In some months, you may play only two or three, in other months none, and you still get paid the same amount. You also get one month's paid vacation each year.

For rent, Dave and Ella paid only about fifty dollars a month for a good-sized two-bedroom apartment. Their rent is only about 5 percent of their income. In America, rent is getting close to 50 percent.

Low rents, guaranteed income, state support for the arts, total medical protection for everybody, including foreigners like us—to me, these were among the many positive things we found out about over there. Not everybody in Russia is dying to get out of that country. And the musicians we met were not all unhappy.

But it's a strange country, too. The average wage, for example, is 140 rubles a month, with a laborer making the same as a doctor, except in Donetsk, a large coal-mining town, where a worker makes *twice* as much as a doctor.

It's a paradoxical country. People have so little over there, but they can't give you enough. When David and Ella invited us over to dinner, we drank a couple of bottles of vodka. That vodka represented one week's pay, which they blew in a single night on some foreign musicians having dinner with them—and they did it with smiles on their faces, never thinking about the hardship.

They and other people we met couldn't give enough. I came back with tons of records people gave me. Folks took paintings off the walls of their homes and gave them to us. Clothes, jewelry, anything—they just wanted to give, give, give.

We were the first American jazz group to have an album recorded in Russia and released on their Melodia label. They recorded every concert we played in Moscow—eight in all—and gave the album a strange title, *Paul Horn: Jazz Compositions*, released in Russia only.

We didn't know Melodia was going to record us, so I brought along a recording engineer from Vancouver and a Sony PCM-Fl portable digital recorder. We taped all eighteen concerts, selected at least one track from each of the four cities we played in, and released *Live from Russia, with Love* on my own Golden Flute label.

I also managed to find a place where I could do another solo flute recording for my "Inside" series.

There are many churches in Vilnius, Lithuania. During the day, we had a lot of free time, so we walked around and visited some of these churches, which then were no longer functional as places of worship. For some time now, Russia has not been religiously oriented. Most of their churches, including this one in Vilnius, have in fact become museums.

In this church, they had enclosed a number of artifacts in glass cases, things like religious clothes and ceremonial objects from past eras. It was a beautiful church, with gorgeous stained-glass windows, a big dome, and a fine sound. I clapped my hands and whistled, listening to the echoes.

A nice-looking blond man in his early thirties came out. His name was Eugene Ivaskevicius. He spoke a little English, which was good, because our interpreters were not with us. I asked him if I could play my flute in there. He looked at me very closely.

"Tell me," he said. "Are you the one who did that recording in the Taj Mahal?"

Amazing. He knew about me in Lithuania. You don't find that album in just any local store over there.

"You want to do another recording like that here?" he asked.

"Maybe. Is it possible?"

"Yes. Come tomorrow morning at nine o'clock. We open to the public at eleven."

We did that, but early morning sounds got in the way. Workers suddenly opened and closed doors. We heard the echoes and had to stop recording. Or somebody would walk on the hard floor, and we would have to stop again. Eugene understood. "Come at night," he said, "and I will open the place for you."

"This is our last night. We're playing our final concert, in Kaunas, 100 miles away. We could drive back here by midnight. Would that be too late for you?"

No problem. He was a beautiful guy. We finished our concert, drove the hundred miles, and arrived at midnight. The cathedral was silent; there were no disturbances. I'm sure Eugene wanted to sit there and watch us, but he was sensitive; he stayed in back where I didn't see him and allowed me to have my space for playing.

The recording came out well, a beautiful sound. It differed from the other "Inside" solo recordings because in addition to flute, I played soprano saxophone and bass flute. I originally called the album *Inside Russia*, but Eckart Rahn of Celestial Harmonies changed it to *Inside the Cathedral*.

The day after I recorded in the Vilnius church, David Friesen, my bassist, said, "Do you know what kind of church that was?" No, I didn't. "It's an agnostic church. It's not even a real church. It's a museum."

David is a spiritual person, along Christian lines, and he was very upset. We had a big discussion about this matter.

"The search for God and the realization of the God within has nothing to do with a physical structure such as a church," I said. "In the West, we put a lot of emphasis on attending church, but we are also very hypocritical. We go to church on Sunday, but the rest of the week we spend our lives in ways that directly contradict what the sermons talk about."

"Yes," said David, "but they are still teaching kids that religion is bad."

"Perhaps the Soviets have realized something that coincides with my own personal view," I replied. "Organized religions have divided humankind. My feeling is that they have not succeeded in realizing the goals set forth at the beginnings of any religion."

I told David how I felt about such enlightened teachers as Jesus, Moses, Mohammed, Buddha, or even Maharishi, and how they have revealed their visions to us. Organized religions came along later and inevitably distorted their messages because it is difficult to hold on to the truth as the years pass by. It has always been this way. As a result, the truth of enlightened masters becomes fragmented and diluted, and a rigid dogma is established by the now-organized religious hierarchy.

We talked about how hierarchies and dogma lead to religious conflicts, which lead to wars and to the madness and horror of the "Holy" Crusades and the "Holy" Inquisition, which say, "I'm right. You're wrong. I want to convert you or kill you." It becomes an endless battle, and humankind is divided. In this kind of thinking, we fail to realize that there is only one Creator. Maybe this reasoning is at the bottom of Russia's decision not to have organized religion, I suggested. It may have nothing to do with "They're atheists" or "They're anti-God."

"Personally," I said, "I can't believe that a different God made Christians than made Jews or Muslims. I think in universal terms. I can't isolate and separate these things. Maybe that's what they are teaching the kids.

"Aside from all that, the Vilnius cathedral was a structure for me to record in, and it had nothing to do with religious terms as far as I am concerned. There was a nice feeling in there, and a fine echo—and we got an excellent recording out of it. That's where it is for me."

It was a good conversation. We often jump back and forth, jostling each other on this issue. He's a spiritual man in his way, and I respect that.

1987: DANCING IN THE AISLES

At the end of our 1983 tour, we were invited to return in the spring of 1986 for a more extensive tour. However, the nuclear disaster at Chernobyl forced us to cancel. It was one of the most painful disappointments of my life.

Then in 1987 I got a call from the Soviet-American Dialogue, a group of citizens in Bellingham, Washington, who have an ongoing dialogue with a citizen group in Moscow called the Peace Committee.

The Soviet-American Dialogue group wanted me to participate in their own exchange program; they could pay no fee but would cover expenses.

The idea was to have me, Dianne Reeves, Kris Kristofferson, some TV people, film producers, film directors, and visual artists get together in Moscow with our Soviet counterparts. We would get to know each other and explore programs we might conceive and pursue jointly. Some performing would be involved, but not a lot. Steven Halpern joined us, too.

Our meeting with the Russian musicians was really interesting. On their side of the table sat some high-powered people—the head of the Moscow Conservatory, one of the great Soviet concert pianists, several music professors, and a number of top modern classical composers. On our side sat Dianne Reeves, Steven Halpern, and myself. Kris had not arrived yet.

At first, the Russians talked only about how much better their system is for the arts. I couldn't deny that. It *is* a better system. Artists are totally supported, and that is wonderful.

But then we countered with, "Don't you think it's time we get on with it and begin to explore the things we have in common? How can we demonstrate to both countries the elements that unite us?"

Once we established that tone, the discussions became positive and productive. Maybe we could do individual concerts in each country. Perhaps we could put together concerts of classical string quartets or jazz groups, combining musicians from both countries. Possibly Soviet and American motion picture people could pool their talents and do projects together, funded by both countries. We also discussed ways that we as artists could utilize the media to help create an atmosphere of understanding and respect, which would help both countries change the images we have of each other.

We played concerts together, too. One took place in the Composers' Guild, which seated about five hundred people. Kris was not there. Steven Halpern opened with some solo piano, then I came on and played with two Russian musicians, bassist Anatoly Sobolev and drummer Eugene Ryaboy, and with Charles Mims, Dianne Reeves's pianist from L.A. After we finished, Dianne came out and sang while our Russian-American group backed her.

Kris came for the big concert, held in a large sports arena in Moscow, which seated some five thousand people. The stage was beautifully decorated, and they had a huge curtain suspended all the way down from the ceiling—thirty or forty feet. Tiny lightbulbs formed a big circle on the curtain, with a butterfly in the center. A Soviet flag formed one wing, an American flag the other. It was a beautiful symbol, one that captured the spirit of the whole concert.

Russian and American musicians performed—jazz groups, rock bands, folk singers, and Kris Kristofferson. Kris is a nice man and very smart. He's a Rhodes scholar, but he's also down-home and straight-ahead, not a prima donna.

He felt a little shy about going out there because he sings lyrics in English. He was afraid the Russians would not understand him. However, by the time he finished his set, he had the people dancing in the aisles.

In 1983 the Soviets would not have allowed that. When the people danced in the aisles in 1987, it was an enormous contrast to the 1983 experience. In just four years, things had loosened up considerably. By now, more groups were going over to the USSR, and many groups from the Soviet Union were touring Canada and the United States. The reserve that the authorities had forced upon the audiences in 1983 was gone.

Now, people were allowed to be much freer. They jumped up on their feet, swayed back and forth to the music, and rushed the stage for me and Kris and some of the Russian groups. It was exciting to see that happen. The concert was a long one, about five hours, and a high evening for all of us. The Russians later showed the videotape all over the Soviet Union.

1988: PROBLEMS, PROBLEMS, PROBLEMS

In 1988 I took a different group over because I wanted to play a different type of music. Miles Black played keyboards, René Worst was on bass, Jim McGillveray played percussion, and Robin played drums once again.

Jazz purists will get all upset with this, but I also like playing fusion music, which is why I took this particular band with me. I don't put down Herbie Hancock, Chick Corea, Michael Brecker, or the late great Jaco Pastorius. Fusion is just another kind of music, that's all. Except for Robin, my musicians on this trip all lived in Vancouver. They looked good onstage, and they played great.

We performed twenty-two concerts from May 15 to June 13, in Moscow,

Kiev, Odessa, and Donetsk. We met some wonderful people, had some good times, and the audiences were very receptive to the music, just as they had been before.

However, I must also say that this was the most difficult tour of my life. Our problems were endless. They just never stopped.

As soon as we arrived, I knew things were different because our interpreters were not very good. Then, we had requested a truck for our equipment—a twenty-four-track soundboard, all the microphones and speakers, and all of our electronic instruments. The equipment truck had not arrived. So, after twenty-four hours' flight time and all of the hassles going through immigration, we now had to wait another two hours for the truck, and the interpreters were no help at all.

Finally we arrived at our hotel, the Minsk—and it was terrible. Reagan and Gorbachev were having their summit meeting. The New York Philharmonic Orchestra, the BBC Symphony Orchestra, the road company of "Cats," and the Harlem Dance Company were touring Russia, too. Luckily, we met someone who was able to cut through the bureaucratic red tape and get us back into the Rossia Hotel, which is where we wanted to be in the first place.

At the time of our tour, some of the *perestroika* changes were emerging, and they were causing confusion. The meeting between Reagan and Gorbachev was bringing even more confusion. And nobody in the Soviet bureaucracy was trained to make an individual decision. They hadn't learned how to deal with that kind of freedom.

The problem was one of delegation of authority. If something comes across a desk at Gosconcerts, the major Russian booking agency we had to deal with, that guy doesn't want to take responsibility for making a decision—even if it's something as simple as going outside and telling the bus driver to take us to the gig. He won't do it. He's afraid to make the decision because nobody has told him he can do that. It's just unbelievable.

My road manager, David Graham, endured frustrations that were totally above and beyond the call of duty. I didn't want to get involved with this sort of thing, but I had to. David had not been to Russia before, so I had to use my previous experience to help him. If I had not gotten involved with making phone calls, stating needs and demands, and telling bureaucrats how things should be done, the tour would have collapsed many times over.

On the positive side, we met some beautiful people from the audiences, several of whom became good friends. We also met a number of first-class musicians.

The changes in music and in the status of musicians over there represent a giant step forward in the way the Russians think today. Jazz was now accepted. Jazz musicians no longer had to play underground. Now jazz clubs existed in all the cities we visited, including Moscow. After performing our concerts, we accepted invitations from the jazz clubs, where we showed up and played with Soviet musicians. As soon as we walked in, everyone stood up and applauded. They had food for us. They gave us presents. It was amazing, even overwhelming.

The state is now loosening up and *allowing* self-expression. Gorbachev doesn't say, "Okay, guys, go ahead and form a jazz club," but he does let you know that it's okay if you do. A few jazz musicians are cherry-picked by the state and employed by the state, but jazz is also above ground now, and a lot of nonprofessional jazz musicians are coming out of the woodwork and playing just for the fun of it, working day jobs to support themselves.

Rock groups are totally new. They are touring around the country, and they are playing outside of Russia, too. Not only do they get paid, but they are allowed to share in the profits.

These young rockers are getting up there and singing lyrics like, "We don't want to be in Afghanistan. We don't want the Cold War. Instead of war, give us peace." And they are saying things like this while the KGB check out the kids in the audience and take pictures of them. The kids themselves are not intimidated at all, as kids won't ever be. They go out there like ours did in the sixties. "We've got something to say, and we're gonna say it." If necessary, they will get shot in the line of duty, the way our kids did at Kent State.

The Soviet government has opened Pandora's box. The country is exploding in many, many ways. On the one hand, there is still paranoia. On the other, the government is saying it's okay to express yourself. A real paradox. It's fascinating to see the confusion—and the progress.

In Moscow, they have three jazz clubs, one of them quite fancy. The night we showed up, a CBS film crew was in the club. Apparently, they were connected with the Reagan-Gorbachev summit, getting background material on Moscow's nightlife. They took some shots of me and the band playing with Russian musicians, and that clip wound up on the Dan Rather "Nightly News" show. This club had a photographic lab downstairs, and before we left, the photographer gave me an 18″ × 20″ color blowup of us playing onstage. They also videotaped each set and played it back during intermission. I thought these were interesting concepts, and they're happening right now on the Soviet jazz scene.

As soon as you leave the main cities, the USSR becomes more colorful. You see curtains and flowers in the windows. Parks are well kept. People wear bright and attractive clothes. The central government is less severe and less restrictive.

They have good jazz clubs in Kiev, Donetsk, and Odessa. We played six nights in Odessa, and after the first concert we met some very interesting people.

Two young women in their thirties came backstage—there were fewer restrictions about that here. The woman who spoke English said she would be honored if I would come by and visit her and her husband, both of whom were artists.

The next day, they came by our hotel and picked us up. They lived in a rather run-down and raggedy section of town, which looked like a poor part of Greenwich Village. We entered their building, a five-story walk-up. They lived on the fifth floor. The staircase was tawdry and dirty. You could smell urine in the hallways. Their apartment was right up at the top—and it was real clean. It was not her studio; it was her apartment, where she lived with her husband. There were paintings all over the walls, handmade drums, several musical instruments. These people and some of their friends were authentic Bohemians; a few of them were Rajneesh followers, complete with red-orange garb and beads.

In the past, abstract modern art had been forbidden in Russia. They tolerated only realistic, socially oriented reproductions of places, things, and people. They wanted images that glorified the Soviet system.

These particular artists and their friends worked in both areas—in spite of the dangers, they had continued to paint, not only realistic images, but abstract images as well. And now, today, many galleries are opening their doors to modern art.

Our Bohemian friends prepared lunch for us and served vodka, too. These folks were not supported by the government. They had chosen to do nothing, even though the government does not pay unemployment or welfare. If you don't do what the government tells you to do, they just say, "Okay, you don't get any money. Find your own way to live." As a result, the women went out and got regular jobs to support themselves and their artist husbands, the way many women do in America.

To me, our friends were sterling examples of people who have nothing but who give from the bottom of their hearts. That meal, complete with fresh vegetables and vodka, must have cost them two weeks' pay—and they did this a couple of times for us.

Their apartment had no running water and no heat. No bathroom, either. Off the one main room, there was a smaller room where they stored their paintings. In that room was a bucket. You did your thing in the bucket, and once a day they carried it downstairs and emptied it. To wash dishes, they had to bring fresh water upstairs by hand. But they had painted their apartment, and the place was nice and clean.

They loved to dance—Sufi dancing. And they loved jazz. They had some records, and they were into Eastern philosophy, and not just intellectually. They were meditators, and they played music and danced. Within the suppressive Soviet system, they had created their own niche and their own life-style. Instead of fighting the system or becoming depressed about it, they'd said, "We'll find a way," and they had found a way.

I asked them what they thought of *perestroika*. They said, "We hope it works. But if it hadn't been for the rigidity of our Soviet system, we would not have found what we have now. We would not have embarked upon our search to find spiritual answers."

It was easy for me to understand that, because it was my own unhappiness that had brought me to the point where it had become necessary to seek some answers. If I had been happy, I might never have found Maharishi.

I don't agree that suffering is necessary for realization, as some people think, but it can certainly be a good catalyst. It forced me to make a serious quest for answers in life. If life is too good, too smooth, you wonder if you would be motivated to go beyond that. But if you have a serious accident or a near-death experience, or if you're just plain miserable and you manage to survive and come out of it, you then have a new perspective on life. That's the way nature operates.

These people looked at the severity of the Soviet system and at the unhappiness of the people around them. Through that they were strongly motivated to seek answers, and as a result, they were beautiful, happy people. They had beautiful smiles on their faces, they didn't complain, and they lived their lives lovingly, peacefully, and joyously, painting their pictures, playing music, going to the beach, doing Sufi dancing, and reading Rajneesh (whose books were probably smuggled in via the Odessa seaport).

Wherever we played in Russia, we had large audiences, which was great, especially for jazz. When the tour was over, we went back to Moscow, took care of business, and returned home.

PROSPECTS FOR THE FUTURE

At this writing, I don't know if Gorbachev can succeed, but I am glad he is there today. Reagan, of course, wanted to take credit for leading the peace process, and Bush wants to take credit, too, but Gorbachev was and is the man who is truly doing it. He is the one leading the way and making the conciliations. He is the one who is willing to make rational and practical compromises, the one who moves forward with vision and courage. He is the one who is confronting the tough right-wing conservative challenges in his own country—ours, too—and dealing with them effectively, so far. My prayers are with him.

The Soviet Union is a superpower. It is the largest territory in the world. They have more than 400 million people. Even if you disagree with them, you can't simplistically sum them up as "the Bad Guys of the Evil Empire." They may be your opponent, so to speak, but you have to treat them as *respected* adversaries and learn how to work with them in civil, rational ways. On both sides, a lack of respect has caused a lot of problems.

The USSR has a very low crime rate. People are free to walk the streets without the fear of getting mugged. They have state-supported medical programs. People are relieved of the struggle of getting enough money to pay their hospital bills. The government pays for all education. The people can pursue their educational goals in areas where they demonstrate talent and ability.

Over here in America, we have many freedoms. But they are infringed upon almost daily. Government is gaining more and more control over individual freedoms. They've got files on almost everybody. Big Brother is watching us—it's "1984" right here in front of us. In the world marketplace, we are losing ground. Unions demand more money when there isn't any more; as the unions escalate wages, we fall further and further behind. All I'm saying is, we have to change, too.

By itself, the word "freedom" means nothing. To be totally free is to be floating around in outer space, unhooked to anything. So what does "total freedom" mean? It means nothing. In order to know what freedom truly is, you have to set parameters and limitations on it. You can give a child total freedom, but it will only feel unloved and unwanted, and it'll wind up in trouble. It is only when a child has sufficient psychological maturity that he or she can handle total freedom. Miles Davis used to talk about "controlled freedom" in music, freedom that comes with reasonable and rational limitations. Maybe we should think about controlled freedom, not only in musical terms, but in American social and political terms as well.

In our country, we are very much like an immature child. We have not grown up enough to be able to handle our freedoms with wisdom and compassion. America's freedoms are great freedoms and great gifts, as conceived by our forefathers, the men who wrote the Declaration of Independence and the Constitution. But if we do not have the psychological and spiritual maturity to handle such freedoms properly, then they can turn against us. Today, greed runs rampant, and a lot of people wind up in the streets homeless; too many people can't pay their bills; our children can't get the proper education to develop their gifts fully for the betterment of themselves and society.

It seems to me that *both* of our countries would do well to analyze in a mature and rational fashion just where we stand as we enter the twenty-first century. We need to see where our basic ideologies should be modified if they are to fit the times. We need to see clearly those things we have in common, things that are constructive and useful and relevant. Gorbachev seems willing to do that. It's important to consider whether *we* are willing to do that. If we are not, then we've got a serious problem. Right now, I think we've got a serious problem. It will get worse if we refuse to face these issues.

Politics always lags behind reality. When change takes place, it occurs first at the level of the people, not at the level of the government. Gorbachev is a good leader, but it is the people themselves who are forcing the changes. The leaders reflect the consciousness of the people.

Today in our country, we have many special groups who are trying to lead the way toward peace. I already talked about the Soviet-American Dialogue group that brought me over in 1987. Another group that is actively taking responsibility for getting things moving in a positive direction is schoolchildren.

There are lots of groups taking kids over to the USSR and bringing Soviet kids over here, and that is important because that's the time when kids should see things and have direct experiences of another country. Once it's in their minds, then when they hear all that stuff about, "That's your enemy," they can reply with conviction, "Wait a minute. I was over in Russia. I saw things for myself. I met other children my age, and they were *not* my enemies. They were my friends." In other words, kids won't buy government propaganda. Tourists go back and forth, too. There is nothing like direct contact.

As for myself, my journeys to the Soviet Union and other countries have been just as fascinating as the music. Ultimately, these experiences find their way into the music—and music is so powerful that it transcends political and ideological barriers. It touches the heart directly, helping us heal the wounds inflicted by politicians and bureaucrats. Music is a great, great power for peace. It is nonverbal. It heals. It unites people in social harmony.

Music also teaches an appreciation for variety. If we are motivated only by fear, then we cannot appreciate and enjoy our differences. When you walk into a garden that has only roses, you will soon feel bored. It is the variety of flowers that makes a beautiful garden. Roses are not better or worse than daisies or orchids. Each flower is lovely in its individuality, and *together* they make a beautiful garden.

Human beings have different-colored skins. They speak many languages, and they have many beliefs politically, sociologically, religiously, and every other way. Why can't we look at ourselves as being flowers in the garden of God? Instead of being frightened, paranoid, and greedy, why can't we look at the variety and scope of human diversity and appreciate it and enjoy it? In other words, why can't we enjoy unity in diversity?

This kind of awareness and awakening should be taught in our homes and our schools. We cannot wait for others to move ahead. We must move forward in terms of our own individual evolution. The more we become evolved, awake, and aware, the more the ripples of higher consciousness spread out to the rest of the community, even to the society and the world.

MEDITATION AND EVOLUTION

I've been meditating twenty-two years now and teaching for twenty-one. When I returned from India and started talking about meditation, I had to be careful—a lot of people thought meditation was some kind of freak show. As a free-lance musician, I didn't have to worry about my job. But I met many people who did.

Executives at Columbia and RCA were interested in meditation. They'd come to me on the side and say, "I can't show up at a public lecture, but is there some way we could get together privately so you can teach me how to meditate?"

If they showed up in public and it got back to the president of RCA or Columbia that one of their executives had attended a public meditation meeting, the reaction would have been, "What are you, some kind of crazy yogi standing on his head? Are you a nut? If this gets out, it will affect our stockholders' confidence—you're fired." There was a tremendous fear of exposing one's interest in meditation.

We've made a lot of progress over the years. Today, it's normal to talk about meditation. Nobody feels ashamed or threatened about going to a meeting. We in the West pretty much understand what meditation is all about by now. The false ideas about it have been dispelled. I see people interested in meditation and spiritual things wherever I travel, all over the world. We have a more holistic and less fragmented attitude about life. Our awareness about mental and physical health and spiritual evolution has greatly improved.

There is a natural law: when you really need to change, you change. People are waking up fast because this is nitty-gritty time. If only 1 percent of the world's population wakes up, the other 99 percent will be swept along with it.

In a way, it's like the Hundredth Monkey principle: an elite minority creates fluctuations within the established system. Then, as connections are made within the system, the new and old parts of the system interact and begin to reorganize. When the fluctuations reach a critical size, the system transforms itself into a higher order. Among small groups of monkeys, when one monkey makes a change, nothing much happens because the system absorbs it. But when one hundred monkeys make the same change, the system cannot absorb that change, and then *all* of the monkeys change. It's the same way with humans. That is, for a significant change to take place between the Soviet Union and America, only a small percentage of awakened people is required.

Then, as the evolution of the planet accelerates, so individual evolution will accelerate. That's why I remain an optimist, even now. The ultimate responsibility remains, not with our leaders, but with ourselves.

SEVENTEEN

TAJ MAHAL REVISITED

In 1989, the twentieth anniversary of the release of *Inside the Taj Mahal*, the idea came to me of returning to the Taj Mahal for a new recording. I had heard that India's prime minister, Rajiv Gandhi, was a fan of mine. I wrote to him to see if he would pave the way for me to record in the Taj Mahal a second time. He granted me a private appointment for February 23 to discuss the matter. Another adventure lay before me.

The following diary gives a day-by-day account of events as they took place.

February 17, 1989—Heavy snowstorm. Taxi didn't show. Missed plane. Had to take a ferry to Vancouver. Ferry ninety minutes late, due to heart-attack victim. Arrived 11:00 P.M. Overnight at Airport Inn.

Feb. 18—Up at 5:30 A.M. United flight to La Guardia, via Chicago; took almost eleven hours. Taxi to Marlen's apartment. Al Schmitt, my sound engineer, arrived with friend (Jack). Dinner, Italian restaurant. Wedding reception taking place.

Feb. 19—Up, out into the city by noon. Window shopping, walking, breakfast at Stage Delicatessen. Great! More walking—bookstores. Back to Marlen's apartment—rest, pack. Plane leaves from JFK at 8:20. Tried to hail cab at 5:45. Couldn't get one for forty-five minutes. Frantic! Arrived JFK at 7:10. Traffic jam around the Air India terminal. Three police ambulances, a dozen squad cars. Street blocked off in front. Carried our bags for a block. Chaos inside. Security everywhere. Bomb scare. Complete check of each piece of luggage. They freak out at our recording equipment, cords, wires. Not allowed to carry on. Ship it below. This worries us. $10,000 worth. No insurance. Pick up ticket. Passport checked four different times at security. Finally on plane, exhausted.

Free business-class seats from Air India. No movie in our section. Very bad food. Arrive in London approximately six hours later. A 1½-hour layover. Walked around till flight time. Flew eight hours to Delhi. Arrived one hour early (Feb. 20); strong tail winds. Thanked God for safe journey. Got VIP escort through immigration. Waited a long time for luggage—mounting anxiety concerning equipment. Finally arrives, all there, whew! By now, 12:30 A.M. Have to register all equipment and instruments with customs. Takes forever. 1:30 A.M. Change money. Get taxi. Arrive at Hyatt Regency, 2 A.M. Double-room too small. Look at suites. $200 per night. Not much choice. Okay. Bags moved. No flutes. Panic. Left in other room. Retrieve. Three A.M., watch TV, "Scar Face." 4:30, sleep.

Feb. 21—Up at nine o'clock. Feel great. Call prime minister's office. Feb. 23rd appointment changed from 5:00 P.M. to 10:00 A.M. Call Holiday Inn. New rooms available, $100 a day for two singles, a special rate, thanks to my German friend Inka Jochum. They send two cars and a beautiful lady to escort us. Check out of Hyatt Regency. First-class treatment at Holiday Inn. Lovely rooms, 21st floor, right in downtown Delhi, on Connaught Place. Basket of fruit and a welcome letter. Al and I walk around Connaught Circus. Eye-opener for Al. Slept five hours. Woke at 10:00 P.M. Ate, back to bed. Slept well.

Feb. 22—After breakfast, sight-seeing. Private car and driver. Mostly old Delhi, which I'd seen before. Al blown away, handling it well. Shopping, then back to hotel for an invitational lunch with resident manager, Rolf Bauer. Sleep. No dinner. Preparing for tomorrow morning's meeting with prime minister. Make notes, review film proposal, script. Lay out CDs, cassettes. Too excited to sleep. Up at 5:00 A.M.—shower, meditate, write in journal.

Feb. 23—Today's the day! Al calls, 7:00 A.M., dressed and ready, shirt, tie, off-white jacket. He couldn't sleep either. Breakfast. I'm wearing comfortable clothes in case I spill tea. Al arranges for car and driver to leave hotel at 9:15. I change clothes, white pants and shoes, rose-colored dress shirt, black tie, bluish sport coat with interwoven subtle colors. Very handsome. Al and I look good for our ages.

Ready. Almost out the door. Phone rings. "Your appointment with the prime minister has been changed to 6:30 this evening." Postponement. Another flexibility test.

Al changes appointment for car to 5:00 P.M. What now? Could always go crazy. Instead, work out at the hotel fitness center. Haven't exercised in six weeks, touring, traveling. Workout feels good. Showered, ate lunch, walked to Connaught Circus in search of headphones for Al and flash batteries for my camera. Got the batteries, not the headphones. We both bought leather bags from street merchants. Bargained to half price each time. Getting used to handling beggars too, but it's always hard, especially the children and the badly crippled.

Returned to hotel, 3:30 P.M., tired. Washed, meditated forty-five minutes. Felt good. No phone calls. Maybe this is it.

Got dressed, met Al. The driver and car are ready, we're off. Arrived at Parliament Building's reception area. Lots of security. X-ray walk-through, personal check, handbag search. Large waiting area with many people, most to see various ministers. We check with a man in charge, verify appointment. He phones PM's secretary, announces our arrival. I tell him to ask permission for Al to accompany me.

We drink tea and wait.

At 6:10, I'm called to the counter, given a slip of paper that has both of our names on it and directions for proceeding inside the Parliament Building. More security at entrance. We have to leave cameras. There go our hopes for photos with the PM. We proceed to room 12, a fairly large room with comfortable chairs. People come and go through another door at the back, where a corridor leads to the PM's office. At 6:40 somebody apologizes for the delay. We get the green light at 6:45. This is it.

PM's door is open. We're shown in. Prime Minister Gandhi stands to greet us. A handsome man; looks much younger than his photos; clear, soft, friendly eyes; a nice smile. He greets us, shakes hands, we sit across from him at his large desk.

I tell him how honored we are to meet him and appreciative of the time he is taking from his busy schedule. (His day begins at 8 A.M., early appointments; then in Parliament all day; then handles private appointments from 6:00 P.M. to 3:00 A.M.)

I present him with six of my CDs and cassettes, *Inside the Taj Mahal* prominently on top. He looks them over briefly, thanks me. I show him the Air India in-flight magazine, with a photo of him as a little boy standing in front of his mother with his grandfather Nehru. I tell him he's changed since then. He laughs.

Down to business. As this is the twentieth anniversary of the release of *Inside*, would he arrange official permission for me to record in the Taj Mahal? He phones his secretary, Mr. V. George, who enters a few seconds later. Which people and instruments are involved? Only me and my flutes. He asks about equipment, mentions DAT (digital audio tape). Al says DAT is what we would be using, small, compact. The PM asks how long we will be in India. One week, till March 3rd. He tells Mr. George to set up an appointment with Mr. G. Parthasarathy, joint secretary to the PM, and Parthasarathy will arrange everything, including permission to take a camera in, normally forbidden these days because of the tension and turmoil in India.

Mr. George leaves. I ask the prime minister if there is anything I can do for him. Perhaps a private concert for his family and friends; a concert for his favorite charity. He smiles, thanks me, stands. Meeting over. He wishes us well, shakes hands. I thank him, say "God bless you," and we leave. The whole meeting takes ten minutes.

Mr. George's office is adjacent to the PM's. We enter and sit. Other people are there. Mr. George on the phone. Finished, he calls me over, tells me I have an appointment with Mr. Parthasarathy at 10:00 A.M., Monday, at the PM's regular office, not at the Parliament. He says he'll follow through; everything will be taken care of.

We meet our driver outside. I don't feel the ground because I'm ten feet up, walking on air. A fantastic experience! Thank you, Lord.

Feb. 24—Feel really good! Spoke to Tryntje at 5:00 A.M. my time (3:30 P.M. in Victoria). Told her about last night's meeting. She was excited. Worked with Al in the gym an hour and a half. Showered, ate breakfast. Went to Connaught Circus; finally found a good pair of headphones.

Hired a car and driver. Headed out to see Maharishi, twenty-four kilometers from here, in a little town called Maharishi Nagar. We cross the umna River. Al sees life in the countryside—water buffaloes, farmland, cow dung drying in the sun for fuel, children riding cart-driven wagons.

After asking directions several times, we find Maharishi's ashram, a huge compound surrounded by a red plaster wall ten feet high. We follow the wall to guardhouses on either side of a big iron gate. Several guards in uniform open the gate, letting vehicles in and out.

We check in. All Indian people—no Westerners. An old man seems amazed that I want to see Maharishi, but he takes my name and country down and gives the slip of paper to another man, who disappears.

In fifteen minutes, a different Indian man arrives, kicks out several people sitting in a small waiting room—motions for Al and me to enter. He sits across from us at a little table and questions us—passports, etc. I tell him I'm an early TM teacher; spent time in the late sixties with Maharishi in Rishikesh; yes, I'm a Siddha; Al is a meditator. We've just visited the prime minister. Would like to see Maharishi for a few minutes.

He leaves, comes back thirty minutes later, says a meeting is not possible. Maharishi is too busy. I half expected this but hoped for a different outcome. It seems ironic. I can have a private appointment with India's prime minister, but not with Maharishi.

We get in our car, head back to the Holiday Inn in Delhi, stopping to take pictures and visit the Old Fort. After lunch, I call a friend, Shree Chakravarti, a famous healer whom I have known for many years. She is happy to hear from me, invites us over.

She is a wonderful person, spiritually oriented, sixty-two years old, long white hair pulled back tightly in a twist. Her husband is older, an intellectual and former army officer.

We enjoy several hours of interesting conversation, ranging from stories of healings to deep philosophical flights. I show her a little cyst on my right inner forearm. She feels it. Her hand starts vibrating. The cyst needs attention. My thymus gland does, too. I'll have a biopsy done when I get back. She calls a taxi. We arrive at the hotel around 11:30. Another nice full day.

Feb. 25—Still awake, 5:00 A.M. I call Tryntje, give her a list of recording equipment for the insurance agent. Al knocks. He has a slight case of diarrhea and is taking pills. I have a lazy morning reading, writing postcards.

Nothing special planned. Killing time until our appointment Monday morning, anxious to get to Agra and do what we came to do—record in the Taj Mahal.

Feb. 26—Time, time, biding time. Hope we're off to Agra tomorrow. Awoke at 5:00 A.M. again. Seem to be needing only five hours sleep. Showered, meditated, read the paper, worked out, ate breakfast, sat by the pool for an hour. To the room, paperwork, arrange a suitcase of things I'll need in Agra. Lunch, Chinese restaurant.

Al and I decide to visit the zoo. A beautiful Chinese lady arrives in the lobby as we're leaving. It is See Foon Koppen from Hong Kong. She is in charge of promotion for all of the Asian and Indian Holiday Inns. She is also the person who got us a 50 percent discount on our rooms and set up the VIP treatment we've been getting, a very pleasant woman.

Grab a taxi, head for the zoo by the Old Delhi Fort (3,500 years old), a nice zoo, natural setting. Sunday afternoon, many people—the children are especially beautiful, and the women look lovely in their colorful saris. We enjoy the lions and the white Bengal tigers most of all. Back to the hotel in a small three-wheel taxi.

Feb. 27—I have a ten o'clock appointment at the PM's office with Mr. G. Parthasarathy, joint secretary to the prime minister. I hope we can be off to Agra today. Didn't sleep much. Want to be early. Arrive at 9:15. Shown to a reception area, announce myself, am told to have a seat. At 10:20, I'm informed the secretary has been detained—but he's on his way. Escorted through security, taken to another waiting room. Fifteen minutes later the phone rings. I pick it up. Mr. Parthasarathy has arrived. Someone escorts me to his office.

He is a pleasant, formal man. I review the train of events for him. He says he will follow through. Time is short. Would like to record tomorrow night. He rings for his assistant, Mr. Bulok Chadderji. He will contact the authorities in Agra and call me at the hotel.

For five hours, I wait anxiously in my room. Finally, he calls. The commissioner in Agra is out of town and will return this evening. He will be in touch with the commissioner tomorrow morning and call me. We decide to leave for Agra tomorrow and record the evening of the next day (Wed.). Timing down to the wire. I had a feeling it would be this way.

Feb. 28—Today's the day. Either I get final permission to record in the

Taj or I don't. Pressed for time. Up at 7:00 A.M.—workout in the gym—breakfast at nine. Now I wait for Chadderji's phone call. And wait. And wait—10, 10:30, 11, 11:30. Anxious, more anxious, very anxious—finally, I call him. He says he should know in just a few minutes.

At 11:45, the phone rings. Okay!!! I'm to see Mr. Harbhajan Singh, the district magistrate in Agra, and he will arrange details. Al and I check out, arrange for a car and driver, we're off.

The drive is unbelievable. I forgot just how crazy traffic is in India. Al is freaked out. We both realize how safe air travel is. Three hours later, we arrive at the Mughal Sheraton Hotel, fancy, but not as warm or well managed as the Holiday Inn. We eat (not very good food), and take a taxi to the Taj Mahal. We have only one hour. It closes at 7:00 P.M.

We enter the outer grounds from the side, which is different than last time. Lots of military, concerned about terrorism. No video or movie cameras allowed. Shoulder bags inspected, checked at the entrance if doubtful or suspicious looking.

We enter the main entrance. Magnificent as ever. Al overwhelmed. But the grounds are not well kept. No water in the reflecting pools. Litter everywhere. Soldiers carrying rifles.

We take photos, walk inside. Lots of tourists. The peace and serenity I remember so well are obliterated. We will be alone tomorrow night; the atmosphere will be different. A busy and special day ahead.

March 1—The events of the next two days were so overwhelming that it is now April 9, five weeks later, and only at this moment can I sort it out and write it down.

It began when I tried to contact Mr. Harbhajan Singh, Agra's chief development officer. The prime minister's office had been in touch with him, and through him all of the arrangements to record in the Taj were to be made. He was my main contact.

I call Singh's office at 9:00 A.M. No answer. Call every fifteen minutes, until 10:30. Still no answer. This is a government office! Somebody is supposed to be there every minute. What could possibly be wrong?

I decide to find Singh myself, but I have no address. The hotel lobby manager finds one, which I give to the driver of my rented car. The address turns out to be wrong. Somebody gives us a new address, directs us to the other side of town. The new address is also wrong. We are at the district magistrate's office, located in a very strange compound, with individual booths spread out over a dirt area. The booths are open on all sides, with thatched roofs and wooden floors. A judge and opposing parties sit in each booth, working out their problems. In a regular building at the far end of the compound, we inquire about Mr. Singh. The verbal directions are too complicated for my driver. A young boy is dispatched to ride with us. Fifteen minutes later, we arrive at another building, almost back where we started. It is 12:30, lunch time, and we might miss Singh—if he's even there.

Somebody shows us to a crowded waiting room. We sit, preparing for a long wait. Surprisingly, in just a few minutes someone says, "This way, please."

A nice looking man in his early thirties sits behind a large desk in a dimly lit office—Mr. Harbhajan Singh! He says the phones aren't working because of an employees' strike; no one is answering them. Pleasant and cordial, he orders his servant to bring tea and spends half an hour visiting with us.

Everything is arranged. Mr. Upadhyay, the assistant district magistrate of protocol, is the officer in charge. Mr. Singh instructed Upadhyay to coordinate things. He would be calling me at the hotel later that afternoon.

I thank him and we leave, visiting Agra Fort on the way back to the hotel. After lunch, we relax by the pool. I send my driver to pick up incense and two garlands of fresh flowers for tonight. At 5:30, Mr. Upadhyay calls and says Mr. Bukesh (another magistrate) will pick us up at seven.

This is it! It is really going to happen. I am excited. Once again, I am getting a chance to play and record inside the Taj Mahal!

Mr. Bukesh arrives with his driver. Al and I are waiting in the lobby with our equipment and instruments. My driver brings two packages of incense and the fresh garlands, beautifully made of roses and assorted flowers. I tell him these are for Shah Jahan and Mumtaz Mahal, to be placed on their tombs tonight before I play. He is so overjoyed that this is what the garlands are for, he throws his arms around me and gives me a kiss on the cheek. The other drivers look on in utter surprise.

We pile in the car and drive to the Taj, about ten minutes away. It is officially closed for the night. A guard recognizes Mr. Bukesh and opens the gates. We drive in, right up to the main entrance. No one is there. A Mr.

Raijada from the department of archaeology meets us. He is in charge of our recording for the evening. Workers help us carry our things.

It is thrilling to walk in the gardens beside the pool in the evening twilight. I notice a few stars appearing and feel the stillness and pleasantly warm air on my skin. As is the custom, we remove our shoes before ascending the steep marble stairs to the platform upon which rests the Taj Mahal.

A soft light hangs suspended over the tombs. I place a garland on each tomb and light the incense. Al sets up his equipment while I unpack my instruments. I play a few notes, listen to them reverberate in the dome. I forgot how truly magnificent the sound is here, totally unique—no other place like it in the world. The soprano sax sounds especially nice. Mr. Bukesh and Mr. Raijada leave. They will return in a couple of hours. Two Indian guards and one or two military men remain. Okay, as long as they're quiet.

One of the guards says to me, "Do you know Paul Horn? I sang with him when he played here many years ago."

"I am Paul Horn."

His face lights up in amazement. "*You* are Paul Horn?"

"Maybe I've changed a little in twenty-one years."

This was extraordinary luck. He could sing on this recording, too.

Testing the microphone and recorder, we hear crackling noises in the headsets, but they seem to go away after a while.

I begin to play. An airplane flies overhead. A soldier coughs. I hear fluttering sounds. Looking up, I see hundreds of pigeons sitting on a ledge about sixty feet above. Every so often, one takes off, flies to the other side. When they coo at the same time, it reverberates in the dome, a strange sound. This situation is quite different than last time.

I manage to get five or ten minutes at a time when things intermittently become quiet. I play the flute, the alto flute, the bass flute, my little Chinese wooden flute, and the soprano sax. Each instrument has its own feeling, its own sound. The guard, Saad Ullah Khan, sings some chants, and we improvise a duet together.

After an hour and a half, we decide to take a break. Our decision comes at the right time. The door bangs open and the officials walk in at just that moment. They put on headsets and listen to playbacks, which they thoroughly enjoy. I estimate I have thirty minutes of recorded music. They decide to stick around for the next session. I am not pleased with that idea, but I say okay, emphasizing they must be extremely quiet. The dome amplifies every little movement or sound, which interferes with recording.

Al starts up his DAT recorder. No sound comes through. He checks the microphone cable connections to the power-supply boxes. Still no sound.

I do not like this situation, but I try not to show anxiety. Al's getting frantic. He checks and rechecks all connections. Nothing works. He starts changing all batteries in the power-supply boxes.

An ugly, disturbing thought enters my mind. The worst nightmare imaginable seems imminent. After all of the seemingly insurmountable obstacles to this project, obstacles that popped up right from the beginning, obstacles that we conquered one by one, could it be possible that I would fail here and now because of malfunctioning electronic equipment? I shudder, hoping it will be all right.

We try the backup recorder. It doesn't help. New batteries don't help. The problem has to be either the microphone or the cables—and Al brought no backups. Our spirits are devastated. It is too bizarre.

Mr. Raijada says, "You can come back. Go to the hotel. Explore the problem. Continue tomorrow night." We have no alternative.

I am thankful he invited us back. That will give us a last-minute opportunity. We return to the hotel, completely dejected. I can't believe this is actually happening. It must be a horrible dream. Unfortunately, it isn't.

We had planned to arrive at the Holiday Inn early tomorrow afternoon after an easy ride back to Delhi. We thought we might spend a leisurely day, a little last-minute shopping, to bed early tomorrow evening, because very early the next morning, at 4:00 A.M., we were to leave for the airport to prepare for our 7:00 A.M. departure. Customs and immigration take a long time in India, especially when you have equipment and instruments.

But with this new, unpleasant twist in our plans, we have to rethink our schedule. At most, allowing for setting up and tearing down, we would have two hours of recording time. At the very latest, we would have to leave the Taj by 10:00 P.M. to arrive at the Holiday Inn by 2:00 A.M. Then we would pick up the rest of our luggage, repack, take a shower (if we were lucky), and split for the airport.

Al goes to his room to keep working on the equipment. In my room, I just sit there in a daze. Neither of us sleep that night.

March 2—Breakfast. The mike is still dead. Can't be fixed. By the grace of God I happen to have two microphones with me—not as sophisticated as the single stereo AKG 422 mike—but we can utilize them, and we can record in stereo. I brought these along in case the prime minister requested a concert. We try them out. They work perfectly. So far so good.

The day passes—very slowly. We bide our time—dozing off a few minutes now and then, too anxious to sleep. Out of the last thirty hours, we have had two hours' sleep at the most.

I line up a car and driver for the night. He will take us to the Taj Mahal with our luggage in the trunk and wait for us while we record, after which he'll drive us to Delhi's Holiday Inn, about four hours away. There, he will turn around and go back to Agra. All of this for sixty-five dollars.

Mr. Bukesh comes by at 6:30 P.M. and we follow his car to the Taj Mahal. The last tourists are clearing out. We set up, ready by 7:30. More people seem to be around tonight—more guards, more military personnel. The pigeons are restless, haven't settled for the night. It is earlier than last night. Pigeons fly and flutter, which interferes with the recording.

I start playing, get a few phrases off, and am forced to stop. When pigeon droppings hit the marble floor from sixty feet above, they sound like hand-claps echoing in the dome. People walk in and out. The big door opens and closes with a bang. This is all getting to be too much.

After an hour of trying, I stop and sigh. Perhaps this recording is not going to happen. Murphy's law in action. What can I do? Maybe it is not meant to be. I sit and meditate for fifteen minutes. When I open my eyes, everything has become very still. Even the pigeons have settled down.

I turn toward the tombs of Shah Jahan and Mumtaz Mahal and say in my mind, "If you don't want me to record here, okay. I can accept that, and I will leave in peace. On the other hand, if you think this recording could be a positive influence in the world and bring some inner peace and spirituality to many people, as the first recording did, then let me have the space to do it."

It happens. The next forty-five minutes are quiet enough for me to get what I need. We leave by ten as planned and take the long, bumpy, noisy, dusty ride back to New Delhi.

CODA

All human beings know and like and relate to music. Music in particular, and sound in general, constitutes our essential nature. We *are* sound. That is what we are made of. Sound is vibration. Human beings are vibrations, solidified in human form. Likewise, each tree is solidified sound in the form of a tree. All of existence is vibration. Sound is fundamental to our physical constitution, and music is the universal language precisely because it touches us at that deep, essential, universal level. It has a unifying and healing power. It creates positive bonds among peoples and nations and cultures. Quiet music holds the greatest and truest power of all.

Like an international passport, music has given me entry into all countries and access to many peoples. No matter how different that culture may be—India, Egypt, the USSR, or China, for example—I feel comfortable and at home. People accept me more readily because of music. Often they confide in me. We get to know each other more easily. Music transcends language, touching our hearts directly. As a result, music gives me the opportunity to see a little more deeply into the life of other countries. I would not normally be able to experience foreign countries and peoples this way if I were simply an ordinary tourist.

Music has taught me how to think in global terms. Today I think of myself, not only as an American or a Canadian, but as a world citizen. Whenever and wherever I see mountains, I enjoy them. They don't have to be American mountains, Canadian mountains, Himalayan mountains, or the Andes. All mountains are beautiful. And the sky is everywhere; so is the sun, the moon, the stars, the grass, the trees, the streams, the lakes, the flowers, the people. It is a beautiful world, a community we share, a spaceship, the Spaceship Earth, and all of us are on it, traveling through the universe together.

Is my corner of the ship better than yours? Why am I attached to the front of the ship, rather than to the rear or the middle? Obviously, it doesn't make sense, because there is only one ship, one world, and there is no place else to be. We must move forward, and we must unite in our efforts to move forward together. In order to survive, we must realize that we are on this ship as one people, one humanity, and we must learn to think in terms of the whole ship, not just its parts. Music has given me the opportunity to experience this realization firsthand.

My life has not been all smooth sailing, but neither have I known the degree of suffering so many others have experienced. I have learned how to see the events of my life in nonjudgmental ways, accepting everything that happens as being a part of the natural order. It is an absolute waste of time to feel guilty about anything. We do the best we can. If something goes wrong, we can learn *why* it went wrong, and do better next time. Everything is perfect in each given moment. There is only the question of experience and what we choose to learn from it. If I could live my life again, I would not change a single thing. *Every* experience contributes to the whole.

Few people enjoy their work. Their frustrated, disappointed state of mind causes unhappiness and physical illness. A disturbed mind, imbalanced and unhappy, creates inner pain, which accumulates and spills over into everyday actions. Personal suffering increases global pain.

In our Western society, we have freedom of choice. The potential for a wonderful existence is spelled out in the Constitution. How sad it is if we choose to be miserable in the midst of such freedom and opportunity.

Our Father is God. We are His sons and daughters. All manifestations of existence are cells in the body of God, including us. Our true identity is God. God lives *in* you *as* you. Self-realization is discovering this and becoming aware of the fact that godliness is our birthright. It is not dignified for the son of a king to be seen walking around in rags. That is, we should be aware of who we truly are and should walk in dignity. When we suffer, we are not aware that we are God, and we are not living our life according to the light and truth of our birthright.

We have 100 percent free will, which means we have the ability to change. And according to the law of karma, every action has its equal and opposite reaction—that means we are responsible for our actions and feelings. What do we choose to do? What kind of a person do we choose to be? How do we use our freedoms?

We need to find what it is in life that we truly enjoy. That desire reveals our natural talents and abilities—musician, firefighter, police officer, poet, artist, secretary, writer, salesperson. It doesn't matter. All work is honorable. We should do what we want, whatever brings us pleasure. We need to enjoy it and do it and be good at it, no matter what it is. This will translate into inner happiness. Individual unhappiness breeds unhappiness in the world. Individual happiness spreads positive feelings, which help the whole earth grow.

The pendulum of life swings back and forth. We have great moments of joy and great moments of dejection. Life is dynamic, never static. It is always moving. Therefore life cannot stay in balance very long—and yet we clearly see the value of balance. A balanced person lives a happier, fuller life.

A balanced person is detached from events and actions. That does not mean desensitized. It means observing and seeing things clearly and accurately, without emotional attachments and their resultant judgments. It means accepting events and actions just as they are and learning from them. It means great sensitivity and great compassion.

Balance means developing our full potential. When the analytical, rational left hemisphere of our brain is fully developed, and the creative, intuitive right hemisphere is fully developed, then both sides of our brain are balanced. A fully developed mind is a balanced mind.

There are two aspects to life. Outer aspects encompass all material things, including our body and surroundings. Inner aspects are spiritual. In a sense, the fullness of life is 200 percent—100 percent outer, 100 percent inner.

Ordinarily, we direct our attention outward and use about 10 percent of our mental capacity. That 10 percent is the conscious thinking mind. When we start developing our inner life, we expand our consciousness. Soon we begin to use 20, 30, or 40 percent. When we use the full potential of our mind, 100 percent, we are in a state of cosmic consciousness, which is a *normal* person, the way we should be—fully developed, both outwardly and inwardly.

If each of us did this, how wonderful life would be. Everyone would act from an enlightened state, and in that state there would be no misery. As we grow inwardly, our days begin with more knowledge and awareness; on all levels, our lives become more productive and joyful and rewarding.

As I view the whole of my life, I accept the fact that there is a purpose to every experience. As long as I keep that in mind, I never have to be devastated by anything that happens. An experience needn't be labeled good or bad. It is just an experience, and there is something to be learned from it. Retrospectively, I can see karmic connections throughout my entire journey.

Out of love for the most part, but also out of ignorance, we are taught many things as children. These things determine our perceptions, which create our attitudes. Perceptions and attitudes determine how we think and what we feel. If we integrate attitudes that are based on ignorance and false assumptions, inevitably we suffer. Truth leads to happiness; ignorance leads to misery.

How do we feel about a rainy day? The rain itself has no thoughts—it just *is*. But this woman says she loves the rain, and that man says he hates it. Each time we judge neutral events—and in essence all events are neutral—the more deeply ingrained do judgmental perceptual patterns become. If we are miserable and unable to change our attitudes, we continue to view life and its events negatively, remaining in ignorance and misery. By going *inside* and *experiencing* direct contact with our essential, higher Self, negativity begins to fade away as we advance along the spiritual path. We learn that our true Self is eternal and perfect. It is God, and we are God.

Self-realization is the prerequisite for the realization of anything else. As our consciousness develops and evolves, so our attitudes change accordingly, and this change leads to a creative, productive, balanced life. Balance is the key.

Self-realization does not come from the intellectual study of anything. Other people can't simply hand it to us. Books and guides can point the way; they can help; they can open certain doors. But ultimately, we have to walk through those doors and do it ourselves. Any form of meditation will enable us to go deeply within, to the point where the ego-self is transcended. Our higher Self is revealed in the process.

Many spiritual teachers have visited us. If we are awake enough to see their potential value as guides, we can enlist their help. In addition to Maharishi, I have met and spent time with Swami Satchidananda, and Swami Muktananda. I enjoy the books of Ram Dass, Krishnamurti, Richard Bock, and others, both Eastern and Western.

Unfortunately, we have the idea that a priest, a minister, a rabbi, or a guru is superhuman. We put them on a pedestal and believe they are supposed to behave in certain ways at all times. They have to be an example of "the right way." We say they are great teachers. Then one day they do something that goes against our conditioned Western, Judeo-Christian ideas about "the right way," and we feel shocked. We reject them—and hurt ourselves in the process.

By setting them up on pedestals, forgetting they are human, and by judging them according to traditional, socially conditioned mind-sets that may be irrelevant to their situation, we do ourselves an enormous disservice. We dismiss all of their knowledge and enlightened awareness and turn away. We think we turn our backs on them, but in truth we turn our backs on ourselves.

At one time or another, gurus have been accused of sexual transgressions. We have this idea that a guru is not supposed to have sex. Suppose he does? So what? Gurus are human beings with the same emotions, desires, and chemical and glandular makeup that we all have. Does that mean he or she is not a "true" teacher? That their vast knowledge and enlightened spiritual insights are just a lie? I don't think so.

We cannot know another person's destiny. We don't even know our own. Someone else performs an action that we condemn. How can we condemn it? They might have to perform that action in order to balance out past debts. All actions are karmic. All of us are doing exactly what we are supposed to do, according to the path we have chosen through thousands of lifetimes. Who are we to judge? Native Americans say, "Do not judge another man until you have walked a mile in his moccasins."

When we make hard and fast judgments of our teachers and guides, we don't hurt them. We just deny ourselves a wonderful opportunity to learn and grow.

We are here precisely for that purpose: to learn and to grow—and to *enjoy* the *gift* of life. We are here to learn who we really are—the God Self within—and to grow in that awareness and live our lives in that fullness. Then it is time to move on—to the next phase of existence, whatever it may be. It is not supposed to take so many lifetimes to learn this. The earth is like a big school. We are supposed to graduate at some point and make way for others. Reincarnation signifies failure. Above all, this wonderful, beautiful, awesome universe was created out of love for only one purpose—for us to enjoy it. Charlie Parker aptly expressed this sentiment in the title of a blues he wrote, "Now is the Time."

A 115-year-old guru from the Himalayas came to speak to the people at Maharishi's ashram one day. He was so beautiful to look at, with his dark brown firm skin offset by his thick, shoulder-length snow-white hair. He summed it all up when he said "the Almighty created only bliss; man created everything else."

The End.

SELECTED DISCOGRAPHY

ABBREVIATIONS

a	arranger	h	harp
afl	alto flute	kybds	keyboards
as	alto saxophone	man	mandolin
b	bass	p	piano
bar	baritone saxophone	perc	percussion
bfl	bass flute	pic	piccolo
cel	cello	sopsx	soprano sax
cl	clarinet	synth	synthesizer
comp	composer	tb	trombone
cond	conductor	tp	trumpet
d	drums	ts	tenor saxophone
elec	electric	vbs	vibraphone
F-hn	French horn	vio	violin
fl	flute	vla	viola
g	guitar	vo	vocal

AS LEADER

HOUSE OF HORN
1957.*Dot DLP-3091

Personnel: Paul Horn (fl, as, pic, cl, afl); Gerry Wiggins (p, celeste); Fred Katz (cel); John Pisano (g); Red Mitchell (b); Forest Thorn (d); Larry Bunker (vbs); Bill Marx (bells); Dan Lube, David Frisina (vio's); David Sterkin (vla).

Compositions: Pony Tale; Day by Day; A Soldier's Dream; House of Horn; The Golden Princess; Sunday, Monday, or Always; To a Little Boy; Siddartha; Interlude.

PLENTY OF HORN
1958. Dot DLP-29002

Personnel: Paul Horn (fl, afl, pic, cl, as); Fred Katz (p); Red Mitchell (b); Billy Bean (g); Shelly Manne (d). *Supporting musicians:* Ed Leddy, Stu Williamson, Ken Bright (tp's); Vince De Rosa, Dick Perissi (F-hn's); Milt Bernhart (tb); Red Callender (tuba); Larry Bunker (claves and vbs); Mongo Santamaria (conga).

Compositions: Chloe; A Parable; Blues for Tom; Romanze; Yesterdays; Moods for Horn; The Smith Family; Tellin' the Truth.

(**House of Horn** and **Plenty of Horn** reissued in 1978 as a two-record set entitled **Plenty of Horn,** on **The Dedication Series, vol. 16**; ABC Impulse, 1A-9356/2.)

IMPRESSIONS
1958. World Pacific WP-1266

Personnel: Paul Horn (fl, as, cl); John Pisano (g); Gene Estes (vbs); Lyle Ritz (b).

Compositions: Maid with the Flaxen Hair; The Little Shepherd; Berceuse; Pavanne for a Dead Princess; Waltz #2 and #3; Greensleeves; Baltimore Oriole; Mist; Green Dolphin Street; Good Bait.

SOMETHING BLUE
(the Paul Horn Quintet)
1960. Hi Fi Jazz J-615

Personnel: Paul Horn (fl, cl, as); Emil Richards (vbs); Paul Moer (p); Jimmy Bond (b); Billy Higgins (d).

Compositions: Dun Dunnee; Tall Polynesian; Mr. Bond; Fremptz; Something Blue; Half and Half.

(**Something Blue** reissued in 1975 as **Paul Horn**, on Everest Records FS-308.)

*Dates refer to the release date of each album.

272

THE SOUND OF PAUL HORN
(the Paul Horn Quintet)
1961. Columbia CS-8477/CL-1677

Personnel: **Paul Horn (fl, afl, as); Emil Richards (vbs); Paul Moer (p); Jimmy Bond (b); Milt Turner (d).**

Compositions: Benny's Buns; Without a Song; Yazz Per Favore; Mirage for Miles; Short Politician; My Funny Valentine; Blue on Blue; Moer or Less.

PROFILE OF A JAZZ MUSICIAN
(the Paul Horn Quintet)
1962. Columbia CL-1922/8722

Personnel: **Paul Horn (fl, afl, as, bfl); Emil Richards (vbs); Paul Moer (p); Vic Gaskin (b); Milt Turner (d).**

Compositions: Count Your Change; Now Hear This; Lazy Afternoon; What Now?; Straight Ahead; Fun Time; Just Because We're Kids; Abstraction.

IMPRESSIONS OF CLEOPATRA
1963. Columbia 2050/8850

Personnel: **Paul Horn (fl, bfl, khaen); Emil Richards (vbs); Victor Feldman (p); Chuck Israels (b); Colin Bailey (d); Larry Bunker (perc).**

Compositions: Caesar and Cleopatra Theme; Cleopatra's Palace Music; Love and Hate; Grant Me an Honorable Way to Die; Antony and Cleopatra Theme; Cleopatra Enters Rome; My Love Is My Master; A Gift for Caesar.

JAZZ SUITE ON THE MASS TEXTS
1965. RCA LSP/LPM-3414

Personnel: **Lalo Schifrin (comp, a, cond); Paul Horn (fl, afl, bfl, pic, cl, as); Lynn Blessing (vbs); Mike Lang (p); Bill Plummer (b); Larry Bunker (d).** *Orchestra:* **Vincent De Rosa (F-hn); Frank Rosolino (tb); Dick Leith (bass tb); Al Porcino, Conte Candoli (tp's); Red Callender (tuba); Dorothy Remsen, Ann Stockton (h's); Ken Watson, Emil Richards, Frank Flynn, Milt Holland (perc).** *Chorus:* **Loulie Jean Norman, Marilyn Powell, Sara Jane Tallman, Evangeline Carmichael, Betty Allen, William Cole, Vern Rowe, Marie Vernon.**

Compositions: Kyrie; Interludium; Gloria; Credo; Sanctus; Prayer; Offertory; Agnus Dei.

CYCLE
(the Paul Horn Quintet)
1965. RCA LPM/LSP-3386

Personnel: **Paul Horn (a, cl, fl, afl, as); Lynn Blessing (vbs); Mike Lang (p); Bill Plummer (b); Bill Goodwin (d, perc); John Turnbull, James Thomson (bagpipes).**

Compositions: Greensleeves; Chim Chim Cheree; Cycle; Shadows #1; Hi-Lili, Hi-Lo; In the Bag; Patterns; Shadows #2 (dedicated to Ravi Shankar).

HERE'S THAT RAINY DAY
(the Paul Horn Quintet with voices)
1965. RCA LSP/LPM-3519

Personnel: **Ralph Carmichael (a, cond, choral director); Paul Horn (cl, fl, bfl, afl); Mike Lang (p); Lynn Blessing (vbs); Bill Plummer (b); Bill Goodwin (d); two harps and chorus unlisted.**

Compositions: Who Can I Turn To; Here's That Rainy Day; How Insensitive; The Shadow of Your Smile; In the Wee Small Hours of the Morning; Girl Talk; Moment to Moment; Ecstasy; Laura; On a Clear Day.

MONDAY, MONDAY
(the Paul Horn Quintet)
1966. RCA LSP/LPM-3613

Personnel: **Oliver Nelson (a, cond); Paul Horn (fl, cl, pic, as); Lynn Blessing (vbs); Mike Lang (p); Bill Plummer (b); Bill Goodwin (d); orchestra unlisted.**

Compositions: Monday, Monday; Norwegian Wood; Acapulco Gold; Girl; Paramahansa; Satisfaction; Karen's World; You've Got Your Troubles; Elusive Butterfly; Guv-Gubi; Eight Miles High.

PAUL HORN IN INDIA
1968. World Pacific WPS-21447

Personnel: **Paul Horn (fl); Gopal Krishan (vichitra veena); Vinay Bharat-ram (vo); Satya Dev Pawar (vio); Gaffar Hyder Khan (tabla); Gopal Verma (tamboura).**

Compositions: Raga Desh; Raga Vibhas; Raga Bihag; Raga Shivaranjani; Raga Tilang; Alap; Manj-Khamaj.

PAUL HORN IN KASHMIR
(Cosmic Consciousness)
1968. World Pacific WP-1445; WPS-21445

Personnel: **Paul Horn (afl); J. N. Shivpuri (sitar); Shri Chunlilal Kaul (dilruba, tamboura, vo); Rajinder Raina (tabla).**

Compositions: Raga Ahir Bhairao; Arti; Prayer Song; Tabla Solo in Teental; Alap in Raga Bhairav; Raga Puira Dhanashri; Raga Kerwani.

(**Paul Horn in India** and **Paul Horn in Kashmir** reissued in 1975 as a two-record set entitled **Paul Horn in India**, Blue Note BN-LA529-H2. Reissued in 1990 as **Paul Horn in India and Kashmir**, Black Sun 15009.)

INSIDE (THE TAJ MAHAL)
1969. Epic BXN-26466

Personnel: **Paul Horn (afl).**

Improvised compositions: Prologue/Inside; Mantra I/Meditation; Mumtaz Mahal; Unity; Agra; Vibrations; Akasha; Jumna; Shah Jahan; Mantra II/Duality; Ustad Isa/Mantra III.

274

(Reissued in 1989 as a two-album set entitled **Inside the Taj Mahal**, including **Inside II**; Kuckuck tape 12062-4, Kuckuck CD 11062-2.)

PAUL HORN AND THE CONCERT ENSEMBLE

1970. Ovation OV/14-05

Personnel: **Paul Horn (fl, pic, afl, cl, as); Libbie Jo Snyder (fl, pic, afl, bfl); Bruce Emarine (fl, afl); Tim Weisberg (fl, afl, bfl); Joyce Collins (p, elec p, harpsichord); Chuck Collazzi (elec g, classical g); David Parlato (b, elec b); Bart Hall (d, perc).**

Compositions: Look of Love; Siciliano (from Bach's Flute Sonata no. 2); Alone Together; Magnificat; Stolen Moments; Presto (from Bach's Flute Sonata no. 1); Paramahansa; Golliwogg's Cake Walk (Debussy); The Gentle Rain; Concerto in D (2nd movement); Light My Fire.

INSIDE II

1972. Epic WKE-31600

Personnel: **Paul Horn (fl, afl, bfl, pic fl w/multivider).**

Compositions: The Mahabhutas (Elements)—Prithivi (Earth), Apas (Water), Vayu (Air), Akasha (Space), Tejas (Fire); Haida; Bach Chorales nos. 10, 13, 164, 270; Centaur—Morning Song, Dance of the Centaur, Flute Pipes, Evening Song; Mass—Kyrie.

(Reissued as **Inside the Powers of Nature** in 1983, Golden Flute Records GFR-2006. Reissued in 1989 as part of a two-album set by Celestial Harmonies with **Inside the Taj Mahal**, CD, Kuckuck Records 12062-4.)

JULY 9 & 10
(LIVE AT GASSY JACK'S)

1973. Pacific North 701

Personnel: **Paul Horn (fl, afl, as, elec p); Lynn Blessing (vbs); Art Johnson (g); Dave Parlato (b); Bart Hall (d, perc).**

Compositions: Pit Crew Promotion; Sunset Painter; Thank You Man . . . Thank You Women; Lucite Wedgies; We Three Kings.

VISIONS

1974. Epic KE-32837

Personnel: **Tom Scott (a, organ); Paul Horn (as, fl, afl); Joe Sample (p); Larry Carlton, Roger Johnson (g's); Max Bennett (b); John Guerin (d, perc); Rubens Bassini (perc); Ms. Lady: Carmen Bryant Kneddy, Kathy Collier, Joni Mitchell (vo's).**

Compositions: Too High; Guinnevere; High Tide; Long Time Gone; Blue; Chelsea Morning; Visions; Song with No Words; Dida; Living for the City.

A SPECIAL EDITION
(two-record set)

1975. Mushroom MRS-5502

Personnel: **Paul Horn (fl, pic, afl, bfl, as, cl, elec p); Lynn Blessing (vbs); Art Johnson (g); Dave Parlato (b); Bart Hall (d, perc).**

Compositions: Prelude; Freedom Jazz Dance; Summertime; Tribute to Jobim—Meditation, Corcovado, Dreamer; Just Because We're Kids; Willow Weep for Me; Rain; Dusk; Dawn; Forms.

(Reissued in 1989 on Black Sun CD, 15003-2.)

PAUL HORN & NEXUS
1975. Epic KE-33561

Personnel: **Paul Horn (fl, pic, afl, bfl, cl, as); Robert Becker, William Cahn, Robin Engelman, Russell Hartenburger, John Wyre, Michael Craden (perc).**

Compositions: Somba; Crystals; Friendship; Nexus; Mbira; Latin Tala; African Funeral Song; Eastern Star; Dharma; Capetown.

(Reissued in 1989 as two-album set with, and under the title of, **The Altitude of the Sun**, on Black Sun 15002-2.)

ALTURA DO SOL
1976. Epic PE-34231

Personnel: **Paul Horn (fl, afl, pic, bfl); Egberto Gismonti (g, p); Roberto Silva (d); Ron Carter (b); Don Salvador (elec p); Dom Um Romao (perc).**

Compositions: Dança das Cabecas (Head Dance); Bodas de Prata (Silver Wedding); Altura do Sol (High Sun); Carmo; Tango; Quarup (Worship Ceremony); Parque Laje (A Park in Rio); Salvador.

(Reissued in 1989 as **The Altitude of the Sun**, a two-record set with **Paul Horn & Nexus**, Black Sun 15002-2.)

INSIDE THE GREAT PYRAMID
1977. (two-record set) Mushroom MRS-5507

Personnel: **Paul Horn (fl, afl, pic, vo).**

Improvised compositions: Initiation—Psalms 1–7, Cheops Pyramid, King's Chamber; Meditation—Psalms 1–6, Cheops Pyramid, King's Chamber; Enlightenment—Psalms 1–6, Cheops Pyramid, Queen's Chamber; Fulfillment—Psalms 1–8, Kephren Pyramid, Burial Chamber.

(Reissued in 1983 by Kuckuck 060/61.)

DREAM MACHINE
1978. Mushroom MRS-5010

Personnel: **Lalo Schifrin (comp, a, cond); Paul Horn (fl, afl); Jim Keltner (d); Abraham Laboriel (b); Dean Parks (g); Ernie Watts, Jim Horn, Charles Loper, Chuck Finley, Oscar Brauscher (horns); Mike Melvoin, Joe Sample, Clark Spangler, Lalo Schifrin (kybds, synth); Emil Richards, Paulinho Da Costa, Robin Horn (perc); Israel Baker (concert master).**

Compositions: Undercurrents; Dream Machine; Vera Cruz; Witch Doctor; Quite Early One Morning; The Juggler.

276

LIVE AT PALM BEACH CASINO, CANNES 1980

1980. Bellaphon BID-155-505

Personnel: **Paul Horn (fl); Mike Garson (p); Marc Michel (b); Umberto Pagnini (d).**

Compositions: Importure; Black Orpheus; Work Song; Here's That Rainy Day; Things; Nature Boy Meets Stan Getz.

CHINA

1982. Golden Flute GFR-2001

Personnel: **Paul Horn (fl, afl, bfl, ti-tze, synth); David M. Y. Liang (cheng, ch'in, sheng, erh-hu); Ron Johnston (p, elec p); Terry Frewer (g); Robbie King (organ, synth); Tom Hazlitt (b); Kat Hendrikse (d, perc).**

Compositions: A Happy Occasion; Autumn Stream in a Desolate Gorge; Melting Snow on a Spring Day; Temple of Heaven; Journey Down South; Reflected Moon; Riding on the Wind; Autumn in North Sea.

(Reissued in 1988 by Kuckuck 080, all formats, with three new titles—"Moon Dance," "Under the Pines," and "In a Sunny Meadow" replace "A Happy Occasion" and "Melting Snow on a Spring Day.")

HEART TO HEART

1983. Golden Flute GFR-2002

Personnel: **Paul Horn (fl, afl, bfl, ti-tze); David Friesen (b, shakuhachi).**

Compositions: Ancient Kings; The Garden at Giverny; A Fantasy; Meditation; Rain Forest; Episodes.

INSIDE THE MAGIC OF FINDHORN

1983. Golden Flute GFR-2003

Personnel: **Paul Horn (fl, afl, ti-tze); Joel Andrews (h); Jim Scott (g); Frank Perry (perc).**

Compositions: Earth Sings; Kingdom of Light; Radiance; Dance of the Devas; Ode to Pan; Dream State; Nature Spirits; Angel of Sound.

JUPITER 8

1983. Golden Flute GFR-2004

Personnel: **Paul Horn (fl, afl, bfl, ti-tze, sopsx); Ralph Dyck (kybds); with Jim McGillveray (perc), Ron Johnston (p), Mike Lent (b), Kat Hendrikse (d).**

Compositions: Benita; Voyager I; Prisms; Voyager II; Jupiter 8; Transitions; Voyager III; Feelin' Good; Voyager IV; Microwave.

JAZZ COMPOSITIONS
(recorded live in Russia)

1984. Melodia C60 20965 002

Personnel: **Paul Horn (fl, afl, sopsx); David Friesen (b); John Stowell (g); Robin Horn (d).**

Compositions: Listed in Russian.

277

LIVE FROM RUSSIA, WITH LOVE
1984. Golden Flute GFR-2007

Personnel: **Paul Horn (fl, afl, sopsx); David Friesen (b); John Stowell (g, man, perc); Robin Horn (d, perc); on "Russian Jam," David Goloschokin (vio) and unidentified Russian (p).**

Compositions: Greetings; Manteca; Billie's Bounce; A Night in Tunisia; Russian Jam; Kaunas Blues.

INSIDE RUSSIA
1984. Golden Flute GFR-2008

Personnel: **Paul Horn (fl, afl, bfl, sopsx).**

Improvised compositions: Song for Friendship; Song for Peace; Moscow Blues; Song for Love; Syrinx; Song for Understanding; Song for Eugene; Song for Edward; Song for Marina; Song for Riya; Oche Chermouiye; Song for Rimsky; Song for Trane.

(Reissued in 1986 as **Inside the Cathedral** on Kuckuck 075.)

IN CONCERT
1984. Golden Flute GFR-2009

Personnel: **Paul Horn (fl, afl, bfl, sopsx); David Friesen (b); Ralph Hooper (organ).**

Compositions: Invocation; Amazing Grace; My Body Is My Temple; Siciliano; Jesu Dulcis Memoria; My Funny Valentine; Inside St. Mary's.

TRAVELER
1986. Golden Flute/Global Pacific GFR-2010

Personnel: **Paul Horn (fl, afl, bfl, ti-tze, sopsx, perc); Christopher Hedge (synth, g, man, p, perc); Pranesh Khan (tablas); Peter Van Gelder (sitar, tamboura); Dimitri Vandellos (elec g); Joey Burt (elec fretless b); Lisa Haley (elec vio); The San Francisco Boys' Chorus.**

Compositions: Traveler; Astral Travel; A Journey; Time Travel; Mini Voyage; Metropolis; Soul Travel; Earth Song.

SKETCHES: A COLLECTION
(selections from the Golden Flute series)
1986. Lost Lake Arts LL-0091

Compositions: Voyager IV, Transitions, Voyager II (from *Jupiter 8*); Earth Sings/Radiance (from *Inside the Magic of Findhorn*); Song for Edward, Song for Marina (from *Inside Russia*); Traveler (from *Traveler*); Riding on the Wind (from *China*); Ancient Kings (from *Heart to Heart*).

THE PEACE ALBUM
1988. Kuckuck 11083-1

Personnel: **Paul Horn (fl, afl, bfl, Conn multivider).**

Compositions: Joyous; Joy to the World; Good King Wenceslas; Air; God Rest Ye Merry, Gentlemen; Christmas Morning Prayer; Ave Maria; Carol of the Bells; Angels We Have Heard on High; Silent Night; The Lord's Prayer; We Three Kings; Magnificat; Little Prelude; What Child Is This.

NOMAD
(Selected Pieces: 1976–1988)
1990. Kuckuck LC 2099

Compositions: Soul Travel, Earth Song, Transitions, Voyager III (from *Traveler*); Song for Trane, Syrinx (from *Inside the Cathedral*); Air (from Suite no. 3 in D Major, BWV 1068) and Magnificat (for four voices, from *The Peace Album*); Jesu Dulcis Memoria (from *In Concert*); Rain Forest (from *Heart to Heart*); Angel of Sound (from *Inside the Magic of Findhorn*); Reflected Moon, Moon Dance, Under the Pines (from *China*); Initiation: Psalm 2; Initiation: Psalm 4; Fulfillment: Psalm 7; Initiation: Psalm 7 (from *Inside the Great Pyramid*).

INSIDE THE TAJ MAHAL II
1990. Kuckuck 11085

Personnel: **Paul Horn.**

Compositions: The Taj Mahal Suite—Part I (Announcement); Part II (sopsx); Part III (sopsx); Part IV (afl); Part V (afl); Part VI (afl, vo); Part VII (afl); Part VIII (fl); Part IX (fl); Part X (fl); Part XI (vo); Part XII (bfl); Part XIII (sopsx); Part XIV (ti-tze); Part XV (vo); Part XVI (sopsx); Part XVII (fl).

FEATURED SOLOIST WITH:

THE SAUTER-FINEGAN ORCHESTRA
Under Analysis
1957 (recorded 1956). RCA LPM-1341/SLP-27

Personnel not listed.

CHICO HAMILTON
Chico Hamilton Quintet
1957. Pacific Jazz PJ-1225

Personnel: **Chico Hamilton (d); Paul Horn (as, ts, fl, cl); John Pisano (g); Fred Katz (cel); Carson Smith (b).**

The Sweet Smell of Success.
1957. Decca DL-86L4

Personnel: **Chico Hamilton (d); Paul Horn (fl, cl, as); John Pisano (g); Fred Katz (cel); Carson Smith (b).**

279

The Chico Hamilton Quintet: Ellington Suite
1958. World Pacific WP-1258

Personnel: Chico Hamilton (d); Buddy Collette (ts, as); Paul Horn (as, fl); Jim Hall (g); Fred Katz (cel); Carson Smith (b).

Chico Hamilton Plays South Pacific in Hi-Fi.
1958. Pacific Jazz PJ-1238

Personnel: Chico Hamilton (d); Fred Katz (cel); Paul Horn (as, fl); John Pisano (g); Hal Gaylor (b).

FRED KATZ
Zen: The Music of Fred Katz
1957. Pacific Jazz JPJ-1231

Personnel: Fred Katz (cel); Chico Hamilton (d, timpani); Paul Horn (as, fl, cl); John Pisano (g); Carson Smith (b). On "Suite for Horn" add Joe Howard, Herbie Harper, Dick Noel (tb's); Harry Klee (fl); Marty Berman (bassoon); Willy Schwartz (cl); Julie Jacobs (oboe).

KEN NORDINE
Word Jazz
1957. Dot DLP-3075

Personnel: Fred Katz (cel, p, cond, comp); Paul Horn (fl, pic, cl, as); John Pisano (g); Jimmy Bond (b); Forest Horn (d); Ken Nordine (vo).

A Somewhat New Medium . . . Word Jazz (a.k.a. *The Son of Word Jazz*)
1957. Dot DLP-3096

Personnel: Fred Katz (comp, cond, cel); Paul Horn (woodwinds); John Pisano (g); Harold Gaylor (b); Red Holt (d); Richard Marx (p).

BUDDY COLLETTE
Buddy Collette's Swinging Shepherds
1958. Emarcy MG-36L33

Personnel: Buddy Collette, Bud Shank, Paul Horn, Harry Klee (fl's); Bill Miller (p); Joe Comfort (b); Bill Richmond (d).

At the Cinema
1959. Mercury MG-20447

Personnel: Buddy Collette, Bud Shank, Paul Horn, Harry Klee (fl's); Bill Miller, John T. Williams (p's); Jim Hall (g); Red Mitchell (b); Shelly Manne, Earl Palmer (d).

HAL MARCH
The Moods of March
1958. Dot DLP 3092

Featuring woodwind solos by Paul Horn. Other personnel unlisted.

MONGO SANTAMARIA
Mongo
1959. Fantasy 3291

Personnel: Paul Horn (fl); Emil Richards (marimba); Al McKibbon (b); José Gamboa (vo); Mongo Santamaria, Willie Bobo, Francisco Aguabella, Juan Cheda, Carlos Vidal (perc).

FREDDIE GAMBRELL
Mikado
1959. World Pacific 1023

Personnel: Freddie Gambrell (p); Paul Horn (woodwinds); Dempsey Wright (g); Ben Tucker (b); Armando Peraza, Ray Mosca (d).

ALLYN FERGUSON
Pictures at an Exhibition Framed in Jazz
1961. Ava Records A-32

Personnel: Allyn Ferguson (cond, a, p); Jules Chaikin, Ollie Mitchell, Stuart Williamson, Jack Feierman, John Audino, Lew McCreary (tp's); Bob Edmondson, Vern Friley, Kenny Shroyer, Bob Knight, Dick Gould (tb's); Paul Horn (as, fl, bfl, pic); Bud Shank (ts, cl, fl); Bill Perkins (ts, cl, fl); Jack Nimitz (bar, contrabass cl); Bill Hood (bar, bass sax, bass cl); John Pisano, Tommy Tedesco, Howard Roberts (g's); Don Bagley (b); Frank Capp (d). *Paul Horn, featured soloist on all woodwinds.*

CAL TJADER
In a Latin Bag
1961. Verve V-8419

Personnel: Cal Tjader (vbs); Armando Peraza (bongos); Paul Horn (fl); Al McKibbon (b); Wilfredo Vicente (congas); Johnny Rae (timbales); Lonnie Hewitt (p).

Latin for Lovers—Cal Tjader and Strings
1962. Fantasy 3279

Personnel: Jack Weeks (a); Cal Tjader (vbs); Paul Horn (cl, fl, as); Vince Guaraldi (p); Al McKibbon (b); Mongo Santamaria, Willie Bobo (d); Boris Blinder, Harry Moulin, Frances Wiener, Eugene Winkler (strings).

Concert by the Sea
1962. Fantasy 3295

Personnel: Cal Tjader (vbs); Paul Horn (fl, as); Lonnie Hewitt (p); Al McKibbon (b); Willie Bobo, Mongo Santamaria (d, timbales).

RAVI SHANKAR
Portrait of Genius
1965. World Pacific 1432

Personnel: Ravi Shankar (sitar); Paul Horn (fl); Dr. Penelope Esterbrook (sitar, tamboura); Harihar Rao (table-tarang, dholak); Alla Rakha (tabla); Sam Chaianis (santoor); Phil Harland (tabla, kartal); N. C. Mullick (tamboura).

BUDDY RICH
Rich à la Rakha
1965. World Pacific WPS-21453

Personnel: Buddy Rich (d, dholak); Alla Rakha (tabla); Paul Horn (fl); Shamim Ahmed (sitar); Taranath Rao (dholak); Nodu C. Mullick (tamboura, manjira); Amiya Das Gupta (tamboura).

DAVID FRIESEN
Amber Skies
1984. Palo Alto Rec. PA 8043-4

Personnel: Chick Corea (p); Paul Horn (fl); Joe Henderson (ts); David Friesen (b); Airto Moreira (perc); Paul Motian (d).

PAUL HORN/STEVEN HALPERN
Connections
1984. Halpern Sounds HS-838

Personnel: Paul Horn (f, afl, bfl, ti-tze); Steven Halpern (p, synth, tp, Vocoder). Side two only—George Marsh (perc); Marc van Wageningen (elec b).

ANTHOLOGIES

DOWN BEAT JAZZ CONCERT
1958. Dot DLP-9003

Groups listed: Pepper Adams; Manny Albam; Don Bagley; Al Cohn; Don Elliott; Paul Horn; Hal McKusick; Frank Rehak; Tony Scott. **"Willow Weep for Me," The Paul Horn Quartet**—Paul Horn (fl); Don Bagley (b); Dick Katz (p); Osie Johnson (d).

DOWN BEAT JAZZ CONCERT, vol. 2
1958. Dot DLP-3188

Groups listed: Manny Albam and his Jazz Greats; Tony Scott Quintet; Steve Allen Quartet; Paul Horn Quartet; Don Elliott Quintet; Steve Allen Trio. **"Give Me the Simple Life," The Paul Horn Quartet**—Paul Horn (fl); Don Bagley (b); Dick Katz (p); Osie Johnson (d).

THE CLASSIC COLLECTION—CONTEMPORARY/THE GREAT JAZZ MEN, vol. 2
1973. Dot DLP-25879

Artists listed: Paul Horn; Tony Scott; Red Norvo; Jimmy Knepper; Kenny Burrell; Paul Motian; Osie Johnson; Milt Hinton; Al Cohn; Charlie Shavers; George Auld; Pepper Adams; Gene Quill; Bob Brookmeyer; Urbie Green; Barry Galbraith; Red Mitchell; Red Callender; Zoot Sims; Donald Byrd; Jimmy Rowles; Shelly Manne; Don Bagley; Jimmy Wyble; Frank Rehak; Eddie Costa; Jan Johansson; Bernie Nierow; Manny Albam; Larry Sonn. **"Exuberance," Paul Horn**—with Ed Leddy, Stu Williamson, Ken Bright (tp's); Vince De Rosa, Dick Perissi (F-hn's); Milt Bernhart (tb); Red Callender, Shelly Manne (d); Red Mitchell (b).

BOBBY TROUP
Bobby Troup and His Stars of Jazz
1959. RCA LPM-1959

Artists listed: Monty Budwig; Benny Carter; Paul Horn; Plas Johnson; Conte Candoli; Pete Candoli; Mel Lewis; Joe Mondragon; Bob Cooper; Bob Enevoldsen; Red Norvo; Shorty Rogers; Chuck Gentry; Bill Holman; Frank Rosolino; Jimmy Rowles; Bud Shank; Stu Williamson. **"Sent for You Yesterday"**—Paul Horn, clarinet solo.

JINGLE BELL JAZZ
1962. Columbia CS-8693/CL-1893

Groups listed: Duke Ellington; Lionel Hampton; Chico Hamilton; Carmen McRae; Pony Poindexter; Paul Horn; The Dave Brubeck Quartet; Lambert, Hendricks and Ross; The Dukes of Dixieland; The Manhattan Jazz All Stars; Marlowe Morris; Miles Davis. **"We Three Kings of Orient Are"**—Paul Horn.

FILL YOUR HEAD WITH JAZZ—25 ALL-TIME GIANTS OF JAZZ
(two-record set)
1970. Columbia G-30217

Artists listed: Charlie Byrd; Mose Allison; Chico Hamilton; Gabor Szabo; Lambert, Hendricks and Ross; Gerry Mulligan; Woody Herman; Art Farmer; Bill Evans-Dave Pike; Duke Ellington; Paul Winter; Paul Horn; George Benson; Charlie Mingus; Herbie Mann; John Handy. **"Count Your Change"**—Paul Horn (as); Emil Richards (vbs); Paul Moer (p); Vic Gaskin (b); Milt Turner (d).

DICK SCHORY—CARNEGIE HALL
(two-record set)
1970. Ovation OV/14-10-2

Artists listed: Gary Burton; Paul Horn; Joe Morello. **"Gentle Rain"**—Paul Horn (fl); Ron Stelle (g).

THE PROGRESSIVES
1973. Columbia KG-31574

Groups listed: The Mahavishnu Orchestra; Weather Report; Matching Mole; Walter Carlos; Ornette Coleman; Soft Machine; Don Ellis; Keith Jarrett; Charles Mingus; Gentle Giant; Compost; Paul Winter Consort; Paul Horn; Bill Evans. **"Haida"**—Paul Horn.

DRUMS AND FLUTES
(four-record set)
1985. The Franklin Mint Record Society 73/74/75/76

Artists listed, Record 73: Jelly Roll Morton; Pee Wee Russell; Red Nichols; Jack Teagarden; Chick Webb; Cab Calloway; Lionel Hampton; Jo Jones Trio; Count Basie Orchestra; Herbie Haymer Quintet; Dexter Gordon Quartet. *Record 74:* Art Blakey and the Jazz Messengers; Max Roach; Roy Haynes; Tadd Dameron; Dave Brubeck Quartet; Shelly Manne Four; Teddy Edwards Quartet; Don Cherry; Tommy Flanagan Trio. *Record 75:* Spike Hughes Orchestra; Ray Linn Orchestra; Frank Wess Sextet; Chico Hamilton Quintet; Herbie Mann Sextet; Tal Farlow Trio; James Moody Quartet; Roland Kirk Quartet; Oscar Pettifor Orchestra; Eric Dolphy Quartet; Paul Horn Quintet; Yusef Lateef Quintet. *Record 76:* Bill Evans Trio (w/ Jeremy Steig); Bud Shank; Charles Lloyd Quartet; Hubert Laws; Elvin Jones Group; Ira Sullivan Quintet; Anthony Davis/James Newton; Ernie Wilkins Group; Herbie Mann/Sam Most; Sam Most/Joe Farrell. **"Now Hear This" (Record 75B), Paul Horn Quintet**—Paul Horn (fl); Paul Moer (p); Emil Richards (vbs); Victor Gaskin (b); Milt Turner (d); from *Profile of a Jazz Musician.* 1962. Columbia CS-8722.

A SPECIAL MEMORY

DUKE ELLINGTON AND HIS ORCHESTRA
Suite Thursday
1960. Columbia CL-1597/CS-8397

Personnel: **Harry Carney, Jimmy Hamilton, Paul Gonzalves, Russell Procope, Paul Horn (saxes); Ray Nance, Willie Cook, Andres Meringuito, Eddie Mullins (tp's); Lawrence Brown, "Booty" Wood, Britt Woodman, Juan Tizol, Mathew Gee (tb's); Sam Woodyard (d); Aaron Bell (b); Duke Ellington (p).**